Stanley Lane-Poole

The People of Turkey

Twenty years' residence among Bulgarians, Greeks, Albanians, Turks, and Armenians. By a consul's daughter and wife.

Stanley Lane-Poole

The People of Turkey
Twenty years' residence among Bulgarians, Greeks, Albanians, Turks, and Armenians. By a consul's daughter and wife.

ISBN/EAN: 9783337299217

Printed in Europe, USA, Canada, Australia, Japan

Cover: Foto ©Andreas Hilbeck / pixelio.de

More available books at **www.hansebooks.com**

THE PEOPLE OF TURKEY:

TWENTY YEARS' RESIDENCE

AMONG

BULGARIANS, GREEKS, ALBANIANS, TURKS, AND ARMENIANS.

BY A CONSUL'S DAUGHTER AND WIFE.

EDITED BY
STANLEY LANE POOLE.

IN TWO VOLUMES.
VOL. I.

LONDON:
JOHN MURRAY, ALBEMARLE STREET.
1878.

[The Right of Translation is Reserved.]

DEDICATED

(By Permission)

TO

THE MARCHIONESS OF SALISBURY,

BY HER GRATEFUL SERVANT

THE AUTHOR.

PREFACE.

No one who has talked with many people on the Eastern Question can have failed to remark the wide difference of opinion held on things which ought to be matters of certainty,—on which two opinions ought to be impossible. This divergence of view is only a very natural consequence of the want of any book of authority on the subject. How is one to learn what manner of men these Bulgarians and Greeks of Turkey really are? Hitherto our information has been chiefly obtained from newspaper correspondents: and it is hardly necessary to observe that the nature of their selected information depends upon the tendency of the paper. There have, of course, been notable exceptions to this common rule of a party-conscience: the world of journalists is but now lamenting the untimely death of one of its most distinguished members, with whose name honour and truth and indefatigable thoroughness must ever be associated. But granting the honesty and impartiality of a correspondent, allowing the accuracy of his report of what he has seen, it must be conceded that his opportunities for observation are short and hurried, that he judges almost solely from the immediate present, and that by the nature of his profession he is seldom able to make a very long or intimate study of a people's character. One accepts his reports as the evidence of an eye-witness; but one does not necessarily pledge oneself to his deductions. For the former he has every necessary qualification: for the latter he may have none, and he probably has not the most important. Especially unsafe is it to trust to estimates of nations formed hastily on insufficient experience in the midst of general disorder such as that in which many summary verdicts have lately been composed.

But if newspaper correspondents are placed at some disadvantage, what can be said for those well-assured travellers who pay a three months' visit to Turkey, spend the time pleasantly at Pera, or perhaps at the country-houses of Pashas, and then consider themselves qualified to judge the merits of each class in each nationality of the mixed inhabitants of the land? It is unpleasant to have to say it: but it is well known that scarcely a single book upon Turkey is based upon a much longer experience than three months.

In this dearth of trustworthy information, it was with no little interest that I learnt that an English lady, who had lived for a great part of her life in various provinces of European and Asiatic Turkey, and whose linguistic powers perfected by experience enabled her to converse equally with Greeks, Turks, and Bulgarians as one of themselves, had formed a collection of notes on the people of Turkey—on their national characteristics, their manners and customs, education, religion, their aims and ambitions. In any case the observations of one who had for more than twenty years enjoyed such exceptional advantages must be valuable. Of the opportunities of the Author there could be as little doubt as of her conscientious accuracy in recording her experience. The only question was not the quality but the quantity of the information. But in this the manuscript surpassed all expectations. Every page teemed with details of life and character entirely novel to all but Eastern travellers, and much that even to them must be entirely unknown. Every subject connected with the people of Turkey seemed to be fully treated, and it was rarely that any need for more ample information was felt.

In editing what, as I have had nothing to do with the matter of it, I may without vanity call the most valuable work on the people of Turkey that has yet appeared, I have strictly kept in view the principle laid down by the Author — that the book was to be a collection of facts, not a vehicle for party views on the Eastern Question, nor a recipe for the harmonious arrangement of South-Eastern Europe. Politically the book is entirely colourless. It was felt that thus only could it commend itself to both, or rather all, the disputing parties, and that only by delicately avoiding the susceptible points of each party could the book attain its end—of generally imparting a certain amount of sound information on the worst-known subject of the day.

The reader, therefore, must not expect to find here a defence of Turkish rule nor yet an attack thereon: he will only find an account of how the Turks do rule, with a few incidental illustrations scattered throughout the book. Comment is, as a rule, eschewed as superfluous and insulting to the intelligence of the reader. Still less must he look for any expression of opinion on the wisdom or folly of the policy of Her Majesty's Government. All these things are apart from the aim of the work. It is wished to provide the data necessary to the formation of any worthy views on the many sub-divisions of the Eastern Question. It is not wished to point the moral. Once conversant with the actual state of the people of Turkey, once knowing how they live, what are their virtues and vices, what their aims and hopes, and it is easy for any rational man to draw his conclusions: easy to criticise favourably or otherwise according to the merits of the case the policy of the British Government towards Turkey and towards Greece, to decide whether after all the supposed rising in Bulgaria (of the details of which little is said here, because everything has already been well said) was ever a rising at all; whether the Turks are or are not incapable of the amenities which many believe them to have then displayed; whether the Bulgarians are friendly to Russia, or are really the very humble servants of the Porte; in short, whether half the questions which have for two years been the subject of perpetual contention admit of debate at all.

The book has been divided into four parts. In the first, the general characteristics of the various races of Turkey are sketched. Very little is said about their history, for it is not the history but the present state of the people—or rather the state just before the war—that is the subject of the book. The Author has tried to bring home to the reader the social condition and the national character of these different races. The Bulgarians, Greeks, Albanians, Turks, Armenians, and Jews, are in turn described; and the, for the time, scarcely less important Circassians, with the Tatars and Gipsies, have their chapter.

In the second part, the tenure of land and the state of the small peasant farmers are explained, and an account is given of houses and hovels in Turkey, including that most superb of Turkish houses, the Seraglio of the Sultan, to which with its inmates a very detailed notice is devoted; and the part ends with an account of Municipality and Police in Turkey, together with the kindred subject of Brigandage.

The third part is occupied with the manners and customs of the races. Few things give such an insight into the character of a people as a study of their customs, and it is believed that these chapters on the extraordinary ceremonies employed in Turkey on the occasion of a birth or marriage or a death, on the dress, food, and amusements, of the Greeks, Bulgarians, Turks, and Armenians will prove of as much value as interest. The fact, for example, that in many parts of Bulgaria the weddings take place not in the church but in the cellar of the bridegroom's house speaks volumes on the insecurity of a woman's person while Turkish governors rule in Bulgarian towns. The custom of the Albanian bridegroom flinging a halter over his bride's neck and dragging her into his house is an interesting relic of capture, and the subsequent knocking of the bride's head against the wall as a warning against infidelity illustrates the general chastity of the people. The indecent exhibitions, again, at Turkish weddings help to explain the want of refinement and womanly feeling among Turkish ladies. The ceremonies of the Greeks are interesting from another point of view, inasmuch as very many of them are identical with those of the ancient Greeks.

The last part is devoted to the education, superstition, and religion of the people of Turkey. It is here that we get to the root of Turkish manners: for we see how the Turk is brought up, how he learns the vices that have become identified with the thought of his race, how he remains, in spite even of a western education, deeply imbued with superstition, and finally how he loses all the energy of the old Othmanli character by the operation of the fatal doctrine of Kismet. The chapters on Education are among the most valuable in the book; whilst those on

Religion will serve to explain some of the difficulties that beset the proper adjustment of affairs in South-Eastern Europe.

The study of the facts thus brought together points to a considerable modification of the views commonly entertained with regard to the characters of the peoples of Turkey. The Author's long experience leaves no doubt of the vast superiority of the Greeks to the other races; yet there is no people that one is more accustomed to hear spoken of with distrust and even contempt. The Greeks are commonly charged with a partiality for sharp practice, and with intolerable vanity; their character is summed up as petty. There is always a grain of truth in a calumny: when plenty of mud is thrown some of it sticks, not because of the quantity of the mud, but because there is sure to be an adhesive sympathy with some part of the object of the attack. The Greeks have in some degree laid themselves open to these charges. It was very unwise of them to take the first rank as merchants in the East, and thus arouse the jealousy of the merchants of all European nations, whom they have eclipsed by their superior business capacities.

Envy will pick holes anywhere, but it is especially easy to criticise the customs of a merchant class. Mercantile morality all over the world is a thing of itself, not generally understanded of the people. But there is nothing to show that the Greek merchants are less scrupulous than the rest, though their temptations are infinitely greater. If a little sharp business is said to be permissible, and even perhaps necessary, at Liverpool for instance, it is *à fortiori* essential in Turkey. It is a perfectly well-understood principle that in Turkey, where everything is done by bribery and corruption, a merchant, unless he wishes to be ruined, must steer a somewhat oblique course. So long as the late Turkish rule extended over Greek subjects, it was necessary to do in Turkey as the Turks do. French and English merchants sin as much as the Greeks in this manner; but the superior commercial ability of the Greeks and their consequent success have drawn on them the whole evil repute. It is not that the Greeks cheat more than other commercial nations: it is merely that they make more money on the same amount of cheating. *Hinc illae lacrumae!*

The Greeks, again, are certainly conceited, and with excellent reason. It would be absurd to expect anything else. They are but newly freed; after centuries of Ottoman tyranny, followed by a generation of Bavarian despotism, they have at last been allowed to enjoy some fifteen years of freedom. Even under the stiff court of Otho, but much more during the last fifteen years, they have made prodigious progress. Having worked out their own freedom, they have been making themselves fit for freedom. From craven slaves of the Turk they have become a liberty-loving people. Their thoughts have been casting back to the noble ancestry which they claim as their own, and looking onward to the great future that is in store for them. They have measured themselves intellectually with the rest of Europe and they have not been worsted. They have spent the last twenty years in the work of self-education, and so successful have been their efforts that it is well known that no nation can compare with Greece in the general education of its people—that to Greece alone can be applied the ambiguous taunt that she is over-educated.

All these things are legitimate subjects of pride. It is no wonder that the Greeks are vain of their adopted ancestors; no marvel that they are proud of their keen wits and facile intelligence. They have formed a justly high estimate of their national worth, and are justly proud of the progress they have already made; and they take no pains to conceal it. Their faults are only exaggerations of national virtues, the outcome of the reaction from a long servitude; they are the necessary but temporary result of the circumstances. A little time for development, a closer association with the other powers of Europe, and a worthier trust on the part of these, and the Greeks will lose their blemishes of youth; conceit will be toned down to a proper pride, and high intelligence will no longer be called over-cleverness. The nation has marched steadily forward in the little time it has been free; it has made great steps in educating itself and in spreading knowledge among its members still subject to the alien; it has shown itself able to govern itself, even to restrain itself under terrible provocation when there was much to gain and little that could be lost. If it is given fair play, the time may yet come when a seventh Great Power shall arise in Europe, when the Greeks shall again rule in Byzantium, and Europe shall know that the name of Hellenes is still a sacred name.

The Author's account of the Bulgarians differs little from the ordinary opinion, except on one important point. She describes them as honest hardworking peasants, rather slow and stupid, but excellent labourers. But she absolutely denies the ferocious character ascribed to them by some writers. Everyone knows that they exacted a terrible vengeance from the Turks, and no man of spirit can blame them for it; though it is much to be regretted that, if the accounts be true, they carried their revenge to the length of Turkish barbarity. But this was an exceptional time: it has had its parallel in most nations, as those who remember the feeling in England at the time of the Indian mutiny can witness. As a rule th Bulgarian is, on the contrary, rather too tame. He is a very domestic animal, lives happily with his family, keeps generally sober, enjoys his dance on the common on feast-days, and goes with perfect willingness and satisfaction to his daily work in the fields or at the rose-harvest. He is an admirable agricultural labourer, with a stolidity more than Teutonic, without the Teuton's energy. Yet these Bulgarians seem to have a good deal of sound common sense, and show many of the qualities necessary in a people that is to govern itself. It has hitherto submitted with curious tranquillity to the Turkish yoke, and the Sultan has probably had few less ill-affected servants than the Bulgarians. On the other hand, it seems that the Bulgarians entertain a very decided hostility to Russia, an enmity second only to their hatred for the Greeks.

The third important element in the future of South-Eastern Europe is the Turks. Of them it is not necessary to say much: most people are fairly enlightened as to the manners and rule of the Turk, and the Author has intentionally avoided crowding her pages with Turkish atrocities; they are all very much alike, and they are not pleasant reading. The official classes meet with scant respect at her hands; but with most writers she speaks favourably of the Turkish peasant. The principal vice he has is his religious fanaticism, which is the result partly of Mohammedanism itself, and partly of the form and manner in which it is inculcated in Turkey. Islam may be broad and tolerant enough; but not the rigid orthodox Islam taught in the primary schools of the Ottoman empire. Islam may be an excellent creed by itself; but a ruling Mohammedan minority in a Christian country is an endless source of trouble. But the religious question is only one of those which have disturbed the position of the Porte. The system of administration, as described in these pages, is enough to overturn any power, and an official class brought up under vicious home influences, educated in fanatical mosque-schools, living the indolent self-indulgent life of Stamboul, getting and keeping office by bribery, administering "justice" to the highest bidder, is a doomed class. When one sees how a Turkish child is brought up he begins to wonder how any Turk can help being vicious and dishonest. It is quite certain that there is no hope for the Turks so long as Turkish women remain what they are, and home-training is the initiation of vice. So far as can be judged, the Turk naturally possessed some of the true elements of greatness; but it is rarely they come to bear fruit: they are choked by the pernicious social system which destroys the moral force of the women and thereafter the men of the empire. It is this carefully inculcated deficiency in all sense of uprightness and justice, and this trained tendency to everything that is a crime against the community, that renders the pasha incapable of governing. It is this fact which compels one to admit that, whatever the decisions of the Berlin Congress, it is a clear gain that the war has won for Europe, to be able to speak of Turkish rule in the past tense.

With full knowledge of the experience and research of the Author, I must yet say there are some points—notably the Greek Church and the Russian policy—in which I cannot bring myself to agree with her; and I must also add that, owing to the haste with which the book has been put through the press, I have allowed a few misprints to escape me.

STANLEY LANE POOLE.

June 20th, 1878.

CONTENTS OF VOLUME I.

PART I.

THE RACES OF TURKEY.

CHAPTER I.

THE BULGARIANS.

PAGE

Sketch of Bulgarian History—The Slav Occupation—Bulgar Conquest—Mixture of the Races—The Bulgarian Kingdom—Contests with Constantinople—Basil Bulgaroktonos—Bulgaria under Ottoman Rule—Compulsory Conversion—The Pomaks—Oppressive Government—Janissary Conscription—Extortion of Officials—Misery of the People—Improvement under Abdul-Medjid—Fidelity of the Bulgarians to the Porte—The late Revolt no National Movement—The Geographical Limits of Bulgaria—Mixture with Greeks—Life in the House of a Bulgarian Country Gentleman—Daily Levees of Elders and Peasants—Counsel of the Chorbadji and Stupidity of the Clients—Instances of Bulgarian Grievances—St. Panteleemon—A Spiritual Elopement—Dentist's Fees—Woman's Work in Bulgaria—Sobriety—Town Life—A Bulgarian Ball—A Night in a Bulgarian Hamlet, and the Comfort thereof—Unity of the Nation—Distrust of Foreigners—Demoralization of the Bulgarians—The Hope for the Future 1

CHAPTER II.

THE GREEKS OF TURKEY.

Importance of the Greeks at the present moment—Their Attitude—The Greek Peasant as Contrasted with the Bulgarian—His Family — Eloquence — Patriotism — Comforts — The Women—A Greek Girl—Women of the towns of the Upper Class—Of the Lower Class—Wives and Husbands—Greek Parties—The Conservatives and the Progressives—A Conversation on Greek Go-a-head-ness—Physical Features of the Modern Greek—Character—General Prejudice—A Prussian Estimate—Greek Vices—An Adventure with Greek Brigands—Adelphé—Unscrupulousness in Business—Causes and Precedents—Jews and Greeks—Summary 35

CHAPTER III.

THE ALBANIANS.

Albania little known to Travellers—Character of the Country—Isolation and Neglect—Products—The Land-holders—Ali Bey's Revolution—Albanian Towns—The Albanian's House his Castle in a Literal Sense—Blood Feuds—Villages—Unapproachable Position—The Defence of Souli—Joannina—Beautiful Site—Ali Pasha's Improvements—Greek Enterprise—The Albanians—Separate Tribes—The Ghegs—The Tosks—Character of the Latter—Superiority of the Ghegs—Respect for Women—An Adventure with a Brigand Chief—Gheg Gratitude—A Point of Honour with an Albanian Servant—Religion among the Albanians—Education among the Tosks—Warlike Character of the Albanians—Use of the Gun—The Vendetta—Women to the Rescue—Albanian Women in General—Female Adornment — Emigration—Mutual Assistance Abroad—The Albanian Character—Recklessness—Love of Display—Improvidence—Pride—Hatred of the Turks, reciprocated to the full 62

CHAPTER IV.

THE TURKS.

PAGE

Turkish Peasants—Decrease in Numbers—Taxation and Recruiting—Relations with the Christians—Appearance—Amusements—House and Family—Townspeople—Guilds—Moslems and Christians—The Turk as an Artisan—Objection to Innovations—Life in the Town—The Military Class—Government Officials—Pashas—Grand Vizirs—Receptions—A Turkish Lady's Life—The Princes—The Sultan—Mahmoud—His Reforms—Abdul-Medjid—Abdul-Aziz—Character and Fate—Murad—Abdul-Hamid—Slavery in Turkey . . 88

CHAPTER V.

THE ARMENIANS AND JEWS IN TURKEY.

Historical Misfortunes of the Armenians—Refugees in Turkey, Russia, Persia—Want of Patriotism—Appearance and Character—Armenian Ladies—American Mission Work—Schools—The Jews of Turkey—Reputed Origin—Classes—Conservatives and Progressives—Jewish Trade—Prejudice against Jews—Alliance with Moslems—Wealth and Indigence—Cause of the Latter—The Jewish Quarter—Education—"L'Alliance Israélite"—Divorce among the Jews merely a Question of the Highest Bidder 128

CHAPTER VI.

THE CIRCASSIANS, TATARS, AND GIPSIES OF TURKEY.

The Circassians.—Their Immigration into Turkey in 1864—Their Camp—Chiefs and Slaves—Origin of the charge of Cannibalism—Assistance of the Government and the Peasantry—Bulgarian Views of the New-comers—A Cherkess Girl—Sale of Circassian Women—Depredations—Cattle-lifting—Circassian fellow-travellers in a Steamer—Appearance and

Character—Scheme of Philanthropy respectfully offered to Russia.

The Tatars.—Their Arrival in the Dobrudcha with a Good Character, which they have since maintained—Their excellent qualities as Artisans—Religion—Women—Dirtiness—Tallow their Specialty—Rivalry of Jewish and Tatar Hawkers.

The Gipsies.—Legend of the origin of the name Chenguin—Abhorrence of them by the Turks—Religion and Superstitions Customs—Nomad Life—Two Classes—Physical Characteristics—Reported Witches—Indiscriminate Pilfering—A Case of Horse-stealing—Gipsy Cunning in the Market—Gipsy Avocations — Character — Gipsy-Soldiers—Town-Gipsies—Agricultural Gipsies 144

PART II.

LANDS AND DWELLINGS.

CHAPTER VII.

TENURE OF LAND.

Three Classes of Land in Turkey—*Vakouf* Lands, their Origin and Growth—Turkish Equivalent of Mortmain—Privileges of Tenants on *Vakouf* Land—Maladministration—Corruption of Charity Agents and Government Inspectors—General System of Embezzlement—Sultan Mahmoud's Attempted Reform—Insufficiency of *Vakouf* Revenues as administered; Supplemented by State—General Decay of *Vakouf* Property, Mosques, Medressés, and Imarets—Misapplication of *Vakouf* Funds intended for the Support of the Public Water-Supply —*Mirié* Lands, Government Grants, Military Proprietors. Growth of a Feudal System—Miserable Condition of the Rayahs—Anxiety of the Porte—Destruction of the Feudal System by Mahmoud and Abdul-Medjid—Reduction of the

Bosnian and Albanian Beys—Present Condition of the Country Boys—*Mirié* Lands reclaimed from the Waste—Title-Inspectors—A Waste-Land Abuse—Similar Difficulties in Connection with Ordinary *Mirié* Tenure—*Mulk* or Freehold Lands—Their Small Extent—Difficulty of Establishing Safe Titles—Descent and Transfer of Land—Tenure of Land by Christians and by Foreign Subjects—Commons and Forests—The Inspectors of the Forest Department . . 171

CHAPTER VIII.

PEASANT HOLDINGS.

Small proprietors *South of the Balkans*—Flourishing State of the Country a few Years ago—A Rose-Harvest at Kezanlik—Bulgarian Villages—Oppressive and Corrupt System of Taxation and of Petty Government—The Disadvantages counterbalanced by the Industry and Perseverance of the Bulgarian Peasant—The Lending Fund in Bulgaria—Its Short Duration—Bulgarian Peasant often unavoidably in Debt—Bulgarian Cottages—Food and Clothing—Excellent Reports of German and Italian Engineers on the Conduct and Working Power of Bulgarian Labourers—Turkish Peasants—Turkish Villages—Comparative Merits of Turkish and Bulgarian Peasants—Land *in Macedonia*—Chiefly Large Estates—*Chiftliks*—The *Konak* or Residence of the Owner—Country Life of the Bey and his Family—His Tenants (*Yeradjis*)—Character of the *Yeradji*—His Wretched Condition—The Metayer System Unfairly Worked—The *Yeradji* generally in Debt—Virtually a Serf bound to the Soil—Difficulty of getting Peasants to become *Yeradjis*—Statute Labour—Cultivation and Crops 195

CHAPTER IX.

TURKISH HOUSES.

The Turkish Quarter—A *Konak*—Haremlik and Selamlik—Arrangement of Rooms—Furniture—The *Tandour*—Turkish Clemency towards Vermin—Bordofska—An Albanian *Konak*

—The Pasha and his Harem—A Turkish *Bas-bleu*—Ruins of *Konaks* outside Uskup—The Last of the Albanian Deri-Beys—A *Konak* at Bazardjik—The Widow of the Deri-Bey—Kiosks—*Koulas*—A *Koula* near Salonika—Christian Quarters—*Khans*—Furniture—Turkish Baths, Public and Private—Cafés 216

CHAPTER X.

THE SERAGLIO.

The Chain of Palaces along the Bosphorus—*Eski Serai*, the oldest of the Seraglios—Its Site and Appearance—Beauty of its Gardens—Contrasts—Its Destruction—*Dolma-Bagché* and *Begler-Bey*—Enormous Expenditure of Abdul-Medjid and Abdul-Aziz on Seraglios—*Yahlis* or Villas—*Begler-Bey* Furnished for Illustrious Guests—Delicate Attentions of the Sultan—Furniture of Seraglios—Mania of Abdul-Aziz—Everything Inflammable thrown into the Bosphorus—Pleasure Grounds—Interior Divisions of the Seraglio—The *Mabeyn*—The Padishah *en négligé*—Imperial Expenditure—Servants, &c.—Food—Wages—Stables—Fine Art—Origin of the Inmates of the Seraglio—Their Training—Adjemis—A Training-School for the Seraglio—Ranks in the Seraglio—The *Bash Kadin Effendi* and other Wives—*Hanoums* or Odalisks—Favourites—Equal Chances of Good Fortune—Ceremonies attending the Sultan's Selection of an Odalisk—A Slave seldom sees the Sultan more than Once—Consequent Loss of Dignity and Misery for the rest of her Life—Precarious Position of Imperial Favourites—Intrigues and Cabals in the Seraglio—Good Fortune of the Odalisk who bears a Child—Fashions in Beauty—Golden Hair—The *Validé Sultana*—The *Hasnadar Ousta*—Ignorance and Vice of the Seraglio Women—The Better Class—The Consumptive Class—The "Wild Serailis"—Amusements of the Seraglio—Theatre—Ballet—Shopping—Garden Parties in Abdul-Medjid's Time—Imperial Children—Foster-Brothers—Bad Training and Deficient Education of Turkish Princes and Princesses . 238

CHAPTER XI.

MUNICIPALITY, POLICE, AND BRIGANDAGE.

PAGE

Municipality.—Improvement at Constantinople—No Improvement in Country Towns—Sanitary Negligence.—*Police.*—The Corruption of the old Police—Formation of the new Corps—Its various Classes—Economical Reductions—The Corruption of the new Police—Voluntary Guards the connecting link between Police and Brigandage.—*Brigandage.*—Ancient and Modern Brigands—Great Diminution of Numbers—Constant Outrages however—Albanians the born Brigands—Systematic Attacks—Uselessness of the Police—My Brigand Guides—Usual Manner of Attack—Danger to *Kheradjis*—Brigands at Vodena repulsed by a Chorbadji and his Wife—Impotence of the Authorities—Outrage at Caterina—Modern Greek Klephts 270

THE PEOPLE OF TURKEY.

PART I.
THE RACES OF TURKEY.

CHAPTER I.

THE BULGARIANS.

Sketch of Bulgarian History—The Slav Occupation—Bulgar Conquest—Mixture of the Races—The Bulgarian Kingdom—Contests with Constantinople—Basil Bulgaroktonos—Bulgaria under Ottoman Rule—Compulsory Conversion—The Pomaks—Oppressive Government—Janissary Conscription—Extortion of Officials—Misery of the People—Improvement under Abdul-Medjid—Fidelity of the Bulgarians to the Porte—The late Revolt no National Movement—The Geographical Limits of Bulgaria—Mixture with Greeks—Life in the House of a Bulgarian Country Gentleman—Daily Levées of Elders and Peasants—Counsel of the Chorbadji and Stupidity of the Clients—Instances of Bulgarian Grievances—St. Panteleemon—A Spiritual Elopement—Dentist's Fees—Woman's Work in Bulgaria—Sobriety—Town Life—A Bulgarian Ball—A Night in a Bulgarian Hamlet, and the Comfort thereof—Unity of the Nation—Distrust of Foreigners—Demoralization of the Bulgarians—The Hope for the Future.

THE Bulgarians, who were completely crushed by the Ottoman Conquest, and whose very existence for centuries was almost forgotten, have been suddenly brought before the world by the late unhappy events in their country.

Much has been written by English and foreign authors respecting them, but few of the writings on the subject appear to agree with regard to the origin, the history, or the present social and moral condition of this much-injured but deserving people. I have no pretensions to throw a fresh light on the first two points. The few remarks I shall make are based upon such authors as are considered most trustworthy, and especially on the recent researches of Professor Hyrtl, reserving to myself the task of describing the moral and social condition of the modern Bulgarians, as fourteen years spent among them enables me to do.

From the Bulgarian Professor Drinov, who appears to have made the Balkan peninsula his especial study, we learn that before the arrival of the Bulgarian tribes into European Turkey, the southern side of the Danube had been invaded by the Slavs, who during four centuries poured into the country and, steadily spreading, drove out the previous inhabitants, who directed their steps towards the sea coasts and settled in the towns there. In the beginning of the sixth century the Slavonic element had become so powerful in its newly-acquired dominions, and its depredatory incursions into the Byzantine Empire so extensive, that the Emperor Anastasius found himself forced to build a wall from Selymbria on the Sea of Marmora to Derkon on the Black Sea in order to repel their attacks. Procopius, commenting on this, relates that while Justinian was winning useless victories over the Persians, part of his empire lay exposed to the ravages of the Slavs, and that not less than 200,000 Byzantines were annually killed or carried away into slavery.

The hostile spirit, however, between these two nations was broken by short intervals of peace and friendly relations, during which the Slav race supplied some Emperors and many distinguished men to the Byzantines. Many Slavs resorted to Constantinople in order to receive the education and training their newly-founded kingdom did not afford them. The migration of the Slavs into Thrace ceased towards the middle of the seventh century, when they settled down to a more sedentary life, and, under the civilizing influence of their Byzantine neighbours, betook themselves to agricultural and pastoral pursuits. According to historical accounts the Slavs did not long enjoy their acquisitions in peace, for about the year 679 A.D. a horde of Hunnish warriors, calling themselves Bulgars (a name derived from their former home on the Volga), crossed the Danube under the leadership of their Khan, Asparuch, and after some desperate fighting with the Slavs, finally settled on the land now known as Bulgaria and founded a kingdom which in its turn lasted about seven hundred years.

From the little that is known of the original Bulgarians, we learn that polygamy was practised among them, that the men shaved their heads and wore a kind of turban, and the women veiled their faces. These points of similarity connect the primitive Bulgarians with the Avars, with whom they came into close contact, as well as with the Tatars, during their long sojourn between the Volga and Tanais, as witness the marked Tatar features some of the Bulgarians bear to the present day. The primitive Bulgarians are said to have subsisted chiefly on the flesh of animals killed in the chase; and it is further related of them that they burnt their dead, and when a chieftain died his wives and servants were also burnt and their ashes buried with those of their master. Schafarik, whose learned and trustworthy researches on the origin of the Bulgarians can scarcely be called in question, remarks that the warlike hordes from the Volga regions, though not numerous, were very brave and well skilled in war. They attacked with great ferocity the patient plodding Slavs, who were engaged in cultivating the land and rearing cattle, quickly obtained the governing power, and after tasting the comforts of a settled life, gradually adopted to a great extent the manners, customs, and even the language of the people they had conquered. This amalgamation appears to have been a slow process, occupying, according to historical evidence, full two hundred and fifty years. It is during this period that the Bulgarian language must have gradually been effaced, and the vanquishing race, like the Normans in England, absorbed by the vanquished.

This fresh mixture with the Slav element constituted the Bulgarians a separate race with no original title to belong to the Slavonic family, beyond that derived from the fusion of blood that followed the long intercourse of centuries, by which the primitive Bulgarians became blended with the former inhabitants of the country. It is evident that they were superior to the Slavs in military science and power, but inferior as regards civilization, and thus naturally yielded to the influence of the more advanced and better organised people. By this influence they created a distinct nation, gave their name to the country, and consolidated their power by laws and institutions.

The Bulgarian kingdom, from its very foundation in 679 until its final overthrow by the Turks in 1396, presents a wearisome tale of battles with short intervals of peace, in the struggle for supremacy between the Emperors of Byzantium and the rulers of Bulgaria. The balance of power alternately inclined from one party to the other; the wars were inhuman on both sides; on the one hand, we read of hundreds of thousands of Byzantines yearly sacrificed by the Slavs; on the other, we have equally horrible spectacles presented to us, like that enacted during the reign of Basil, surnamed Βουλγαροκτόνος (The Bulgarian-killer), on account of the great number of Bulgarians killed by his order. This savage, having on one occasion captured a large number of Bulgarians, separated 15,000 into companies of 100 each, and ordered ninety-nine out of each of these companies to be blinded, allowing the remaining hundredth to retain his sight in order to become the leader of his blind brethren.

In the midst of such scenes and at the cost of torrents of blood, successive kingdoms were constituted in this unhappy land of perpetual warfare. Raised into momentary eminence by the force of arms, they were again hurled to the ground by the same merciless instrument. Supreme power has been alternately wielded by the savage, the Moslem, and the Christian; each of whom to the present day continues the work of destruction.

The condition of Bulgarians did not improve under the Ottoman rule. Their empire soon disappeared, leaving to posterity nothing but a few ruined castles and fortresses, and some annals and popular songs illustrating its past glory. The Turkish conquest was more deeply felt by the Bulgarians than by their brethren in adversity, the Byzantines and the neighbouring Slav nations. These, owing to the more favourable geographical position of their countries and other advantages, were able to save some privileges out of the general wreck, and to retain a shadow of their national rights. The Byzantines were protected by a certain amount of influence left in the hands of the clergy, while the Slav nations were enabled to make certain conditions with their conqueror before their complete surrender, and were successful in enlisting the sympathies and protection of friendly powers in their behalf, and in obtaining through their instrumentality at intervals reforms never vouchsafed to the Bulgarians. This nation, isolated, ignored, and shut out from the civilized world, crouched under the despotic rule of the Ottomans, and submitted to a life of perpetual toil and hardship, uncheered by any of the pleasures of life, unsupported by the least gleam of hope for a better future.

This sad condition has lasted for centuries; and by force of misery the people became grouped into two classes: the poor, who were constant to their faith and national feeling, and the wealthy and prosperous, who adopted Islam in order to escape persecution and save their property. To this latter class may be added the Pomaks, a predatory tribe inhabiting a mountainous district between the provinces of Philippopolis and Serres. They live apart, and pass for Mussulmans because they have some mosques; but they have no knowledge of the Koran nor follow its laws very closely. Most of them to this day bear Christian names and speak the Slav language. The men are a fine race, but utterly ignorant and barbarous.

Upon the poor and therefore Christian class fell all the weight of the Ottoman yoke, which made itself felt in their moral and material condition, and reached even to the dress, which was enforced as a mark of servility. They were forbidden to build churches, and beyond the ordinary annual poll-tax imposed by Moslems on infidel subjects, they had to submit to the many illegal extortions of rapacious governors and cruel landlords; besides the terrible blood-tax collected every five years to recruit the ranks of the Janissaries from the finest children of the province. Nor were the Bulgarian maidens spared: if a girl struck the fancy of a Mohammedan neighbour or a government official, he always found means to possess himself of her person without using much ceremony or fearing much commotion.

The depressing and demoralizing effect of such a system upon the Bulgarians may be imagined; it was sufficient to brutalize a people far more advanced than they were at the time of the conquest. It cowed them, destroyed their brave and venturous spirit, taught them to cringe, and weakened their ideas of right and wrong. It is not strange that a people thus demoralized should, under the pressure of recent troubles, be said in some instances to have acted treacherously both towards their late rulers and present protectors; but the vices of rapacity, treachery, cruelty, and dishonesty, could not have been the natural characteristics of this unhappy people until misery taught them the lesson.

The laws promulgated in the reign of Sultan Abdul-Medjid with respect to the amelioration of the condition of the rayahs were gradually introduced into Bulgaria, and their beneficial influence tended greatly to remove some of the most crying wrongs that had so long oppressed the people. These reforms apparently satisfied the Bulgarians—always easily contented and peacefully disposed. They were thankful for the slight protection thus thrown over their life and property. They welcomed the reforms with gratitude as the signs of better days, and, stimulated by written laws, as well as by the better system of government that had succeeded the old one and had deprived their Mohammedan neighbours of some of their power of molesting and injuring them, they redoubled their activity and endeavoured by industry to improve their condition. Such changes can be only gradual among an oppressed people in the absence of good government and easy communication with the outer world. The Bulgarians, inwardly, perhaps, still dissatisfied, seemed outwardly content and attached to the Porte in the midst of the revolutionary movements that alternately convulsed the Servian, Greek, and Albanian populations. A very small section alone yielded to the influence of the foreign agents or *comitats*, who were using every means to create a general rising in Bulgaria, or was at any time in the Bulgarian troubles enticed to raise its voice against the Ottoman Government and throw off its allegiance. The late movement is said to have received encouragement from the Bulgarian clergy acting under Russian influence, and from the young schoolmasters, whose more advanced ideas naturally led them to instil notions of independence among the people. But these views were by no means entertained by the more thoughtful and important members of the community, and no organised disaffection existed in Bulgaria at the time the so-called revolt began. The action of a few hotheaded patriots, followed by some discontented peasants, started the revolt which, if it had been judiciously dealt with, might have been suppressed without one drop of blood. The Bulgarians would probably have continued plodding on as faithful subjects of the Porte, instead of being made—as will apparently be the case—a portion of the Slav group. Whether this fresh arrangement will succeed remains to be seen; but according to my experience of Bulgarian character, there is very little sympathy between it and the Slav. The Bulgarians have ever kept aloof from their Slavonic neighbours, and will continue a separate people even when possessed of independence.

The limits of Bulgaria, which must be drawn from an ethnological standpoint, are not very easily determined. The right of conquest and long possession no doubt entitles the Bulgarians to call their own the country extending from the Danube to the Balkans. South of that range and of Mount Scardos, however, *i.e.*, in the northern part of Thrace and Macedonia, their settlement was never permanent, and their capital, originally established in Lychnidos (the modern Ochrida), had to be removed north of the Balkans to Tirnova. The colonies they established were never very important, since they were scattered in the open country as better adapted to the agricultural and pastoral pursuits of the nation. These settlements, forming into large and small villages, took Bulgarian names, but the names of the towns remained Greek.

The Bulgarians south of the Balkans are a mixed race, neither purely Greek nor purely Bulgarian; but their manners and customs and physical features identify them more closely with the Greeks than with the Bulgarians north of the Balkans. There the Finnish type is clearly marked by the projecting cheek bones, the short upturned nose, the small eyes, and thickly-set but rather small build of the people.

In Thrace and Macedonia, where Hellenic blood and features predominate, and Hellenic influence is more strongly felt, the people call themselves Thracians and Macedonians, rather than Bulgarians; the Greek language, in schools, churches, and in correspondence, is used by the majority in preference to the Bulgarian, and even in the late church question in many places the people showed themselves luke-warm about the separation, and the bulk remained faithful to the Church of Constantinople.

The sandjak of Philippopolis, esteemed almost entirely Bulgarian by some writers, is claimed for the Greeks by others upon the argument that Stanimacho, with its fifteen villages, is Greek with regard to language and predilection, and Didymotichon, with its forty-five villages, is a mixture of Greeks and Bulgarians. As a matter of fact, however, in this sandjak, in consequence of its proximity to Bulgaria proper, and to its developed and prosperous condition, the Bulgarian element has taken the lead.

The revival of the church question and the educational movement have stayed and almost nullified Greek influence, which is limited to certain localities like Stanimacho and other places, where the people hold as staunchly to their Greek nationality as the Bulgarians of other localities do to their own. While dispute waxed hot in the town of Philippopolis between the parties of Greeks and Bulgarians, each in defence of its rights, no spirit of the kind was ever evinced in Adrianople, where the population is principally Greek and Turkish, with a small number of Armenians and Bulgarians. In Macedonia the sandjak of Salonika, comprising Cassandra, Verria, and Serres, numbering in all about 250,000 souls, is, with few exceptions, Greek, or so far Hellenised as to be so to all intents and purposes. The inhabitants of Vodena and Janitza, and the majority in Doïran and Stromnitza, and a considerable portion of the population of Avrat Hissar, on the right bank of the Vardar, claim Greek nationality. The Greeks in this part of the country have worked with the same tenacity of purpose and consequent success in Hellenising the people, as the Bulgarians of the kaza of Philippopolis in promoting the feeling of Bulgarian nationality there. This mission of the Greeks here has not been a very difficult one, as the national feeling of the bulk of the population is naturally Greek.

Notwithstanding the marked tendency of the people towards Hellenism, the language in Vodena and other places is Bulgarian; but the features of the people, together with their ideas, manners, and customs, are essentially Greek; even the dress of the Bulgarian-speaking peasant is marked by the absence of the typical *potour* and the *gougla* or cap worn in Bulgaria.

Most of the authors who have written on the populations of these regions have, either through Panslavistic views or misled by the prevalence of the Bulgarian language in the rural districts, put down the whole of the population as Bulgarian, a mistake easily corrected by a summary of the number of Greeks and Bulgarians conjointly occupying those districts, separating the purely Greek from the purely Bulgarian element, and taking into consideration at the same time the number of mixed Greeks and Bulgarians.

If the wide geographical limits projected by Russia for Bulgaria be carried out, there will be a recurrence of all the horrors of the recent war in a strife between the Greeks and Bulgarians, in consequence of the encroachment of the future Bulgaria upon territory justly laid claim to by the Greeks as ethnologically their own and as a heritage from past ages. The question would be greatly simplified and the danger of future contests between the two peoples much lessened if not entirely removed, by the Bulgarian autonomy being limited to the country north of the Balkans.

The Greek Government might not be equal at first to the administration of their newly-acquired kingdom, but if united in close alliance with some friendly power and placed under its tutelage, an honest and stable empire might be established with every probability of soon rising into a flourishing condition in the hands of a people whose intelligence, activity, and enterprising spirit give them an incontestable superiority over the other races of Turkey.

The Bulgarians south of the Balkans being, as before said, of a mixed race engrafted upon the Hellenic stock, would not be found to offer any serious opposition. They are closely incorporated with the Greek element in some districts; while in others, where Bulgarian feeling predominates, the people would willingly migrate to Bulgaria proper, as the Hellenised Bulgarians under such an arrangement would draw nearer to Greece; whilst in parts of Macedonia, where Hellenism has the ascendancy, very little difficulty would be met with from the Bulgarian settlements.

My recollections of Bulgarian social life are to a great extent derived from a three months' stay I made under the hospitable roof of a Bulgarian gentleman, or *Chorbadji*, as he was called by his own people. He was the most wealthy and influential person in the town of T——, where his position as member of the *Medjeiss* constituted him the chief guardian and advocate of the Bulgarian people of the district. I mention this in order to show the reader that in his house the opportunity of making important observations and of witnessing national characteristics were not wanting. These observations embraced the social features I was allowed to study in the midst of the home and family life both of the educated and thinking Bulgarians and of the peasants who daily flocked to the house of my friend from the towns and villages to submit to him their wrongs and grievances, and, as their national representative, to ask his advice and assistance before proceeding to the local courts.

These levées began sometimes as early as six o'clock in the morning, and lasted until eleven. The *Kodja-bashi*, or headmen, would come in a body to consult about the affairs of the community, or to represent some grave case pending before the local court of their respective towns; or groups of peasants of both sexes, sometimes representing the population of a whole village, would arrive, at the request of the authorities, to answer some demand made by them, or plead against an act of gross injury or injustice. Whatever the cause that brought them daily under my notice, the picture they presented was extremely curious and interesting, and the pleasure was completed by the privilege I enjoyed of afterwards obtaining a detailed account of the causes and grievances that brought them there. When the interested visitors happened to be elders of their little communities or towns, they were shown into the study of my host. After exchanging salutes and shaking hands, they were offered *slatko* (preserves) and coffee, and business was at once entered into. At such moments the Bulgarian does not display the heat and excitement that characterises the Greek, nor fall into the uproarious argument of the Armenians and Jews, nor yet display the finessing wit of the Turk; but steering a middle course between these different modes of action, he stands his ground and perseveres in his argument, until he has either made his case clear or is persuaded to take another view of it. The subjects that most animated the Bulgarians in these assemblies were their national affairs and their dissensions with the Greeks: the secondary ones were the wrongs and grievances they suffered from a bad administration; and although they justly lamented these, and at times bitterly complained of the neglect or incapacity of the Porte to right them in an effective manner and put a stop to acts of injustice committed by their Mohammedan neighbours and the local courts, I at no time noticed any tendency to disloyalty or revolutionary notions, or any disposition to court Russian protection, from which, indeed, the most enlightened and important portion of the nation at that period made decided efforts to keep aloof.

When it was the peasants who gathered at the Chorbadji's house, their band was led by its Kodja-Bashi, who, acting as spokesman, first entered the big gate, followed by a long train of his brethren. Ranged in a line near the porch, they awaited the coming of the master to explain to him the cause of their visit. Their distinguished-looking patron, pipe in hand, shortly made his appearance at the door, when caps were immediately doffed, and the right hands were laid on the breast and hidden by the shaggy heads bending over them in a salaam, answered by a kindly "Dobro deni" (good morning), followed by the demand "Shto sakaty?" (what do you want?) The peasants, with an embarrassed air, looked at each other, while the

Kodja-Bashi proceeded to explain matters. Should his eloquence fall short of the task, one or two others would step out of the ranks and become spokesmen. It was almost painful to see these simple people endeavouring to give a clear and comprehensive account of their case, and trying to understand the advice and directions of the Chorbadji. A half-frightened, surprised look, importing fear or doubt, a shrug of the shoulders, accompanied by the words "Né znam—Né mozhem" (I do not know, I cannot do), was generally the first expression in answer to the eloquence of my friend, who in his repeated efforts to explain matters frequently lost all patience, and would end by exclaiming "Né biddy magari!" (Don't be donkeys!)—a remark which had no effect upon the band of rustics further than to send them off, full of gratitude, to do as he had counselled.

Perhaps the reader may be curious to know the details of some of the cases daily brought under my notice. I will mention a few not connected with Turkish oppression and maladministration; for by this time the English public has been pretty well enlightened on that subject. My list will include some rather more original incidents which took place in the community: disputes between all non-Mussulmans are generally settled by the temporal or spiritual chiefs, and seldom brought before the Courts of Justice.

While Greeks and Bulgarians in the heat of controversy were snatching churches and monasteries from each other, the priests and monks who were attached to these sacred foundations found themselves unpleasantly jostled between the two hostile elements. To be a Greek priest or monk and be forced to acknowledge the supremacy of an anathematised and illegal church was a profanation not to be endured; and, on the other hand, to be a Bulgarian and be forced to pray day by day for a detested spiritual head rejected by his nation was an insupportable anomaly. In the midst of the difficulty and confusion at first caused by this state of affairs, some of the good fathers and monks had to remove their quarters and betake themselves to a wandering life, visiting their respective communities and encouraging the people by their exhortations to hold fast to their church and oppose with all their might the claims and usurping tendencies of the others. Among these a Bulgarian monk, more venturous and evidently endowed with a greater amount of imaginative eloquence than the rest, and rejoicing in the title of Spheti Panteleemon, regarded himself as the prophet of the Bulgarian people. This Saint Panteleemon was a man of middle age and middle height, with a jovial face, a cunning look, and an intelligent but restless eye, by no means indicative of an ascetic view of life.

Contrary to the saying that no man is a prophet in his own country, Spheti Panteleemon was acknowledged as such by a considerable class of his people, consisting entirely of the gentle sex, and his success among them was as great as ritualism appears to be in England.

The preaching of this prophet, intended solely for the Bulgarian women, became so pronounced in its tenets, so eloquent in its delivery, and was rendered so impressive by the different means he employed to instil his precepts into the hearts and minds of his hearers, that their number soon increased into a vast congregation, which flocked from all parts of the country to hear the words of their favourite saint. On such occasions, this false prophet, who had managed to usurp possession of a small monastery, would stand forth amid thousands of women, who at his approach would cross themselves and fall down almost to worship him. Spheti Panteleemon, in acknowledgment of this mark of devotion, would raise his voice and rehearse his doctrines to the devotees. These doctrines included strange principles, asserted by their author to be the best and surest way to Paradise; but they scarcely conduced to the satisfaction of the husbands. Women, according to this man, were to be free and independent, and their principal affections were to be bestowed upon their spiritual guide; their earnestness was to be proved by depositing their earthly wealth (consisting chiefly of their silver ornaments) at his feet. The practical Bulgarian husbands, however, were by no means admirers of this new spiritual director, whose sole object appeared to be to rob them of the affections of their wives along with their wealth, and they soon raised their voices against his proceedings. After holding counsel on the subject, they decided to give notice of his doings to the local authorities, and by their influence to have him sent out of the country. The prophet was arrested one fine morning, while addressing a congregation of 500 women, by a body of police, and brought to the prison of the town of S——, whilst all the women devoutly followed, weeping, beating their breasts, and clamouring for the release of their saint. The husbands, on the other hand, pleaded their grievances against this disorganiser of society, and proved his dishonesty by displaying to the authorities a quantity of silver trinkets of all descriptions taken from his dwelling, to the great indignation of his devotees. The imagination of some of these ignorant and superstitious peasant women had been so worked upon that they solemnly declared to me that the feet of their prophet never touched the ground, but remained always a distance of two feet above it, and that his sole sustenance was grass. While his fate was still undecided, amidst the wailings of the women, the protests of the husbands, and the embarrassment of the authorities, the fellow got out of the difficulty by declaring himself a "Uniate" and a member of the Church of Rome. This avowal could not fail to excite the interest of the agents of that body: they claimed the stray sheep as redeemed, took him under their immediate protection, but (it is to be hoped) deprived him of his pretended attribute of sanctity and the power of making himself any longer a central object of attraction to the *beau sexe*.

Another incident was of a nature less sensational but equally repulsive to the feelings and notions of the strict portion of the Bulgarian nation, and had also a monk for its hero. It consisted of an elopement, and if there is one crime that shocks and horrifies orthodox people more than another, it is that of a monk who, taking the vows of celibacy, perjures himself by adopting the respectable life of a married man. Such events are of very rare occurrence, and when they take place cause a great commotion.

This monk, at the time of the disputed church rights, lost his solitary retreat, and was once more thrown in contact with the world he had forsworn. Sent adrift, he set out in search of an unknown destiny, without hope or friends, uncertain where his next meal was to come from. After a long day's march, he lay down to rest under a tree in a cultivated field, and, overcome by fatigue, fell asleep. He was about twenty-five years of age, tall, with regular features, a startlingly pale complexion, and coal black eyes, hair, and beard; his whole appearance, indeed, rather handsome than otherwise. Such, at least, was the description given of him by the rustic beauty who surprised him while driving her father's cattle home.

A Bulgarian monk in those stirring times was always an object of interest, even to a less imaginative person than a young maiden. She, therefore, considered it her duty to watch over his slumbers, and refresh him with bread and salt on awaking. Quietly seating herself by his side, she awaited the arousal of the unconscious sleeper. When he awoke, his eyes met those of the girl, and in that exchange of looks a new light dawned upon these two beings, who, though they had never met before, were now to become dearer to each other than life itself. The monk forgot his vows, and poured forth his tale of love to a willing listener, who immediately vowed to follow his fortunes and become his wife, or end her days in a convent. This illustrates the definition of love once given to me by a Bulgarian gentleman: "Chez nous l'amour n'a point de préliminaires; on va droit au fait." The adventurous couple forthwith eloped, and wandered about the country, until the monk was discovered, in spite of his disguise, by the scandalised Bulgarians, by whom he was once more sent to a monastery, imprisoned in a dungeon, condemned to live upon dry bread and to undergo daily corporal chastisement for his sins. But the adventurous maiden, determined to effect his release, contrived to make friends with the Kir Agassi, or head of the mounted police in the district where the monastery was situated, and through his instrumentality the monk was again set at liberty. The subject was discussed in all its bearings at the house of my friends, until the couple wisely adopted Protestantism, and after being married by a minister of that church settled down to a peaceful life of domestic bliss.

A third incident illustrates the Bulgarian appreciation of surgical art. The name of surgeon was unknown in the country villages, and that of dentist, even in a large town like S——, until an adventurous spirit belonging to the latter profession, in the course of a speculative tour, established himself there. The inhabitants, on passing his house, used to stop and gaze in wonder at the sets of teeth displayed under glass cases. Conjecture ran wild as to how these were made and could be used. Some imagined them to be abstracted from the jaws of dead persons, salted, and prepared in some mysterious way for refitting in the mouths of the living.

The fame of the dentist's art began to be noised abroad throughout the district, and many became desirous, if not of procuring new teeth, at least of having some troublesome old stumps extracted. Among these was a well-to-do Bulgarian peasant, who presented himself in the surgery for this purpose. The dentist relieved him of his tooth with great facility, to the man's exceeding astonishment. On leaving, he took out his long knitted money-bag, carefully counted out five piastres (10*d*.), and handed them to the dentist, who returned them, saying that his fee would be half a lira. "What!" exclaimed the indignant Bulgarian; "do you mean to say that you will charge me so much, when last week I underwent the same operation at the hands of my barber, and after a struggle of two hours over an obstinate tooth, during which I had several times to lie flat on my back and he and I were both bathed in perspiration until it finally yielded, I paid him five piastres, with which he was quite contented; and you, who were only a few minutes over it, demand ten times that sum! It is simply monstrous, and I shall forthwith lodge a complaint against you!"

As good as his word, in a fever of excitement he arrived at the Chorbadji's house to denounce the extortionate Frank. When quietly asked if it were not worth while to pay a larger sum and get rid of his tooth without loss of time and trouble, instead of spending two hours of suffering and violent exertion for which he was charged only five piastres, he admitted that such was the case, and that the Frank was a far cleverer man than the barber could ever hope to be.

Social life among the Bulgarians differs little from that of the Greeks, save in the greater ascendancy the Bulgarian wives of the working classes have over their husbands. This advantage is probably derived from the masculine manner in which they share in the hardy toil, working by the side of their husbands, and by their personal exertions gaining almost as much as the men do. The care of clothing the family also devolves entirely upon them, besides which they have to attend to their domestic duties, which are always performed with care, cleanliness, and activity. Simple as these tasks may be, they require time, which the housewife always manages to find. The well beaten earthen floor is always neatly swept, the rugs and bedding carefully brushed and folded up, and the copper cooking utensils well scoured and ranged in their places. The cookery is simple but very palatable, especially the pastry, which is excellent; whilst the treacle and other provisions stored away for the winter are wholesome and good.

Some uninformed authors have, I believe, stated that not only are the Bulgarian men seldom to be seen in a state of sobriety, but that the women also indulge to a great extent in the vice of drunkenness. So far as I am able to judge, this statement is utterly groundless; for no woman in the east, whatever her nationality, disgraces herself by drinking to excess in the shops where spirituous drinks are sold, or is ever seen in the streets in a state of intoxication. The man certainly likes his glass, and on occasions freely indulges in it; but excesses are committed only on feast-days, when the whole village is given up to joviality and merriment.

The townspeople seldom indulge in these festivities; but tied down to a sedentary life, cheered by no view of the open country, nor by fresh air and the rural pursuits congenial to their nature, they lead a monotonous existence, divided between their homes and their calling. The women on their side fare no better, and with the exception of paying and receiving calls on feast-days, or taking a promenade, keep much within doors, occupying themselves with needlework and taking an active part in their domestic affairs. This quiet uniform life is occasionally brightened by an evening party, or even a ball, if the deficiency in the arrangement of the rooms, the refreshments, and especially the *sans gêne* observed with regard to dress, permit of the name. One of these festive scenes was illuminated by large home-made tallow candles, supported by candelabra of Viennese manufacture, further supplemented by another innovation in the shape of a pair of elegant snuffers, which fortunately obviated the usual performance with the fingers, by which the ball-rooms are usually perfumed with the odour of burnt mutton chops. Setting aside minor details, my attention was much attracted by the queer versatility of the band, which suddenly changed from the national *hora* to an old-fashioned polka which had just been introduced as a great novelty, but was indulged in only by married couples, or timid brothers and sisters, who held each other at so respectful a distance that another couple might easily have passed between them. But the greatest charm of the gathering was the *coup d'œil* that embraced dress, deportment, and decorations. The dress was as varied in shape and material as the forms of the wearers. Double and triple fur coats, according to age and taste, safely sheltered the majority of the gentlemen from cold and draughts; well-fitting frock coats distinguished the few *comme il faut* officials; while dress coats of Parisian cut distinguished the quiet and apparently gentlemanlike youths brought up in Europe, and contrasted with the less elegant toilettes of their untravelled brethren dressed *à la Bulgare*.

The variety in the dress of the ladies was equally diverting. Some wore their fur jackets over rich silk dresses, others, more fashionable, dispensed with the weight of this unnecessary article; while the heads of all of them sparkled with jewelry. Crinoline, often heard of under the name of "Malakoff," but unseen in the town before 1855, was supposed to be introduced into the room by a German Jewish lady, an old resident in the town, and was so proudly displayed by her in all its proportions, that it attracted the attention of a homely old Bulgarian *gospoyer*, who, in a simple manner, quietly turned up the hem of her dress and displayed to a small section of the astonished assembly an ingenious substitute for the crinoline made of *The Times* newspaper!

The chapter on Peasant-holdings treats at some length of the Bulgarian peasant, of his capacity for work, and the amount of ease and prosperity he is able to attain in spite of the many drawbacks that surround him. His prosperity is due to two sources—the modesty of his wants, and the activity of his whole family. The fruits of such a system are naturally good when the soil, climate, and other natural advantages favour it.

But some parts of Bulgaria are far from being the Utopia some newspaper correspondents have represented it, with vines hanging over every cottage-door, and milk and honey flowing in the land. Nothing but long residence and personal experience can enable one to arrive at a true estimate of such matters.

Though in some parts I found the scenery delightful, the prosperity of the inhabitants astonishing, and Moslems and Christians rivalling each other in hospitable kindness to the traveller, some spots were anything but romantic or prosperous, and far from happy-looking. Some villages, in particular, I noticed in the midst of a dreary plain, such as the traveller may see on the road from Rodosto to Adrianople, where the soil looks dry and barren, and the pastures grow yellow and parched before their time, and where flying bands of Circassian thieves and cut-throats hover about like birds of prey. I was once travelling through the country, riding the whole of one day on such bad roads, that the mud often reached up to my horse's knees, and the carriage containing my maid and the provisions often came to a dead stop, while the rain poured incessantly. The journey appeared interminable, and as darkness crept on and several miles of road still separated us from our projected halting-place, I made up my mind to stop at an isolated village for the night. So traversing fresh pools of mud we entered the hamlet, and were met by the Kodja-Bashi, a poorly-clad, miserable-looking individual, who led our party into his farmyard. On alighting from my horse I was ushered into a dark, bare, dismal hovel, without windows, and lighted only by a hole in the roof, through which escaped some of the smoke from a few dung-cakes smouldering in a corner. One or two water-jars stood near the door, and an earthen pot, serving for all culinary purposes, was placed by the fire, in front of which was spread a tattered mat occupied by a few three-legged stools. A bundle of uninviting rags and cushions, the family bedding, was stowed in a corner, and in another were seen a few pots and pans, the whole "table-service" of the occupants.

This hovel was attached to a similar one opening into it, where I heard some bustle going on. I was told that a member of the family who occupied it and was seriously ill was being removed to a neighbour's house. Much annoyed at having caused so much trouble and disturbance to the unfortunate sufferer, I asked my host why he had not placed me in another cottage. "Well, *gospoyer*," answered he, with an apologetic gesture, "poor and wretched as my home is, it is the best the village possesses. The rest are not fit to kennel your dogs in. As for my daughter, I could not but remove her, as her cries during the night would prevent your sleeping." I inquired her complaint, and was told that she was in high fever, and suffered from sharp pains all over her body. There was no doctor to attend her, nor had she any medicine but the decoctions prepared for her by the old *bulkas*.

I visited the poor creature and gave what help I could; but, being by no means reassured as to the nature of her malady, and unwilling to sleep in the vicinity of an infected room, I ordered the carriage to be placed under a shed and proposed to pass the night in it. The host, however, on hearing this, told me that it was quite impracticable, as the village dogs were so famished that they would be sure to attack the carriage for the sake of the leather on it. "I have taken the precaution," he added, " of removing every part that is liable to be destroyed, but there is no telling what these animals will do." I then ordered the hamper to be brought in and supper to be prepared; but on sitting down on the floor to partake of it we discovered that our provision of bread was exhausted, and learnt that not a morsel was procurable in the village. Our host explained this by saying, "You see, *gospoyer*, our village is so poor and miserable that we have no drinkable water, and our *bulkas* have to fetch it from a distance of three miles. We have no fuel either, for the village has no forest, and we content ourselves with what you see on the hearth. As for bread, it is a luxury we seldom enjoy; millet flour mixed with water into a paste and baked on the ashes, is our substitute for it; it does for us, but would not please you."

In the meantime the women and children had gathered round me in the little room, all looking so poor, fever-stricken, and miserable, and casting such looks of eager surprise at the exhibition of eatables before me, that I felt positively sick at heart; all my appetite left me, and distributing my supper among the hungry crowd, I contented myself with a cup of tea, and endeavoured to forget in sleep the picture of misery I had witnessed. I was thankful to get away in the morning, and am happy to say, that neither before nor since have I witnessed such poverty and misery as I saw in that village.

The marked slowness of perception in the character of the Bulgarian peasants, and their willingness to allow others to think and act for them in great matters, is not so apparent when the immediate interests of the village or community are concerned. Before referring these to the higher authorities, they meet and quietly discuss their affairs, and often settle the differences among themselves. The respect the Bulgarian entertains for the clergy and for the enlightened portion of his fellow-countrymen is so great that he allows himself to be entirely guided by them, evincing in small things as well as great the feeling of harmony and union that binds the whole people together. But the reverse of this disposition is manifested by the Bulgarians, more especially the peasants, towards any foreign element, and particularly towards the Turkish authorities. Obedient and submissive as they have generally shown themselves under the Ottoman rule, they have inwardly always disliked and distrusted it, saying that the government with regard to their country, its richest field of harvest, has only one object in view—that of getting as much out of it as possible.

This prevalent idea, not altogether ill-founded, gave to the Bulgarian character that rapacity and love of gain which, being developed by late events, in the midst of general ruin and loss of property, tempted him to try to get what he could of what had been left, without much scruple as to the means. When unmerited calamities befall a people, and oppression long weighs heavily upon them, the sense of justice and humanity is gradually lost and replaced by a spirit of vindictiveness which incites to ignoble and cruel actions. This ought not to surprise the world in the case of the Bulgarians, when their national life during the last two years is taken into consideration; for what is it but a series of unspeakable outrages by their enemies, and destruction by those who professed themselves their friends?

The Bulgarians, however, as I have known them in more peaceful times, never appeared to possess as national characteristics the vices that hasty and partial judges arguing from special instances have attributed to them. On the contrary, they seemed a peace-loving, hard-working people, possessing many domestic virtues which, if properly developed under a good government, might make the strength of an honest and promising state.

CHAPTER II.

THE GREEKS OF TURKEY.

Importance of the Greeks at the present moment—Their Attitude—The Greek Peasant as Contrasted with the Bulgarian—His Family—Eloquence—Patriotism—Comforts—The Women—A Greek Girl—Women of the towns of the Upper Class—Of the Lower Class—Wives and Husbands—Greek Parties—The Conservatives and the Progressives—A Conversation on Greek Go-a-head-ness—Physical Features of the Modern Greek—Character—General Prejudice—A Prussian Estimate—Greek Vices—An Adventure with Greek Brigands—Adelphé—Unscrupulousness in Business—Causes and Precedents—Jews and Greeks—Summary.

ALL eyes are now turned upon the Greek race as one of the most important factors in the Eastern Question. The future of South-Eastern Europe is seen to lie in the balance between Greek and Slav, and people's opinions incline to one side or the other as dread of Russia or distrust of "Greek guile" gets the upper hand. I have nothing to say here about the people of free Hellas: I have only to tell what I have witnessed of the character and condition of the subject Greeks in Turkey. These, though they shared in the national effort of 1821-9, reaped little of the fruits. The Greeks of Macedonia, Thessaly, and Thrace did not gain the freedom accorded to the people of "Greece Proper," though their condition was somewhat improved. But they are only biding their time. They know that their free countrymen are anxious to share with them the results of the glorious struggle of 1821. They know that centuries of subjection and oppression have demoralised and debased the nation; and they have long been striving with their whole strength to prepare themselves for freedom. They have employed the time of transition with great moderation and judgment. Those whom the Porte has appointed to high offices have filled their posts with conscientiousness, fidelity, and dignity. Taught worldly wisdom in the school of adversity, they have avoided premature conspiracy and rebellion, and have directed all their energies to educating the race for its future. "Improve and wait patiently" is the motto of the Greeks in Turkey.

The Greek peasant differs greatly from the Bulgarian. Agriculture is not all the world to him; his love for the pursuit is decidedly moderate unless he sees an opening for enterprise and speculation, as in the growth of some special kind of produce which he can sell in the raw condition or as manufactured goods. Unlike the Bulgarian, his whole family is not chained to the soil as the one business of life. When the paterfamilias can dispense with the services of some of his daughters, they leave their home in pursuit of occupation, and his sons in the same manner are allowed to quit the paternal roof in search of some more lucrative employment elsewhere. It is thus that the Greek is to be found in every nook and corner of Turkey, established among his own kindred or with foreigners, and following various professions and callings, as doctors, lawyers, schoolmasters; whilst, descending to a lower scale, we find him employed in every town and village as a petty tradesman, mason, carpenter, shoemaker, musician, in all which occupations he manages by dint of energy, perseverance, and address, to obtain a modest competence, or sometimes even to reach prosperity.

I remember, among other instances of the kind, the case of a Greek peasant family in the district of B——. The father was a respectable man, who owned a small property in his native village, and whose quiver was filled with eight children. The eldest remained to assist on the farm; two others of tender age also remained under the mother's care; the other five, including a girl, left their home, and came to the town. One of the boys and the girl took service with me; a second boy apprenticed himself to a photographer, another became a painter of church pictures, and the fourth a cigarette maker. The salaries these young peasants received were at first very meagre; but all the same the four boys clubbed their savings together, and after a time sent for their younger brother to live in town in order to enjoy the benefit of receiving a good education. Six years passed, during which the boy and his pretty and intelligent sister remained in my house; both learned to speak English, the boy having studied the language grammatically in his leisure moments. They are now honest, intelligent servants, perfect in the performance of their duties, and devoted to my family. The three apprentices, through their steadiness, good conduct, and energy, have become proficient enough in their different callings to set up for themselves, while the boy at school is one of the most advanced students of the *Gymnasium*.

The intellectual position of the Greeks is far superior to that of the Bulgarians. They are cleverer, and they and their children are more advanced in education. They display a great interest in passing events, as well as in politics, a knowledge of which they obtain by means of the numerous Greek newspapers they receive from Athens, Constantinople, and all the large towns of Turkey. These journals find their way to the remotest hamlets, one or two being sufficient to make the round of a village. They also possess other literature in the shape of the history of their country, biographies of some of their illustrious ancestors, and national songs in the vernacular. All these make a deep impression upon the entire population, who, after the conclusion of the labours of the day, gather together in the taverns and coffeehouses to discuss matters, talking excellent sense over the coffee-cup, or waxing hot and uproarious over their wine and *raki*.

The Greek peasant displays none of the embarrassment and tonguetiedness of the Bulgarian. I have often met with instances of this: one especially struck me which happened in the early part of last summer in the vilayet of B——. Some Bashi-bazouks had entered a village, and committed some of their usual excesses; but the peasants had found time to send away their wives and daughters to a place of safety. On the following day a body of fifty Greeks came to complain to the authorities. In order to render their claims more effective, they applied for protection at the different Consulates. I happened to be at luncheon at one of these Consulates, and the Consul ordered the men to be shown into the dining-room to make their statements. One at once stepped forward to give an account of the affair, which he related with so much eloquence and in such pure modern Greek that the Consul, suspecting him to be some lawyer in disguise, or a special advocate of Greek grievances, set him aside, and called upon another to give his version. Several looked questioningly at each other, but with no sign of embarrassment; on the contrary, the expression on each face betokened natural self-confidence, and meant in this instance to say, " We can each tell the tale equally well, but I had better begin than you."

Patriotism is highly developed among the Greek peasants, who are fully aware of the meaning of the word *patris,* and taught to bear in mind that half a century ago free Hellas formed part of the Ottoman Empire; that its inhabitants, like themselves, were a subject people, and owe the freedom they now enjoy to self-sacrifice and individual exertion. "They are our elder brothers," say they, "who have stepped into their inheritance before us. There is a just God for us as well!"

The wants of the Greek are more numerous than those of the Bulgarians. Their dress, for instance, is not limited to a coarse suit of *aba* and a sheepskin *gougla,* but is sometimes made of fine cloth and other rich materials, and includes shoes and stockings. The culinary department also demands more utensils; besides which, tables, table-linen, knives and forks are often seen at their meals. The bedding they use is more complete, and does not consist solely of rugs, as with the Bulgarians. Their houses are better built, with some regard to comfort and appearance, frequently with two stories, besides possessing chimneys and windows (when safe to do so). The village schools are better organised, and kept under the careful supervision of the Society for their direction, and the churches are more numerous. The women are less employed in field work, and consequently more refined in their tastes, prettier in appearance, and more careful and elegant in their dress. The Greek peasant girl knows the value of her personal charms, and disdains to load herself with the tarnished trinkets, gaudy flowers, and other wonderful productions in which the Bulgarian maiden delights. A skirt of some bright-coloured silk or mixed stuff and a cloth jacket embroidered with gold form the principal part of her gala costume, covered with a fur-lined pelisse for out-of-door wear. Her well-combed hair is plaited in numerous tresses, and surmounted by the small Greek cap, which is decorated with gold and silver coins like those she wears as a necklace. She is not to be bought, like the Bulgarian, for a sum of money paid to her father as an equivalent for her services; but according to her means is dowered and given in marriage, like the maidens of classical times. Still the peasant girl is neither lazy nor useless; she takes an active part in the duties of the household, is early taught to knit and spin the silk, flax, wool, or cotton which the mother requires for the different home-made tissues of the family. She leads her father's flock to the pasture, and under the title of *Voskopoula* kindles a flame in the heart of the village youth and inspires the rustic muse. On Sundays and feast days she enters heartily into all the innocent pleasures of her retired and isolated life. She has more pride than the Bulgarian; and although in married life she is submissive and docile, she possesses a greater depth and richness of love. I have known instances of peasant girls exchanging vows with youths of their village who are leaving their home in search of fortune, and patiently waiting for them and refusing all offers in the meantime. In most cases this devotion is requited by equal constancy on the part of the lover; but should she be deserted, her grief is so terrible that she not seldom dies from the blow.

If there is more than one daughter in a family, some from the age of twelve or fourteen are usually sent to town and placed out as servants, with the double object of giving them the opportunity of seeing more of the world and the means of earning something for their own maintenance. These earnings as they are acquired are converted into gold coins and strung into necklaces.

When these girls are honest and good, and fall into proper hands, they are usually adopted by the family with whom they take service, under the title of ψυχόπαιδα. On reaching the age of twenty-five or twenty-seven a trousseau is given to them with a small dowry, and they are married to some respectable artisan. Those simply hired as servants either marry in the towns or do so on returning to their native village.

The Greek peasant women are as a rule clean and industrious, fond mothers and virtuous wives. The best proof of their morality is in the long absences many husbands are obliged to make from their homes, which are attended by no unfaithful results. In some instances for a period of even twenty years the wife becomes the sole director of the property, which she manages with care and wisdom, and the only guardian of the children left in her charge.

The peasants who still cling to the soil plod away at their daily toil in very much the same way as the Bulgarians, but show a greater aptitude for rearing the silkworm and growing olives and grapes. The Greek peasants are not models of perfection; but as a body, they are better than any other race in Turkey, and under a good government they are certain to improve and develope much faster than either the Bulgarians or the Turks.

The Greek women of the towns, according to their station and the amount of refinement and modern ideas they have been imbued with, display in their manners and mode of living the virtues and faults inherent in the Greek character. I must in justice state that the former exceed the latter; their virtues consist principally in their quality of good honest wives, and in the simple lives they are usually content to lead in their homes. The enlightenment and conversational talents of some of the better class do not fall far short of those of European ladies. Those less endowed by education and nature, have a quiet modest bearing, and evince a great desire to improve. The most striking faults in the Greek woman's character are fondness of dress and display, vanity, and jealousy of the better circumstances of her neighbours. The spirit of envious rivalry in dress and outward appearance is often carried to such a pass that the real comforts of home-life are sacrificed, and many live poorly and dress meanly on ordinary occasions in order to display a well-furnished drawing-room and expensive holiday costumes to the public. When living in the town of N——, I was taken into the confidence of the Archbishop's niece, who was my neighbour. She confessed to me that on promenade days she regularly stationed her servant at the end of the street in order to inspect the toilette of her rival, the wife of the richest *chorbadji*, so that she might be able to eclipse her.

Greek ladies are fond and devoted mothers, but they are not systematic in rearing their children. This has, however, been remedied in many cases by children of both sexes being placed from a very early age in the care of governesses, or at school, where the more regular training they receive cannot fail to have beneficial results.

The life of women of the working classes is still more homely and retired, as it is considered an impropriety to be seen much out of doors, especially in the case of young girls, whom prejudice keeps very secluded, even to the length of seldom allowing them to go to church. When abroad, however, their fondness for display is equal to that of their richer sisters, whose toilettes, however novel or complicated, in cities like Constantinople and Smyrna, are sure to be copied by the fishermen's or washerwomen's daughters. In provincial towns like Rodosto and Adrianople, the love of dress finds its satisfaction in bright colours and wreaths of artificial flowers, especially the much coveted carnation, when out of season, which is worn by some as a love-trophy: for it must have been given by some lover on the feast-day. Greek girls are very clever at needlework and embroidery; but their life is nevertheless monotonous, and they have little variety of occupation and amusement. This is owing in part to the exclusion of women of all races in Turkey from occupations in shops, and to the absence of manufactories, which, with the exception of some silk factories, do not exist in the country. Those in the silk-growing districts, however, give employment to a number of Greek girls, who show great aptitude for this branch of industry and often become directresses of establishments in which Armenian and other women are employed.

The affection of a Greek wife for her husband is joined to a jealous care of his interest; she will strive to hide his faults and weaknesses, and the disinterested devotion with which she will cling to him in prosperity and adversity is astonishing. A woman belonging to the town of S——, on hearing that her husband had been arrested on a charge of complicity with brigands, left her home and five children to the care of a blind grandmother, and set out on foot on a three days' journey to the town where he was to be tried. He was condemned to seven years' imprisonment, and sent to the prison at A——, whither she followed him. Young and pretty, entirely friendless, and without means of subsistence, she lingered about the Greek quarter until her sad tale gained her an asylum in a compassionate family. She toiled hard to gain a small pittance, which she divided between herself and her unhappy partner shut up in the common prison. The dreadful news was brought to her that three of her children were dead, that her house was falling to pieces, and that her aged and afflicted mother was unable to take care of the two surviving little ones. Unmoved by these calamities she refused to quit the town of A—— until, through the instrumentality of some influential persons whose sympathies she had enlisted, her husband's period of punishment was shortened.

Greek society may be divided into two classes, the conservative party and the progressive. The former, in the provincial towns, are jealous of their rights and privileges as elders of the community and representatives of the nation in the *Medjliss*. In many instances these side with the authorities in acts of injustice, sometimes from timidity and sometimes from interested motives. This small retrograde class is also strongly opposed to the progress of education and often hinders it by stint of money and general hostility to all changes.

The second class consists of the educated members of the community, who earn their fortunes in much the same way as the rest of the civilized world, and spend it liberally in comforts and luxuries, and for the benefit of the nation—an object to which every Greek tries to contribute in some degree. The motto of this party is *Embros!* (Forward!) They are stopped by no difficulties and overcome by no drawbacks, either in their personal interests or those of the nation. Their success in enterprise should no longer (as formerly) be attributed to disloyalty, dishonesty, and intrigue—in these respects there is no reason for believing them worse than their neighbours—but to the wonderful energy and ability they show in all their undertakings. I heard a conversation some time ago between two medical celebrities of Constantinople with reference to the Greek spirit of enterprise and ambition. One praised their enterprise as a promising quality, and to use his own expression, said, "There is an immense amount of 'go' in the Greek."

"Go!" repeated the other, waxing hot, "Too much so, I believe: there is no telling where a Greek's enterprising spirit may not lead him, or where his ambition will stop! Listen to my experience on the subject and judge for yourself. Some years ago I was asked by a good old Greek I know very well to take his son, a youth of twenty, into my service. According to the father's recommendation, he was a good Greek scholar and knew a little Latin. I asked the father in what capacity I was to engage him. 'Any you like,' was the reply: 'let him be your servant—your slave.' 'Very well; but he will have to clean my boots and look after my clothes!' 'πολὺ καλὰ' was the response, and I engaged his son.

"On the following day my new valet entered upon his duties. He was a good-looking, smart, and intelligent fellow, and at first exact and able in the performance of his functions; but gradually he became lax, absent in manner, and negligent; although steady and quiet in his conduct. One day the mystery of this change was revealed on my returning home unexpectedly, and finding the fellow, instead of cleaning my boots, which he held in his hand, deeply plunged in one of the medical works on my table. In my anger at seeing my papers and books meddled with, I brought my boots into contact with his head, telling him that if ever I caught him again at that sort of thing, he would be punished more severely. 'Forgive me,' said he, in a very penitent manner, and walked demurely out of the room. He showed, however, no signs of improvement, and subsequently I discovered him committing no less a piece of impertinence than copying some prescriptions that lay on my desk. This was too much; so, as a punishment, I made him take one of the potions; but on the next day he calmly told me that the *iatrico* had done him good, having calmed his blood and cleared his head! Of course, I dismissed the fellow and replaced him by an Armenian, who answered my purpose better, though he did dive now and then rather extensively into the larder. For some years I lost sight of my former valet and had forgotten his very existence till it was brought to my recollection in the following unexpected manner. I one day received a pressing message to go at once to the house of D— Pasha to see a sick child and hold a consultation with his new *hekim bashi* (doctor) on its case. At the appointed hour I went, and on entering the konak was ushered into the selamlik to await the arrival of the other doctor who was to lead me into the harem. In a few minutes my supposed colleague walked in, hat and gold-headed stick in one hand, while the other was extended to me, with the words 'καλημέρα, ἰατρέ' (good morning, doctor). The face and voice transfixed me for a moment, but the next presented to me the fact that my former valet stood before me, claiming the right of holding a consultation with me. Whereat I was on the point of giving vent to my indignation, by seizing him by the collar and ejecting him from the apartment, when he quietly said, 'Excuse me, ἰατρέ, but I stand before you in right of the diploma I have obtained from Galata Serai. Allow me to submit it to your learned and honourable nspection.' There was no denying the fact; the fellow's diploma was in perfect order. My anger cooling, I consented to consult with him, when he again incensed me by venturing to take a view of the case opposed to mine. His opposition, however, was only momentary; for, taking the upper hand, I dictated my directions to him, and he, yielding with a good grace to my experience, carried out my orders with great precision. I had subsequently many opportunities of meeting him, and must in justice say that he turned out one of the best pupils of Galata Serai, and the most grateful man I have ever known. He is at present attached to the Red Cross Society, to which he gives the greatest satisfaction."

In feature and build the modern Greek still possesses the characteristic traits of his ancestors. Scientific researches and anatomical observations made upon the skulls of ancient Greeks are said to prove that if art had glorified to a slight extent the splendid models of statues, it could not have strayed very far from the originals. Such pure and perfect types are constantly met with at the present day in the modern Greeks, who, as a rule, possess fine open foreheads, straight noses, and fine eyes full of fire and intelligence, furnished with black lashes and well-defined eyebrows; the mouths are small or of medium size, with a short upper lip; the chin rather prominent, but rounded. The entire physiognomy differs so essentially from the other native types, that it is impossible to mistake it. In stature the Greek is rather tall than otherwise, well-made and well-proportioned; the hands and feet are small in both sexes. The walk is graceful, but has a kind of swagger and ease in it, which, although it looks natural in the national costume, seems affected in the European dress.

The distinct Greek type, so noticeable in certain localities, has in others suffered from the admixture with foreign elements; but we find it again in all its perfection in the inhabitants of the coast of Asia Minor, where the Greeks were at one epoch so crushed and denationalised as to have lost the use of their mother-tongue. Some of the finest specimens of the Greek race may be found in Smyrna, Gemlek, and Philadar, as well as in more inland places, such as Mahalitch, Demirdesh, and Kellessen.

The influence and effects of the last and most important change must be carefully followed and the transformation already wrought upon the nation taken into consideration before a fair and impartial estimate of the character of the present Greeks can be arrived at. The nation in its present scattered condition presents great variety and dissemblance; but even these points, in my opinion, constitute its force and guarantee its future prosperity. No person well acquainted with modern Greece can contest the vast improvement in the national character during the last half century, the moral development already gained, and the prosperous condition the little kingdom has now entered upon. The educated and enlightened *rayah* follows closely in the footsteps of his liberated kinsmen, and bids fair some day to catch them up. Until recent times the real advance in the Greek character seems to have escaped the notice of European critics, and in obedience to ancient prejudice it is still the fashion to cry down the future queen of South-East Europe. A charitable Prussian diplomatist, writing with more zeal than knowledge, gave the following flattering portrait of the Greeks of Constantinople at the end of the last century:—"Le quartier est la demeure de ce qu'on appelle la noblesse grecque, qui vivent tous aux dépenses des princes de Moldavie et de Valachie. C'est une université de toutes les scélératesses, et il n'existe pas encore de langue assez riche pour donner des noms à toutes celles qui s'y commettent. Le fils y apprend de bonne heure à assassiner adroitement son père pour quelque argent qu'il ne saurait être poursuivi. Les intrigues, les cabales, l'hypocrisie, la trahison, la perfidie, surtout l'art d'extorquer de l'argent de toutes mains, y sont enseignés méthodiquement!"

An English author of more recent date, but neither more enlightened nor animated with a greater sense of justice or impartiality, denies their right to a national history or their possession of an ancestry, furnishing them instead with one out of his fertile imagination. According to him several millions of Greeks are nameless homeless upstarts, who have invariably made their fortunes by following the trade of *bakals* or chandlers, and, with the enormous and illegal profits of their business, send their sons to Athens to be educated and receive a European varnish, then to return to Turkey full of pretension and bad morals, to sow discord and create mischief among their less enlightened brethren. Such absurd statements carry their own refutation; but they mislead people who are already prejudiced and ready to believe anything bad of the Greeks. The general currency such erroneous assertions receive, even in England, the country of Byron and the seamen of Navarino, struck me in a remark lately made by an intelligent English boy of twelve, who, happening to hear the Greeks mentioned at the luncheon table, asked his mother if all the Greeks were not cut-throats?

These fallacies are gradually being cleared away. As a nation the Greeks possess undeniable virtues and talents, which, properly encouraged and guided, have in them the making of a strong progressive people—such as one day the Greeks will assuredly be. Their faults are as distinct and prominent as their virtues. In the careful and impartial examination a long residence has enabled me to make of the character of this people, I discovered a good deal of vanity, bravado, and overweening conceit. They are vain of their ability, and still more vain of the merits and capacity of free Hellas, of which they are so enamoured as to consider this little kingdom, in its way, on a level with the Great Powers. The spirit of bravado is often shown in animated disputes and controversies, for which they have a great partiality. They are subtle, extremely sensitive, fond of gain, but never miserly. Their enthusiastic nature, given free scope, will lead them into the doing of golden deeds; and, in the same way, bad influence will make of some the most finished rogues in creation. No Greek thief of Constantinople will be beaten in daring or in the art of carrying out a *coup de main*. No assassin will more recklessly plunge his knife into the heart of an enemy, no seducer be more enticing, no brigand more dashing and bold. And yet in the worst of these there is some redeeming quality; a noble action polluted by many bad ones; crimes often followed by remorse and a return to a steady and honest life. Gratitude for a good service is always met with among the Greeks, as among the Albanians. An example of this may be seen in an adventure that more than twenty years ago happened to an Englishman in the Government employ, who was travelling in a province infested by brigands. Armed and accompanied by a good escort, Mr. F. had set out during the night for the town of L——, and following the impulse of an adventurous spirit, he strayed away from his companions in a dense forest. The light of a full moon made the path quite distinct, and he had proceeded some distance, when his bridle was suddenly seized by some fierce-looking fellows, who appeared by his side as if by magic. Mr. F.'s surprise was as great as the action was menacing; but he instantly seized his revolver, and thought on the prudence of using it, when the "capitan," a regular *leromenos*,* sprang forward, and a struggle ensued for its possession, in which the weapon was broken. The moment was critical, the danger imminent, for self-defence was out of the question with a broken revolver. In this emergency, with the presence of mind which characterises him, Mr. F. thought of another means of protection, and removing the white cover of his official cap, pointed out the crown on it, and declared himself a servant of the British Government. This had the desired effect, for the chief released his hold of the bridle, and retired a short distance with his companions to hold a consultation, the result of which was his again stepping forward, and inquiring if the gentleman was the son of the consul of the town of T——, and being answered in the affirmative, the "capitan," with much feeling,

---

* *Leromenos* signifies *soiled*, which among the Greeks is the highest title of a brigand bravo, evinced in the filth of his long worn and unwashed *fustanalla*.

declared he was free to pursue his way, for his father had rendered many good and noble services to the Greek families of Thessaly and Epirus, and had saved the lives and property of many others. "Besides," added he, "we love and respect the English. But a few miles hence you will fall in with the camp of old A. Pasha, who, with 800 troops and two guns, intends to surround yonder mountain, where he expects to entrap and chase us like wild beasts. The price of your freedom is your word of honour not to reveal to him your meeting with us until to-morrow; when that is given, your escort will be allowed to pass unmolested." Mr. F. then continued his journey, and a couple of hours brought him to the camp of his friend the brigand-chasing Pasha, who gave him an excellent supper, and entertained him with the plan of his next day's assault on the brigand band, to which he had patiently to listen, bound as he was by his word not to reveal what he knew of their whereabouts until the next day. As the game the Pasha expected to entrap escaped him on the morrow, the revelation naturally annoyed him; but he was too well aware of the value an Englishman placed upon his pledged word, even to a brigand, to find fault with the reticence of his friend on that occasion.

The Greek aristocracy has almost disappeared, and the nation seems now eminently democratic, though fond of giving titles to persons of position, such as "Your Worship," "Your Honour," "Your Highness," etc., and "Your Holiness" to the clergy. Such terms are smoothly introduced in epistolary addresses or used in conversation, so long as this is carried on with calmness and reflection; but directly discussion becomes animated, and the speaker, whatever his condition, excited, all such highflown phrases are discarded and exchanged for that more natural to the Greek fraternal feeling, the word "Adelphé" (brother), which never fails to grate upon the ear of Englishmen in the East.

It certainly had this effect upon one of our old consuls who had rather a hasty temper and was a strict observer of etiquette. On one occasion he had to listen to an excited Greek who had a dispute with another, and heard the title of Adelphé addressed to him by the complainant, who, to make matters worse, was by no means such a respectable person as could be wished. The indignant consul exclaimed in Greek, "Brother! I am no brother of yours!" and was proceeding to render his assurance more effectual by a vigorous and unexpected movement of his foot, when he lost his balance and was stretched on the floor. This unforeseen aspect of affairs appeared so comical to him that he indulged in a hearty peal of laughter, in which the Greek, though politely asking after his injuries, joined—in his sleeve.

The charges raised most frequently against the Greeks are their want of honesty in their dealings with strangers, and their general unscrupulousness in business transactions. These accusations, in great part well founded, are due to the unnatural position in which the rayah is placed. Every Greek, who is truly a Greek in heart, (and I have known few who were not so,) must detest and dislike his rulers, and direct his energies to promoting, openly or secretly, the interest of his nation. In order to do this, however, he must work in the dark, and strive to undermine the interests of his masters: consequently the mask of hypocrisy has to be worn by all in the same way. To cheat the Turks in small matters when he can, in revenge for grosser injuries he is liable to receive from them, becomes one of his objects. His is not the only subject race that evinces a laxity of principle and want of morality in the transaction of business. He is sharp in its dispatch, perhaps sharper than some others, but no worse than they in the manner in which he carries on his trade.

I have often heard this subject discussed in all its bearings, and the statements of European as well as native merchants appeared to agree on the main point—that with the corrupt administration, and the perpetual necessity of having recourse to bribery in order to facilitate the course of business, honest and straightforward dealing was out of the question. "We must," said a wealthy French merchant, "do in Turkey as the Turks do, or else seek a fortune elsewhere."

The following incident out of innumerable others will give an idea of how enterprise is encouraged and business carried on in this country.

Some Jews in the town of L—— had established a soap factory, producing a bad article and selling it at high prices. Subsequently some Cretan Greeks set up a rival establishment in the same town. The Cretans enjoyed a great repute in Turkey for this branch of industry, and offered their soaps to the public at a lower price than the Jews, who were thrown into the shade; these therefore had to invent some plan to ruin their rivals. Both factories imported their own oil from the Greek islands, and paid the duties in kind or in cash. The Greeks adopted the former method, and the Jews, aware of the fact, presented themselves at the customhouse, estimated the oil the Greeks received at double its value, and transported a portion of it to their premises, thus obliging the Greeks to pay double duty—a serious matter, which, if not remedied, would ruin their business. They decided upon offering the Jews privately half of the extra duty they were called upon by them to pay to the revenue. But on a second cargo of oil being imported they abstained from paying that sum to the Jews, who thereupon made them pay double duty a second time, which so exasperated the Greeks that they resolved to have their revenge. So sending a fresh order for oil, they instructed their agent to have two of the barrels filled with water, and marked with some sign. This cargo on arriving was left by the Greeks in the custom-house until the Friday afternoon, when they went to clear it. The Jews, made aware of this fact by their spies, also presented themselves, estimated the oil, as formerly, at double its value, and offered to purchase the two barrels left as payment of duty. The Greeks prolonged the affair until there was only just time for the Jews to take away their purchase, but not to inspect it without breaking the Sabbath. On the following evening the Jews discovered the trick that had been played upon them, and exposed it to the custom-house officials, demanding redress. The Greeks, summoned to appear and answer the charge, denied that the swindle had been practised by them, and exposed the dishonest dealings of the Jews towards them, saying that it must have been they who abstracted the oil and replaced it with water, with the object of cheating the Customs. The authorities, unwilling to take further trouble about the matter, sent away both parties, and would have nothing more to do with the case. The Jews in the meantime were inconsolable; and when the Cretans thought they had been sufficiently punished, they confessed the trick, and offered to make amends by refunding the money they had paid for the casks if they would go with them to the Rabbi and take an oath to make no more attempts to injure their business by dishonest means.

The principal Greek merchants trade under foreign protection, as it affords them greater security and freedom from the intrigues of the ill-disposed.

To sum up. The subject Greek of Turkey has his vices: he is over-ambitious, conceited, too diplomatic and wily; and, in common with most merchants, European or Eastern, in Turkey, he does his best to cheat the Turks—and occasionally extends the practice further, not without excellent precedent. But these are the vices of a race long kept in servitude and now awaking to the sense of a great ancestry: the servitude has produced the servile fault of double-dealing and dishonesty; and the pride of a noble past has engendered the conceit of the present. Such vices are but passing deformities: they are the sharp angles and bony length of the girl-form that will in time be perfected in beauty. These faults will disappear with the spread of education and the restoring of freedom long withheld. The quick intellect and fine mettle of the Greek, like his lithe body, descended from a nation of heroes, are destined to great things. The name alone of Hellenes carries with it the prescriptive right of speaking and doing nobly: and the modern Hellenes will not disown their birthright.

CHAPTER III.

THE ALBANIANS.

Albania little known to Travellers—Character of the Country—Isolation and Neglect—Products—The Land-holders—Ali Bey's Revolution—Albanian Towns—The Albanian's House his Castle in a Literal Sense—Blood Feuds—Villages—Unapproachable Position—The Defence of Souli—Joannina—Beautiful Site—Ali Pacha's Improvements—Greek Enterprise—The Albanians—Separate Tribes—The Ghegs—The Tosks—Character of the Latter—Superiority of the Ghegs—Respect for Women—An Adventure with a Brigand Chief—Gheg Gratitude—A Point of Honour with an Albanian Servant—Religion among the Albanians—Education among the Tosks—Warlike Character of the Albanians—Use of the Gun—The Vendetta—Women to the Rescue—Albanian Women in General—Female Adornment—Emigration—Mutual Assistance Abroad—The Albanian Character—Recklessness—Love of Display—Improvidence—Pride—Hatred of the Turks, reciprocated to the Full.

THE Albanians, like most of the races of minor importance inhabiting European Turkey, are little known to the civilised world. Albania, with its impassable mountains, broken by deep and precipitous ravines, the footways of torrents, has been visited only by those few travellers who have had enough courage and adventurous spirit to penetrate into its fastnesses. This country, occupying the place of the ancient Illyria and Epirus, was in the middle ages called Arvanasi, and later on Arnaoutlik by the Turks and Arvanitia by the Greeks; but in the native tongue it is called Skiperi, or "land of rocks." It is divided into Upper and Lower Albania, and forms two vilayets, that of Scutari (comprising the provinces of Berat, El Bassan, Ochrida, Upper and Lower Dibra, Tirana, Candia, Duratzo, Cruia, Tessi, Scutari, Dulcigno, and Podgoritza), and that of Joannina, in Epirus (comprising Joannina, Konitza, Paleopogoyani, Argyrokastro, Delvino, Parakalanio, Paramythia, Margariti, Leapourie or Arbar, and Avlona).

Owing to the mountainous character of the country, and the turbulent and warlike disposition of its inhabitants, it is still unexplored in many parts, poorly cultivated in others, and everywhere much neglected in its rich and fertile valleys. Unfortunately agriculture, still in a very primitive and neglected condition throughout Turkey, is especially so in Albania. This neglect, however prejudicial to the well-being of the inhabitants, rather heightens the wild beauty of the scenery, the changing grandeur and loveliness of which alternately awes and delights the traveller.

Shut out from the civilised world by the want of roads and means of communication, all the natural advantages the country possesses have remained stationary, and its beauty and fertility turned to little account by the wild and semi-savage population that inhabits it.

The principal productions of Illyrian Albania are

horses, sheep, and oxen, reared in the valleys of the Mousakia; grain is extensively grown at Tirana; and rye and Indian corn are grown in El Bassan; and in some parts of Dibra a coarse kind of silk is manufactured into home-spun tissues, and used for the elaborate embroidery of the picturesque national costume. A stout felt used for the *capa*, or cloak, is made of wool. A kind of red leather, and other articles of minor importance, are also manufactured in these parts.

Epirus, or Lower Albania, owing to its more favourable situation and the mildness of its climate, is by far the more fertile and better cultivated of the two vilayets. In addition to the above-mentioned products, it grows rice, cotton, olives, tobacco, oranges, citrons, grapes, and cochineal. Though agriculture is carried on in the same primitive manner, richer harvests are produced, and, as shown by the yearly returns, there is a steady increase of the export trade.

Albania abounds in minerals, but the mines are little known, still less worked. Hot springs, possessing valuable medicinal qualities, are also to be found in many places, but the country people are totally ignorant of their properties, and take the waters indiscriminately for any ailments they may happen to have, and, in obedience to the old superstitious reverence for the spirits of the fountains, even drink from several different sources in the hope of gaining favour with their respective nymphs.

The large landowners, both in Upper and Lower Albania, are Mohammedans, often perverted from Christianity. They still exercise a despotic and unlimited control over the peasants, and show the convert's proverbial spirit of intolerance towards their brethren who hold fast the faith of their fathers. At the beginning of this century, and before Ali Pasha had made himself the complete master of Joannina, much of the landed property in Lower Albania was held by Christians, and many semi-independent villages, entirely inhabited by Christians, were to be found scattered all over the country. Their number was sadly diminished during the revolutionary convulsion that upset the country. The property of many Christian landholders experienced the same fate. Their estates were snatched from their lawful owners by the wily, avaricious, and hypocritical despot, who, employing by turns the three methods of force, fraud, and nominal compensation, drove away the owners and appropriated the lands to himself. After his death all these lands passed to the crown as *Imlak* property, and were never restored to their former possessors.

The landed property in both Upper and Lower Albania still retains much of the characteristics of the species of feudal system which once prevailed throughout Turkey; but instead of the rule of a few powerful Beys or one single despot, a legion of petty tyrants hold the people in bondage. Yet there may be found among the landholders a few, poorer than the rest, who are respected for their integrity and for their paternal treatment of the peasants on their estates.

The general aspect of the towns and villages in Upper Albania differs very little from that of other towns and villages in Turkey. The same want of finish and clumsiness of workmanship prevail in all the Albanian houses, which are usually detached from one another and stand in court-yards surrounded by high walls. Some of these dwellings are complete fortresses; but this is not on account of the terrible never-ending blood-feuds transmitted from generation to generation, which make each man's life (out-of-doors) the least secure of his possessions. In times of peace his house can be left with open gates, and is held sacred and respected even by the vilest and most desperate characters: for it is a point of honour with an Albanian never to incur the disgrace of shedding a man's blood in his own house; but the moment he crosses the threshold, he is at the mercy of his foe.

An Albanian chieftain, who had a deadly quarrel with a neighbour and consequently was in terror of his life, was compelled to stay within doors for twelve long years, knowing the risk he ran if the threshold were crossed. Finally, craving a little liberty, he obtained an armistice and was allowed perfect freedom for a short space of time.

In times of open contention the houses are fortified

and guarded by armed bands, who conceal themselves in strongholds attached to some of the buildings, watch for the approach of the enemy, and open fire upon them from the loop-holes with which the walls are pierced.

The furniture of their dwelling-houses is scanty, poor, and comfortless. Some valuable carpets, a gorgeously embroidered sofa in the reception-room, and a few indispensable articles, are all they possess. The streets are narrow and badly paved, and look dismal and deserted. The bazars and shops are inferior to those of most of the towns of Turkey. They contain no variety of objects for use or ornament beyond those absolutely necessary for domestic purposes.

The villages are far more curious and interesting to the traveller than the towns. Some of these in Upper Albania, in mountainous districts, are at a great distance from each other, and are perched up on the summits of high rocks that tower above each other in successive ranges, in some places forming a natural and impassable rampart to the village, in others trodden into steep paths where the goat doubtless delights to climb, but where man experiences any but agreeable sensations.

Lower Albania, better known to travellers, is less rugged and wild in appearance. But here and there we meet with mountainous districts—such as the far-famed canton of Souli, which in the time of Ali Pasha numbered eleven villages, some scattered on the peaks of mountains, others studding their skirts; while the terrible Acheron gloomily wound its way through the deep gorges that helped to secure the river its victims.

Souli, defended by its 13,000 inhabitants, withstood the siege of the dreaded pasha's armies, held them in check for fifteen years, and acquired undying fame in the history of the war of Greek independence for heroism hardly surpassed by the most valiant feats of the ancients, and with which nothing in modern warfare can compare. Every Souliot, man, woman, and child, was ready to perish in the defence. The women and children who had fought so long by the side of their husbands and fathers, at the last extremity, preferring death to captivity and dishonour, threw themselves from the rocks into the dark stream below, while the few that survived the final destruction cut their way through their enemies, and were scattered over Greece to tell the sad tale of the fall of Souli.

The plateau of Joannina is entirely surrounded by wooded mountains, and is from 1,200 to 1,500 feet above the level of the sea. On this table land is a lake about fourteen miles in length and six in breadth, on the rich borders of which rises the town of Joannina, like a fairy palace in an enchanted land. This town, which contains 25,000 inhabitants, became the favourite abode of Ali Pasha, who transformed and embellished it to a considerable extent, and founded schools and libraries.

The edifices erected by him were partly destroyed by his followers, when his power was supposed to have reached its end, together with the gilded kiosks and superb palaces built for his own enjoyment. All that Joannina can boast of at the present day is the exceeding beauty of its situation, and the activity that Greek enterprise has given to its commerce, and the excellent schools and syllogae that have been established and are said to be doing wonders in improving and educating the new generation of Epirus.

The Albanians are divided into several distinct races, each presenting marked features of difference from the other and occupying separate districts. Those of Upper Albania are called Ghegs, and inhabit that portion of the country called Ghegueria, which extends from the frontiers of Bosnia and Montenegro to Berat.

These men are broad-chested, tall, and robust, have regular features, and a proud, manly, independent mien. Their personal attractions are not a little enhanced by their rich and picturesque national costume—a pair of cloth gaiters; an embroidered jacket with open sleeves; a double-breasted waistcoat; the Greek fustanella (white calico kilt), surmounted by a cloth skirt opened in front; a kemer, or leather belt, decorated with silver ornaments, and holding a pistol, yataghan, and other arms of fine workmanship. The whole costume is richly worked with gold thread. On the head is worn a fez, wider at the top than round the head, and ornamented with a long tassel.

The Tosks inhabiting Lower Albania, in the sandjaks of Avlona and Berat, and the Tchames and Liaps of the sandjaks of Delvina and Joannina, designate their country Tchamouria and Liapouria.. These latter are supposed to be direct descendants of ancient Hellenes, as they speak the Greek language with greater purity than the rest; and certainly some of their characteristic features bear a great resemblance to those of the ancient Greeks. All the Albanians of Epirus use the Greek language, and are more conversant with it than with Turkish, which in some places is not spoken at all.

The Tosks are tall and well built, and extremely agile in all their movements; their features are regular and intelligent, but like most Albanians they have a fierce, cruel, and sometimes cunning cast of countenance, and a swagger in their gait, by which they can easily be distinguished from the other races, even when divested of their national costume. They are of a warlike and ferocious disposition, yet they have noble qualities which atone in some measure for their ferocity and produce a very mixed impression of the national character. They are a constant source of dread to strangers, but objects of implicit confidence and trust to those who have gained their friendship and earned their gratitude.

In bravery, trustworthiness, and honour, the Ghegs bear the palm. No Gheg will scruple to "take to the road" if he is short of money and has nothing better to do. If any man he may meet on the high road disregards his command, "*Des dour*" (stand still), he thinks nothing of cutting his throat or settling him with a pistol-shot: but if a Gheg has once tasted your bread and salt or owes you a debt of gratitude or is employed in your service, all his terrible qualities vanish and he becomes the most devoted, attached, and faithful of friends and servants. Generally speaking, the Ghegs are abstemious and not much addicted to the vices of Asiatics. Women are respected by them and seldom exposed to the attacks of brigands or libertines.

These characteristics are so general and so deeply rooted in the character of the Gheg, that consuls, merchants, and others, who need brave and faithful retainers, employ them in preference to men of any other race.

I was once making a journey across country to a watering-place in Albania, and set out for this deserted and isolated spot with a capital escort; accompanied moreover by a wealthy Christian dignitary of the town in which I had been staying. During a short halt we made in a mountain gorge to refresh ourselves with luncheon, near a ruined and deserted *beklemé* or guard-house, suddenly a fine but savage-looking Albanian appeared before us. He was followed by several other sturdy fellows, all armed to the teeth. My friend turned pale, and the escort, taking to their guns, stood on the defensive.

But the feeling of fear soon vanished from my people, as the Albanians approached them, and instead of uttering the dreaded " *Des dour!* " gracefully put their hands on their breasts and repeated the much more agreeable welcome word " *Merhaba!* " The band chatted with my men, whilst their chieftain approached my travelling companion, and entered into conversation with him, every now and then giving a glance at me with an expression of wonder on his face. At last, he inquired who I was, and declared he was astonished at the independent spirit of the *Inglis* lady, who, in spite of fatigue and danger, had ventured so far.

He willingly accepted our offer of luncheon; first dipping a piece of bread in salt and eating it. My horse was then brought up; the chief stood by, and gallantly held the stirrup while I mounted. I thanked him, and we rode off at a gallop. After we had gone some distance on our road, my friend heaved a deep sigh of relief, and said to me, "Do you know who has been lunching with us, holding your stirrup, and assisting you to mount? It is the fiercest and most terrible of Albanian brigand chiefs in this neighbourhood! For the last seven years he and his band have been the terror of this kaza, in consequence of their robberies and murders, respecting none but those of your sex,—guided, I presume, in this, by the superstition, or let us say point of honour, some Albanians strictly observe, that it is cowardly and unlucky to attack women."

An adventure that lately happened to a friend of mine will show the manner in which Ghegs remember a good service rendered them. Some years ago, a few Albanians, personally known to the gentleman in question, who owns a large estate in Macedonia, heard that three of their fellow-countrymen had got into trouble. Through the influence Mr. A. possessed with the local authorities, their release was obtained. The incident had almost passed out of his memory when it was unexpectedly recalled at a critical moment. Some Albanian beys, who had a spite against Mr. A., in consequence of a disputed portion of land, resolved to take advantage of the present state of anarchy and disorder in the country to have him or his son assassinated the next time either of them should visit the estate. The villanous scheme was entrusted to a band of Albanian brigands that were known to be lurking in the vicinity of Mr. A.'s estate. At harvest time, as he was about to start for the country, he received a crumpled dirty little epistle, written in the Greek-Albanian dialect, to this effect :—

"Much esteemed Effendi, and venerated benefactor.

"Some years ago your most humble servant and his companions were in difficulties. You saved them from prison and perhaps from the halter. The service has never been forgotten, and the debt we owe to you will be shortly redeemed by my informing you that the robber band of Albanians in the vicinity of your chiftlik have received instructions and have accepted the task of shooting you down the first time you come in this direction. I and my valiant men will be on the look-out to prevent the event if possible, but we warn you to be on your guard, for your life is in danger.

"Kissing your hand respectfully,

"I sign myself,

"A MEMBER OF THE VERY BAND!"

Another friend related to me a strange adventure he had with an Albanian ex-brigand, who for some time had been in his service. This gentleman was a millionaire of the town of P., who in his younger days often collected the tithes of his whole district, and consequently had occasion to travel far into the interior and bring back with him large sums of money. During these tours the faithful Albanian never failed to accompany his master. On one occasion, however, when they had penetrated into the wildest part of his jurisdiction, his servant walked into the room where he was seated, and after making his *temenla*, or salute, said, " Chorbadji, I shall leave you ; therefore I have come to say to you *Allah 'semarladu* (good-bye)."

" Why," said the astonished gentleman, " what is to become of me in this outlandish place without you ? "

" Oh," was the response, " I leave you because I have consented to attack and rob you, and as such an act would be cowardly and treacherous while I eat your bread and salt, I give you notice that I mean to do it on the highway as you return home, so take what precautions you like, that it may be fair play between us." This said, he made a second *temenla* and disappeared.

He was as good as his word; going back to his former profession, he soon found out and joined a band of brigands and at their head waylaid and attacked his former master, who, well aware of the character of the man he had to deal with and the dangers that awaited him, had taken measures accordingly and provided himself with an escort strong enough to overpower the brigands.

The Albanians before the Turkish conquest professed the Christian religion, which, however, does not appear to have been very deeply rooted in the hearts of the people ; from time immemorial they were more famous for their warlike propensities and adventurous exploits than for their good principles.

After the conquest, Islam, finding a favourable soil in which to plant itself, made considerable progress in some districts, where the inhabitants willingly adopted it in order to escape persecution and oppression. This progress, however, was not very extensive until the time of the famous Iskander Beg, or Scanderbeg, who played so prominent a *rôle* in the history of his country, and whose desertion of the Mohammedan and adoption of the Christian religion so exasperated Sultan Murad, that he forthwith ordered that most of the Christian churches should be converted into mosques and that all Epirots should be circumcised under pain of death.

The second impulse Mohammedanism received in Albania was under the rule of Ali Pasha, when whole villages were converted to Islam, though their inhabitants to this day bear Christian names and in some cases the mother or wife is allowed to retain the faith of her fathers and will keep her fasts and feasts and attend her Christian church while her husband joins the Mussulman congregation. In those parts of Epirus, however, where the Greek population was in the majority and its ignorant though devout clergy had influence with the people, they held fast to their religion as they did to their language.

The Mirdites were equally steadfast to their faith

and purpose, and have remained among the most faithful and devout followers of the Pope. The number of Roman Catholic Mirdites is reckoned at about 140,000 souls, scattered in the different districts of Albania. They have several bishoprics, and their bishops and priests are sent from Rome or Scutari. The Mirdites make fine soldiers, and have often been engaged by the Porte as contingent troops, or employed in active service. They take readily to commerce and agriculture, and on the whole may be considered the most advanced and civilised of the Illyrian Albanians. They might, however, progress much more rapidly if their pastors, to whose guidance they submit themselves implicitly, would follow the example of the Greeks in Epirus, and introduce a more liberal course of instruction; for the education is at present very limited beyond the religious branches. There can be no doubt that excessive religious teaching among ignorant people, though a powerful preservative of the faith, tends inevitably to render them narrow-minded, bigoted, and incapable of self-development.

The Mohammedanism of the Albanians is not very deeply rooted, nor does it bear the stamp of the true faith. Followers of the Prophet in Lower Albania especially may be heard to swear alternately by the *Panaghia* (blessed Virgin) and the Prophet, without appearing disposed to follow too closely the doctrines of either the Bible or the Koran. It is an undoubted fact that the Moslems of Albania contrast very unfavourably with the Christians.

The Tosks are held in ill-repute on account of the difficulty they seem to experience in defining the difference between treachery and good faith. They are clever, and have made more progress than the Ghegs in the civilisation that Greece is endeavouring to infuse among her neighbours. Some of their districts are worthy of mention, on account of the taste for learning displayed by their inhabitants, the earnestness with which they receive instruction, and the good results that have already crowned their praiseworthy efforts.

Zagora, for instance, famous as having afforded shelter to many Greeks after the conquest of Constantinople, is renowned for the intelligence and general enlightenment of its inhabitants. The sterile and unproductive soil induces the men to rely less upon the fruits of their manual toil than upon their mental labour, consequently most of them migrate to other countries, seeking their fortune. Some take to commerce, others to professions, and after realising a competence they return to their native land and impart the more advanced ideas their experience has given them to their compatriots who have not enjoyed the same privileges.

The women of Zagora are much esteemed for their virtues and enlightenment. Such facts as these make a refreshing contrast to the dark cloud of ignorance which, in spite of the pure sky of Albania and the beauty of the scenery, still hangs thickly on the land, and casts a shadow where Nature meant all to be sunshine.

The warlike instincts of the Albanian find more scope for action in the Mohammedan than in the Christian religion. They gladly accept an invitation to fight the battles of the Porte or those of any nation that will pay them. This help must, however, be given in the way most agreeable to themselves, *i.e.* as paid contingents under the command of their own chieftains, to whom they show implicit obedience and fidelity. Under the beloved banner of their Bey, legions will collect, equally ready to do the irregular work of the Bashi-bazouks or to be placed in the regular army.

But, as a rule, the Albanian objects to ordinary conscription, and avoids it, if possible, by a direct refusal to be enrolled, or else makes his escape. When on the road to the seat of war, a regiment of Albanians is a terrible scourge to the country it passes through; like locusts, they leave nothing but naked stalks and barren ground behind them.

The principal merits of the Albanian soldier are his rapidity in motion, steady aim, carelessness of life, and hardy endurance in privation. An Albanian's gun is his companion and his means of subsistence in peace or war. To it he looks for his daily bread more than to any other source, and he uses it with a skill not easily matched.

When travelling in Upper Albania, we halted one day in a field which appeared quite uncultivated and waste, and were making arrangements for our mid-day meal, when an Albanian *bekchi* (forest-keeper) appeared on the scene and ordered us to quit the spot, as it was cultivated ground. Our escort remonstrated with the fellow, saying that it was the only convenient place near for a halt, and that now we had alighted we should remain where we were until we had finished our meal.

The Albanian, entirely regardless of the number of the escort and the authority of government servants, became more persistent in his commands, and the guards lost patience and threatened to arrest him and take him before the Mudir of the town that lay a little further on. "The Mudir," scornfully repeated the mountaineer, "and who told you that I recognise the authority of the Mudir?" Then taking his long gun from his shoulder, he held it up and said, "This is my authority, and no other can influence me or acquire any power over me!"

The social relations of the Albanians are limited to two ideas, *Vendetta* and *bessa* (peace).

In cases of personal insult or offence the vendetta is settled on the spot. Both parties stand up, the insulted full of indignation and thirsting for revenge, the offender repentant, perhaps, or persistent. The aggrieved person, even in the former case, seldom yields to persuasion or softens into forgiveness; he draws a brace of pistols and presents them to his antagonist to make his choice. The little fingers of their left hands are linked together and they fire simultaneously. A survivor is rare in such cases, and the feud thus caused between the relatives of both parties is perpetuated from generation to generation.

It takes very little to provoke these terrible blood-feuds, and one or two instances that have come under my direct notice will suffice to give an idea of their nature and the violence with which real or fancied insult is avenged.

One happened while I was at Uskup. The cause was nothing more weighty than a contention between two Albanian sportsmen, who were disputing the possession of a hare that each maintained he had shot. The dispute became so violent that a duel was resorted to as the only way to settle it. It came off on the common in the presence of the combatants' relatives and friends, who joined in the quarrel; and a general battle ensued, in which the women fought side by side with their husbands and brothers. A girl of seventeen, a sister of one of the two sportsmen, fought with the courage of a heroine, and with a success worthy of a better cause. Fourteen victims fell on that day.

The Governor of Uskup, who related the story to me, said that he despaired of ever seeing these savage people yield to the influence of their more refined neighbours, or become entirely submissive to the Sultan's government. But great changes have taken place since then with respect to their submission to the Porte. The Government is now able almost safely to send governors and sub-governors into Albania to collect taxes from such as choose to pay them, and even draw a certain number of recruits from the most turbulent and independent districts.

Another of these lamentable blood-feuds happened in Upper Dibra, and was witnessed by one of my friends then living there.

It originated in two lads at the village fountain throwing stones and breaking the pitcher of an Albanian girl who had come to fetch water. This was considered an insult to her maidenhood and was at once made the cause of a serious quarrel by the friends of the two parties. A fight ensued in which no less than sixty people lost their lives. Women's honour is held in such high esteem in these wild regions that so trivial an accident suffices to cause a terrible destruction of life.

Albanian women are generally armed, not for the purpose of self-defence—no Albanian would attack a woman in his own country—but rather that they may be able to join in the brawls of their male relatives, and fight by their side. The respect entertained for women accounts for a strange custom prevalent among Albanians,—that of offering to strangers who wish to traverse their country the escort of a woman. Thus accompanied, the traveller may proceed with safety into the most isolated regions without any chance of harm coming to him.

The Albanian women are lively and of an independent spirit, but utterly unlettered. Very few of the Mohammedans in Lower Albania possess any knowledge of reading or writing. They, are, however, proud and dignified, strict observers of the rules of national etiquette; and they attach great importance to the antiquity of their families, and regulate their marriages by the degrees of rank and lineage.

The natural beauty of the Albanian girl soon disappears after she has entered upon the married state. She then begins to dye her hair, to which nature has often given a golden hue, jet black; she besmears her face with a pernicious white composition, blackens her teeth, and reddens her hands with henna; the general effect of the process is to make her ugly during youth, and absolutely hideous in old age. The paint they use is not only most destructive to the complexion, but also to the teeth, which decay rapidly from its use. I believe they blacken their teeth artificially to hide its effects. On my inquiring the reason of this strange custom of some Albanian ladies, they laughed at my disapproval of it, and told me that in their opinion it is only the fangs of dogs that should be white!

Both Christian and Mohammedan Albanians, dissatisfied with the poverty of their country and their incapability of developing its natural resources or profiting by them, often leave it and migrate to other parts of Turkey in search of employment. Large numbers seek military service in Turkey, Egypt, and other countries, or situations as guards, herdsmen, etc. Some of the Christians study and become doctors, lawyers, or schoolmasters. The lower classes are masons, carters, porters, servants, dairymen, butchers, etc.; their wives and children seldom accompany them, but remain at home to look after their belongings, and content themselves with an occasional visit from the assiduous bread-winner.

All Albanians call themselves *Arkardash* (brothers), and when away from their homes will assist and maintain the *Kapoussis* or new-comers, until they obtain employment through the instrumentality of their compatriots already established in the town. Thus assistance is given in small towns to the *Kapoussis* to defray the expenses of his maintenance and lodging in the Khan. When he obtains a place, he repays the money in small instalments until the debt is acquitted.

The Albanian, generally a gay, reckless fellow, is always short of money: many among the better conditioned carry their fortune on their person in the shape of rich embroideries on their handsome costumes and valuable arms. In their belt is contained all the money they possess. When the fortune-seeker has to wait a long time for the fickle goddess to smile upon him, and the forbearance or generosity of his friends is exhausted, and the *kemer* becomes empty, he sells his fine arms and the splendid suit of clothes follows to the same fate. But the Albanian, though externally transformed, will be by no means crushed in spirit or at all less conceited in manner, even when a tattered rag has replaced the gaudy fez, and a coarse *aba* his *fustanella* and embroidered jacket. With shoes trodden down at heel he patiently lounges about under the name of *Chiplak* until the expected turn of fortune arrives. Should it be very long in coming, our Albanian turns the tables upon the goddess, shoulders his gun, and takes to the high road.

The *bessa* or truce is the time Albanians allow themselves at intervals to suspend their blood feuds; it is arranged by mutual consent between the contending parties, and is of fixed duration and strictly observed: the bitterest enemies meet and converse in perfect harmony and confidence.

The character of the Albanians is simply the mixed unhewn character of a barbarous people; they have the rough vices but also the unthinking virtues of semi-savage races. If they are not civilised enough not to be cruel, at least civilisation has not yet taught them its general lesson that honour and chivalry are unpractical relics of Middle-Age superstition, quite unworthy of the business-like man of to-day, whose eyes are steadily fixed on the main chance. The Albanian, too, can plunder, but he does it gun in hand and openly on the highway; not behind a desk or on 'Change. His faults are the faults of an untrained violent nature, they are never mean; his virtues are those of forgotten days, and are not intended to pay. He is more often abused than praised, but it is mostly for want of knowledge; for his faults are on the surface, whilst his sterling good qualities are seen only by those who know him well, and know how to treat him.

. The ties that bind this nation to its rulers have never been those of strict submission, or of sympathy. The Turkish government cannot easily forget the troubles and loss of life the conquest of Albania occasioned, nor can it feel satisfied with the manner in which imperial decrees are received by the more turbulent portion of the inhabitants with regard to the enrolment of troops and the payment of taxes; nor pass over the insolence and even danger to which its officials are often exposed.

The Mohammedan Albanians on their side deeply resent the loss of their liberty, and the forfeiture of their privileges, and reciprocate to the full the ill-feeling and abusive language of the Turks. The Turk

calls the Albanian *Haidout Arnaout!* or *Tellak!* *
The Albanian regards the Turk as a doubtful friend, and a corrupt and impotent master; and if this antipathy exists between the Turks and the Albanian Moslem, it is scarcely necessary to say that it is felt far more strongly between the Turks and the Albanian Christians of Epirus and the Mirdites, who, feeling doubly injured by the oppressive rule to which they are forced to submit, and the loss of their freedom, ill-brook the authority of the Porte. The Mirdite turns his looks and aspirations towards the Slavs, while the Albanian hopes finally to share the liberty of the Greek.

The Porte, under these circumstances, had a difficult mission to fulfil in controlling this mixed multitude, and was not unjustified in looking upon it with distrust and suspicion. It now seems probable, however, that it may be relieved of the weight of this responsibility.

* " Brigand Albanian ! " " Bath-boy ! "

CHAPTER IV.

THE TURKS.

Turkish Peasants—Decrease in Numbers—Taxation and Recruiting—Relations with the Christians—Appearance—Amusements—House and Family—Townspeople—Guilds—Moslems and Christians—The Turk as an Artisan—Objection to Innovations—Life in the Town—The Military Class—Government Officials—Pashas—Grand Vizirs—Receptions—A Turkish Lady's Life—The Princes—The Sultan—Mahmoud—His Reforms—Abdul-Medjid—Abdul-Aziz—Character and Fate—Murad—Abdul-Hamid—Slavery in Turkey.

The Turkish peasants inhabiting the rural districts of Bulgaria, Macedonia, Epirus, and Thessaly, although the best, most industrious, and useful of the Sultan's Mohammedan subjects, everywhere evince signs of poverty, decrease in numbers, and general deterioration. This fact is evident even to the mere traveller, from the wretchedness and poverty-stricken appearance of Turkish villages, with their houses mostly tumbling to pieces. The inhabitants, unable to resist the drain upon them in time of war when the youngest and most vigorous men are taken away for military service, often abandon their dwellings and retire to more populous villages or towns: the property thus abandoned goes to ruin, and the fields in the same manner become waste. This evil, which has increased since the more regular enforcement of the conscription, may be traced to three principal sources:—The first is the unequal manner in which the conscription laws are carried out upon this submissive portion of the people; the second is the want of labourers, the inevitable consequence of the recruiting system, whereby the best hands are drawn away annually at the busiest and most profitable time of the year, to the great and sometimes irreparable injury of industry; the third is the irregular and often unjust manner in which the taxes are levied. Under these unencouraging circumstances the disabled old men, the wild boys, and the women (who are never trained to work and are consequently unfit for it), are left behind to continue the labour of the conscripts, and struggle on as well as indolent habits and natural incapacity for hard work will allow them. The large villages will soon share the fate of the small ones and be engulfed in the same ruin, unless radical changes are introduced for the benefit of the Turkish peasants. Their condition requires careful and continued attention at the hands of a good and equitable administration.

The Turkish peasant is a good, quiet, and submissive subject, who refuses neither to furnish his Sultan with troops nor to pay his taxes, so far as in him lies; but he is poor, ignorant, helpless, and improvident to an almost incredible degree. At the time of recruiting he will complain bitterly of his hard lot, but go all the same to serve his time; he groans under the heavy load of taxation, gets imprisoned, and is not released until he manages to pay his dues.

He is generally discontented with his government, of which he openly complains, and still more with its agents, with whom he is brought into closer contact; but still the idea of rebelling against either, giving any signs of disaffection, or attempting to resist the law, never gets any hold upon him. His relations with his Christian neighbours vary greatly with the locality and the personal character of both. In some places Christian and Turkish peasants, in times of peace, live in tolerable harmony, in others a continual warfare of complaints on one side and acts of oppression on the other is kept up. The only means of securing peace to both is to separate the two parties, and compel each to rest solely upon its own exertions and resources, and to prove its worth in the school of necessity. An English gentleman owning a large estate in Macedonia, used to assert that until the Christian peasant adopts a diet of beer and beef nothing will be made of him; in the same manner I think that until the Turk is cured of his bad habit of employing by hook or by crook Petcho and Yancho to do his work for him, he will never be able to do it himself.

The Turkish peasant is well-built and strong, and possesses extraordinary power of endurance. His mode of living is simple, his habits sober; unlike the Christians of his class he has no dance, no village feast, and no music but a kind of drum or tambourine, to vary the monotony of his life. His cup of coffee and his chibouk contain for him all the sweets of existence. The coffee is taken before the labours of the day are begun, and again in the evening at the *cafiné*. His work is often interrupted in order to enjoy the chibouk, which he smokes crouched under a tree or wall. His house is clean but badly built, cold in winter and hot in summer, possessing little in the way of furniture but bedding, mats, rugs, and kitchen utensils. He is worse clad than the Christian peasant, and his wife and children still worse; yet the women are content with their lot, and in their ignorance and helplessness do not try, like the Christian women, to better their condition by their individual exertions; they are irreproachable and honest in their conduct, and capable of enduring great trials. Some are very pretty; they keep much at home, the young girls seldom gather together for fun and enjoyment except at a wedding or circumcision ceremony, when they sing and play together, while the matrons gossip over their private affairs and those of their neighbours. The girls are married young to peasants of their own or some neighbouring village. Polygamy is rare among Turkish peasants, and they do not often indulge in the luxury of divorce.

On the whole the Turkish peasant, though not a model of virtue, is a good sort of man, and would be much better if he had not the habit in times of national trouble to take upon him the name of Bashi-Bazouk, and to transform himself into a ruffian.

Turks, generally speaking, prefer town to country life: for in towns they enjoy more frequent opportunities of indulging in that *dolce far niente* which has become an integral part of the Turkish character and has entirely routed his original nomadic disposition.

The tradespeople of the towns are ranged into *esnafs*, or guilds, and form separate corporations, some of which include Christians when they happen to be engaged in the same pursuits. Thus there are the *esnafs* of barbers, linendrapers, greengrocers, grooms, etc. These bodies, strange to say, in the midst of general disunion and disorganisation, are governed by fixed laws and regulations faithfully observed by Christians and Turks alike, and the rival worshippers, bound only by the obligation of good faith and honour towards each other, pull together much better and show a greater regard for justice and impartiality than is evinced by any other portion of the community. Every corporation elects one or two chiefs, who regulate all disputes and settle any difficulties that may arise among the members. These *Oustas*, or chiefs, are master-workmen in their different trades. The apprentices are called *Chiraks*, and obtain promotion, according to their ability, after a certain number of years. When considered sufficiently advanced in their business, the master, with the consent and approval of the corporation, admits them into the fraternity, and gives them the choice of entering into partnership with him or beginning business on their own account.

The grooms yearly elect a chief in each town called *Seis Bashi*, through whom, for a small fee, grooms may be obtained with greater security than otherwise for their good behaviour and capability. The meetings, or *lonjas*, of this *esnaf*, are held pretty frequently in coffee-houses, where the affairs of the corporation are regulated, and the meeting generally terminates in an orgie; after which the grooms retire to their stables, much the worse for the wine and *raki* they have drunk.

Once a year each of the associations gives a picnic, either on the feast of the patron saint or at the promotion of an apprentice. On such occasions a certain sum is collected from the members or taken from the reserve fund which some of the *esnafs* possess, for the purchase of all kinds of provisions needed for a substantial and sometimes even sumptuous meal, to which not only all the members of the guild are invited, irrespective of creed and nationality, but also all strangers who may happen to pass the place where the feast is held. The amusements include music and dancing for the Christians, and a variety of other entertainments, always harmless and quite within the bounds of decorum, and joined in with the spirit of joviality that characterises these gatherings; disputes are of rare occurrence and the greatest harmony is displayed throughout the day between Christian and Mussulman. When the interests of the Mohammedans are closely connected with those of the Christians, both willingly forego something of their usual intolerance in order to further the cause of business. It is strange and regretable that this spirit of association among the lower orders should receive so little encouragement from the Government and the higher classes.

Though the Mohammedans in certain localities and under such circumstances as those I have mentioned, are just in their dealings with the Christians, and maintain a friendly feeling towards them; in others, especially in inland towns, the growing prosperity of the Christians excites a bitter feeling among their Turkish neighbours, who often offer open hostility and inflict irreparable injury on their business and property. Many incidents of this nature have come under my notice, and lead me to the conclusion that the non-progressiveness of the Turks and the rapid decline of their empire is partly due to the unfortunate and insurmountable incongeniality existing between the Turks and Christians. The Turks, as the dominant race, assumed total ascendancy over the Christians, got into the habit of using them as tools who acted, worked, and thought for them in an irresponsible fashion, and thus lost the power of doing for themselves, together with the sense of seeing the necessity of dealing with justice, generosity, and impartiality, which alone could have guaranteed enterprise or secured confidence and sympathy between the two classes. Unfortunately for the Turks this has brought about a state of permanent antipathy between the two that can never be corrected; nor can any reconciliation be arrived at unless these classes become entirely independent of one another. Any arrangement short of this, as any person well-informed as to the actual relations of Turks and Christians, be they Greeks or Bulgarians, will admit, must be of short duration, and before long there could not fail to come a recurrence of outbreaks, revolutions, and the usual atrocities that accompany disorder among these races.

The Turks, generally speaking, are not active or intelligent in business, and do not venture much into speculation or commercial transactions of any great importance. For example, one never hears of their undertaking banking, or forming companies for the purpose of working mines, making railways, or any other enterprise involving risk and requiring intelligence, activity, system, and honesty to ensure success.

The first reason for this strange neglect in a people who possess one of the finest and most productive countries in the world is a naturally stagnant and lethargic disposition; another is the want of the support of the Government, which has never shown itself earnestly desirous of aiding private enterprise or guaranteeing its success by affording disinterested protection. Until very recent times no pains have been taken either by individuals or by the Government to introduce those innovations and improvements which the times demand. The consequence is that the Turkish tradespeople gradually find the number of their customers decrease, while the Greeks, Franks, and others successfully supply the public with the new articles, or the old ones improved and better fashioned. To give an instance of this I will repeat an incident related to me by a Turkish bey of. "La Jeune Turquie" as a lamentable proof of the non-progressiveness of the masses. "When at Stamboul," said he, "I had during some time to pass by the shop of a Turkish basketmaker who, with two of his sons, one grown up and the other a boy, might be seen working at the wicker hampers and common baskets which have been used in the country from time immemorial, but are now less used by reason of the superiority of those brought from Europe or made in the school for mechanical arts in Stamboul, an institution not much appreciated by the artisans who enjoy the liberty of going themselves or sending their children to learn the innovations in their different branches of industry. The basketmaker and his sons were evidently a steady-going set, representing the honest Turks of olden time, but seemed to be struggling for a livelihood. Feeling an interest in them, I one day stopped and asked the old man what he realized per diem by the sale of his baskets? He heaved a deep sigh, glanced round his dismal shop, ornamented only with dust-covered baskets, and said, 'Very little, from three to six piastres (6*d*. to 1*s*.); for my business, once a thriving one, is now cast into the shade, and few customers come to buy the old Turkish baskets.' 'Why then do you not give it up and take to something else?'

"'No, it did very well for my father, who at his death recommended me to continue it and leave it to my sons and grandsons, who should also be brought up to the trade. I have done so, but it is a hard struggle for three of us to live by it.'

"I then suggested that one or more of his sons should learn the new method of basket-making, which would improve his business at once. This idea did not seem to be received favourably by the old man and the eldest son; but the boy caught at it and asked if he could go and learn. Encouraged by his evident willingness, I prevailed upon the father to allow me to place his son in the Industrial School, where I hear he has made certain progress in his art." The Turkish mechanic has no power of invention, and his work lacks finish; but he is capable of imitating with some success any design shown to him.

The life led by the Turkish tradespeople is extremely monotonous and brightened by no intellectual pleasures. The shopkeeper, on leaving his house at dawn, goes to the coffee-house, takes his small cup of coffee, smokes his pipe, chats with the *habitués* of the place, and then proceeds to his business, which is carried on with Oriental languor throughout the day. At sunset he again resorts to the coffee-house to take the same refreshment and enjoy the innovation of having a newspaper read to him—a novelty now much appreciated by the lower classes. He then returns to the bosom of his family in time for the evening meal. His home is clean though very simple; his wife and daughters are ignorant and never taught a trade by which they might earn anything. Embroidery, indispensable in a number of useless articles that serve to figure in the *trousseau* of every Turkish girl, and latterly coarse needle and crochet-work, fill up part of the time, while the mothers attend to their household affairs. The young children are sent to the elementary school, and the boys either go to school or are apprenticed to some trade.

A considerable proportion of the Turks belong to

the army. The officers, however, unlike those of their class in Europe, do not enjoy the prestige or rank to which the merits of the profession entitle them. It follows that the individuality of the officer is not taken into account: if he possesses any special ability it is overlooked so long as superiority of rank does not enforce it and obtain for him proper respect from soldiers and civilians. A Turkish captain does not receive much more consideration from his senior officer than does a common private; and in a moment of anger his colonel or general may strike and use foul and abusive language to him: a major is barely secure from such treatment. There are certainly men of merit and education among the officers of the Turkish army, whose behaviour, like that of the soldiers, is much praised by those who have had the opportunity of seeing the admirable manner in which they conducted themselves in the late war. Unfortunately it is principally in individual cases that this can be admitted, and it can by no means apply to the whole body of officers.

When not in active service Turkish officers generally have their wives and families in the towns in which they are stationed. The pay of an officer under the rank of a general is very inadequate and is irregularly received—a fact sadly evident in their neglected and disordered appearance. With boots down at heel and coats minus half the buttons, they may often be seen purchasing their own food in the market and carrying it home in their hands.

The young officers who have pursued their studies in the military schools present a marked contrast to these. They are well dressed and have an air of smartness, and in military science they are said to be far more advanced than those who have preceded them. The training they receive, however, is by no means a perfect one, and much will be needed before the Turkish officer can rise to a level with the European.

Their wives are women from the towns; as they generally follow their husbands to the different stations allotted to them, they obtain some knowledge of the world by travelling in various parts of the country, and are conversable and pleasant to associate with.

The sons of all good and wealthy families in the capital are either placed in the military schools, or sent to the *Kalem* (Chancellerie d'État), where the majority of the upper class Turkish youth are initiated into official routine and receive different grades as they proceed, the highest rank accorded corresponding with that of *Serik* (general of division). The officials who pass through this school are generally more polished in manner, more liberal in their ideas, and superior in many respects to the mean creatures who in former times were entrusted with offices for which they were quite unfit. This practice of appointing *Chiboukjis* (pipe-bearers) and other persons of low origin as *Mudirs* (governors of large villages) and *Kaimakams* (governors of districts), is now less in force, and is limited to Governors-general, who sometimes send their servants to occupy these positions. A Mudir may become a Kaimakam, and a Kaimakam a Pasha, but the top ranks can be obtained without passing through the lower grades. The inferior official placed over each village is the *Mukhtar*. He may be Christian or Moslem, according to the population; in mixed villages two are generally chosen to represent the respective creeds. These functionaries are entrusted with the administration of the village; they collect the taxes, and adjust the differences that arise among the peasants. They are too insignificant to do much good or much harm, unless they are very vicious. The Mudirs are at the head of the administration of their villages and of the medjliss or council, in which members chosen by the people take part. *Mutessarifs* are sub-governors of *Kazas* or large districts, and *Valis*, Governors-general of vilayets.

All this body of officials, together with the *Defterdars* (treasurers), *Mektebjis* (secretaries of the Pashalik), *politico memours* (political agents), etc., taken as a whole, are seldom fitted for their posts: they are ignorant and unscrupulous and much more bent upon securing their personal interests than the welfare of their country.

It must, however, in justice be said that, owing to the large sums the higher officials have to disburse in order to obtain their appointments, the great expense entailed in frequently moving themselves and their families from one extremity of the empire to the other, and the irregular and meagre pay the minor officials receive, it is impossible for them to live without resorting to some illicit means of increasing their incomes. And it must be admitted that praiseworthy exceptions are to be found here and there among both the higher and the lower officials.

The case is very simple. A man has to pay a vast sum of money to various influential people in order to get a certain post. His pay is nothing much to speak of. He is liable to be ejected by some one's caprice at any moment. If he is to repay his "election expenses" and collect a small reserve fund, he must give up all idea of honesty. An honest official in Turkey means a bankrupt. Under the system of favouritism and bribery no course but that of corruption and extortion is open to the official. *Il faut bien vivre:* and so long as the old system exists one must do in Turkey as the rest of the Turks do. It is utterly corrupt: but it must be reformed from the top downwards.

People in the east never think of asking what was

the origin of pashas or in what manner they have attained their high station. Genealogical trees in Turkey are not cultivated; most of the old stems (as explained in Part II., Chap. I.) were uprooted at the beginning of the present century; their branches, lopped off and scattered in all directions, have in some instances taken fresh root and started into a new existence; but they no longer represent the strength of the ancient trunk. The important body of beys, pashas, etc., thus abolished, had to be replaced by a new body selected without much scrutiny from the crowd of adventurers who were always awaiting some turn of fortune whereby they might be put into some official position and mend their finances.

Yusbashi A., one of the chief leaders of the Bashi-Bazouks, who performed the work of destruction at the beginning of the Bulgarian troubles, was subsequently sent to Constantinople by the military authorities to be hung; but being reprieved and pardoned, he was promoted to the rank of Pasha. He had come, when a boy, to the town of T—— as an apprentice in a miserable barber's shop; later on he left his master and entered the service of a native bey. During the Crimean war he joined the Bashi-Bazouks, and when peace was made returned to the town with the rank of captain and a certain amount of money, which he invested in land. By extortion and oppression of every kind exercised upon his peasants, he soon became a person of consequence in the town. Later on this man found his way to the Konak, was appointed member of the council, and was placed upon some commission by which he was enabled, through a series of illegal proceedings, to double and triple his fortune at the expense of the Government revenues. The misdeeds of this man and some of his associates becoming too flagrant to be longer overlooked, the Porte sent a commission to examine the Government *defters* or accounts. The captain, by no means frightened, but determined to avoid further trouble in the matter, is said to have set fire to the Konak in several places, so that all the documents that would have compromised him were destroyed and the Pasha and commission who came to inspect his doings barely escaped with their lives. Knowing the desperate character of the man they had to deal with, they were alarmed, and unfeignedly glad to get away and hush the matter up.

Thus the illustrious line of Pashas and Grand Vizirs, like the Kiprilis, was put aside and replaced by a long list of nonentities who, with the exception of a few such as Ali and Fuad Pashas, cannot be said to have benefited their country in any remarkable degree, or to have shown any special qualifications as statesmen.

The title of Grand Vizir, now nominally abolished, was one of the oldest and the highest given to a civil functionary. His appointment, being of a temporal nature, depended entirely upon the will of the Sultan, who might at his pleasure load the Vizir with honours, or relieve him of his head. This unpleasant uncertainty as to the future attached to the Vizir's office gradually almost disappeared as the Sultans began to recognise the indispensible services rendered to them by an able Grand Vizir. They began to appreciate the comfort of having ministers to think for them, make laws, and scheme reforms in their name: and this confidence, so agreeable to an indolent Sultan, and so convenient to an irresponsible minister, was the ruling principle of the constitution during the reign of Sultan Abdul-Medjid, who was affable to his ministers, changed them less frequently than his ancestors did, and loaded them indiscriminately with decorations and gifts. Not so his wayward and capricious brother and successor Abdul-Aziz, who scrupled not, on the slightest pretext, to dismiss his Grand Vizir. A trifling change in his personal appearance, a divergence of opinion, timidly expressed by the humble minister—who stood with hands crossed, dervish-fashion, on his shoulders, in the attitude of an obedient slave—just as much as a more serious fault, such as casting difficulties in the way of his Imperial Majesty with regard to his exorbitant demands on the treasury, were sufficient to seal the fate of the daring *Sadrazam*. But in spite of the difficulties and drawbacks and humiliations of the post, a Grand Vizir continued to be, after the Sultan, the most influential person in the country. The gates of his Konak were at once thrown open, and the other ministers and functionaries flocked to pay their respects to him. The governors of districts telegraphed their felicitations, while the antechamber and courts of his house and office were rarely free from the presence of a regular army of office-hunters, petitioners, dervishes, old women, and beggars, waiting for an audience or a chance glimpse of the minister on his exit, when each individual pressed forward to bring his or her claim to his notice. *Pek aye, bakalum olour,** were the words that generally dropped from the mouths even of the least amiable Vizirs on such occasions—words of hope that were eagerly caught by the interested parties, as well as by the numerous *cortége* of *kyatibs*, servants, and favourites of the great man who, according to the importance of the affairs or the station of the applicant, willingly undertook to be the advocate of the cause, guaranteeing its success by the counter-guarantee of receiving the *rushvets* or bribes needed in all stages of the affair. This method of transacting business, very general in Turkey, is called *hatir*, or by favour; its extent is unlimited, and its application varied and undefined; it can pardon the crime of murder, imprison an innocent person, liberate a condemned criminal, take away the property of one

* " Very well, we shall see, it may be done."

minister to present it to another, remove governors from their posts just as you change places in a quadrille, or simply turn out one set, as in the cotillon, to make room for another. Anything and everything can in fact be brought about by this system, except a divorce when the plea is not brought by the husband.

I have particularised the Grand Vizir as doing business in this way merely because it was he who was more appealed to in this manner than the other ministers, not because the others do not follow closely in his steps. Their duties are extensive and important, and demand for their proper and exact performance not only intelligence, but also high educational qualifications, which, with rare exceptions, Turkish officials do not possess—a capital defect, which, added to the uncertainty of the period they are likely to remain in office, and the systematic practice, pursued by each successive minister, of trying to undo what his predecessor had done for the country, and of dismissing most of the civil officials and provincial governors to replace them by some from his own set, greatly contributes to increase mal-administration, and to create the disorder that has long prevailed in Turkey.

About honesty I need not speak, for no business of any kind is undertaken without bribery; even if the minister should be above this, there are plenty of people surrounding him who would not be so scrupulous. Kibrizli Mehemet Pasha was one of the few high officials against whom no charge of the kind could be brought, but his *Kavass-Bashi* condescended to take even so small a sum as five piastres as a bribe. This Pasha was a thorough gentleman, high-minded both in his administrative affairs and family life. After he lost his position as Grand Vizir, I had occasion to see a great deal of him; he took the reverses of fortune with great calmness and *sang-froid:* so do all Turks meet " the slings and arrows of outrageous fortune."

The fall of a Minister was generally rumoured some time before it took place, during which period he and those around him tried to make the most of the opportunities left to them, while the opposition continued their intrigues until the blow finally fell. When this happened the *Sadrazam* remained at home, the gates of his Konak were closed, and the world, including his best friends, would pass without venturing to enter; the only visitors would be his banker, doctor, and creditors, who in prosperity and adversity never neglect this duty.

During the administration of a Grand Vizir, his harem was also called upon to play its part and take the lead in the female society of Stamboul. The *salon* of the chief wife, like that of her husband, would be thrown open, and crowds of visitors, including the wives of the other ministers, would arrive to offer their respects and felicitations, and demand favours and promotions for their sons, or posts for their husbands. All these visitors, on their arrival, were ushered into the antechamber according to their respective stations, where they took off their *feridjés* and refreshed themselves with sweets, coffee, sherbets, etc. The interval between this and their reception, sometimes of several hours' duration, was spent in conversation among the visitors, in which some of the ladies of the household, or some visitors staying in the house, would join, until they were requested to proceed to the drawing-room. When the hostess appeared all would rise from their seats, walk towards the door, make *temenlas* and deep obeisances, and endeavour to kiss her foot or the hem of her garment, an act of homage which she would accept, but gracefully and with much dignity try to prevent in those of high rank by saying *Istafourla* (excuse me—don't do it). The conversation, started afresh, would depend for subjects upon the disposition and tact of the mistress of the house; but would chiefly consist in flattery and adulation, carried sometimes to a ridiculous extent. The manner of the *hanoum effendi* would be smooth and friendly towards the partizans of her husband, curt towards those of the opposition, but patronising and protecting in its general tone towards all. Should the Vizir's lady be of the unprincipled type, the conversation would bear a different *cachet*. I was told by some distinguished Turkish ladies that when they paid a visit to the wife of a short-lived Vizir, the lady, both old and ugly, entertained them with a recital of the follies and weaknesses of her husband and exposed some of her own not more select proceedings into the bargain.

The wife of a Grand Vizir also played a great part with regard to the changes, appointments, and dismissions which followed each new Vizirate, by the influence she exercised both over him and also in high quarters, where she often found means to make herself as influential as at home.

I have often been asked what a Turkish lady does all day long? Does she sleep or eat sugar-plums, and is she kept under lock and key by a Blue-Beard of a husband, who allows her only the liberty of waiting upon him? A Turkish lady is certainly shut up in a harem, and there can be no doubt that she is at liberty to indulge in the above-mentioned luxuries should she feel so disposed; she has possibly, at times, to submit to being locked up, but the key is applied to the outer gates, and is left in the keeping of the friendly eunuch. Besides, woman is said to have a will of her own, and "where there is a will there is a way" is a proverb to which Turkish ladies are no strangers. I have seldom met with one who did not make use of her liberty; in one sense she may not have so much freedom as Englishwomen have, but in many others she possesses more. In her home she is perfect mistress of her time and of her property, which she can dispose of as she thinks proper. Should she have cause of complaint against any one, she is allowed to be very open spoken, holds her ground, and fights her own battles with astonishing coolness and decision.

Turkish ladies appreciate to the full as much as their husbands the virtues of the indispensable cup of coffee and cigarette; this is their first item in the day's programme. The *hanoums* may next take a bath, the young ladies wash at the *abtest* hours: the slaves when they can find time. The *hanoum* will then attend to her husband's wants, bring him his pipe and coffee, his slippers and pelisse. While smoking he will sit on the sofa, whilst his wife occupies a lower position near him, and the slaves roll up the bedding from the floor. If the gentleman be a government functionary the official bag will be brought in, and he will look over his documents, examining some, affixing his seal to others, saying a few words in the intervals to his wife, who always addresses him in a ceremonious manner with great deference and respect. The children will then trot in in their *gedjliks* with the hair uncombed, to be caressed, and ask for money with which to buy sweets and cakes. The custom of giving pence to children daily is so prevalent that it is practised even by the poor.

The children, after an irregular breakfast, are sent

to school or allowed to roam about the house; the *effendi* proceeds to perform his out-of-door toilet and leaves the *haremlik*, when the female portion of the establishment, freed from the pleasure or obligation of attending to his wants, begin the day's occupation. If this should include any special or unusual household work, such as preserve-making, washing or ironing, or general house-cleaning, the lady, be she of the highest position, will take part in it with the slaves. This is certainly not necessary, for she has plenty of menials, but is done in order to fill up the day, many hours of which necessarily hang heavily on her hands when not enlivened by visiting or being visited. In the capital, however, less of this kind of employment is indulged in by the fashionable *hanoums*, who are trying to create a taste for European occupations by learning music, foreign languages, and fine needle-work. The time for dressing is irregular. A lady may think proper to do her hair and make herself tidy for luncheon, or she may remain in her *gedjlik* and slippers all day. This fashion of receiving visitors *en négligé* is not considered at all peculiar unless the visit has been announced beforehand.

Visiting and promenading, the principal amusements of Turkish ladies, are both affairs of very great importance. Permission has previously to be asked from the husband, who, if liberally disposed, freely grants it; but if jealous and strict, he will disapprove of seeing his family often out of doors. When a walk or drive is projected the children all begin to clamour to go with their mother. Scarcely is this question settled by coaxing or giving them money, than another arises as to which of the slaves are to be allowed to go. Tears, prayers, and even little quarrels and disturbances follow, until the mistress finally selects her party. The details of the toilette are very numerous; the face has to be blanched, then rouged, the eyebrows and lashes to be blackened with *surmé*, and a variety of other little coquetries resorted to requiring time and patience before the final adjustment of the *yashmak* and *feridgé*.

Then comes the scramble for places in the carriage, the *hanoums* naturally seat themselves first, the rest squeeze themselves in, and sit upon each other's knees. It is wonderful to see how well they manage this close packing, and how long they can endure the uncomfortable postures in which they are fixed.

If the excursion is solely for visiting, the occupants of the carriages make the best of the time and liberty by coquetting with the grooms and *agas* in attendance, should these be young and handsome, and sending salaams to the passers by, mingled with laughter and frolic. But when the excursion has a picnic in prospective, or a long drive into the country, the gaiety and fun indulged in is bewildering; and the *hanoums* can only be compared to a flock of strange birds suddenly let loose from their cages, not knowing what to make of their new freedom. Flirting, smoking, eating fruits and sweets, walking about, running, or lounging on the carpets they bring with them, varied by music and singing, fill the day. They usually set out early and return before sunset in time to receive their master on his visit to the harem before dinner. When this meal is over, the company, comfortably dressed in their *négligé* costume, indulge in coffee and cigarettes, and the events of the day are discussed. The ladies then retire to rest at an early hour, and rise the next day to go through the same routine.

At the foot of the imperial throne we see the princes, who, like children at dessert, are to be seen, not heard. They now enjoy a degree of freedom before unknown, and their wants and caprices are to a certain extent satisfied by allowances from the Sultan. In childhood and youth they are masters of their own time, and employ it as they please. On emerging from boyhood they are furnished with harems; some more distantly related to the reigning Sultan are allowed to have children; but the others are denied that privilege. All these members of the imperial family live a very secluded life. They are not allowed to take any part in the administrative, hold commissions in the army or navy, or enter the civil service.

The only exception to this rule was the son of the late Sultan Abdul-Aziz, who, at the age of ten, was, I believe, a captain in the army, and a few years later was made a general. This is said to have given the occasion for a reproach made to the prince by his father, who at the moment of his deposition turned to him and said, " My son, I placed you in the military school where you remained three years without making a single friend; see what this has now led to ! "

This reproach of being friendless addressed to any of the princes is unjust, as they are not allowed to make friendships. Friends for a prince mean a party, and a party means cabals and conspiracies, so all such dangerous connections are carefully suppressed, and the prince, under the influence of the suspicion and espionage by which he is surrounded, is as little disposed to have any friends among the influential classes and men of rank as they are to court his friendship or approach him too closely. A personal friend of the ex-Sultan Murad told me that in early youth that prince and he had been very much thrown together, and a sincere affection had sprung up between them, which, however, on Sultan Abdul-Medjid's death, had to be entirely given up. Rare meetings between them could only be arranged when the prince went to Pera on shopping expeditions. Thus the Ottoman princes, spoilt in childhood, secluded from active public life, are left to vegetate in their respective homes.

The Princes of the Blood and all relations of the late Sultan used always to be cleared out of the way on the accession of a new Padishah; but the custom has fallen into disuse since the time of Mahmoud II., who found it necessary to order the strangulation of the deposed Sultan, the drowning in sacks of 174 of his wives and odalisks, and also the decapitation of a great number of other persons. This measure, considered needful to ensure the inviolability of his person, as the only remaining representative of the house of Othman, soon put an end to the rebellion that had occasioned his ascension to the throne. On the day of his proclamation as Sultan, thirty-three heads were exposed at the gate of the Seraglio to bear evidence to the fact. Rebellion, fire, and murder, it was said, could not be otherwise put down than by counter-violence, and the extreme measures adopted by the new sovereign ended in the restoration of order in the capital.

Notwithstanding this black page in the history of Mahmoud, this Sultan, to whom history has not yet done justice, was one of the best, most enlightened, and powerful of Ottoman sovereigns.

Unlike most of his predecessors, he had not wasted the long years of captivity in idleness and frivolous occupations, but had seriously employed them in study. He originated the material changes that have since been made in the life of seraglio inmates, and also endeavoured to better the condition of his Christian subjects. Whatever progress has been made by the Turkish Mohammedans in the road of civilisation must also be attributed to his efforts. Amid wars without and revolts within, the discontent of the Moslems at the attempted innovations, the clamouring of the Christians for the amelioration of their condition, the Sultan struggled on for thirty years with a perseverance worthy of the cause, till death put an end to his work. He was succeeded by his son, the liberal but weak-minded Abdul-Medjid.

The young Sultan was well imbued with the ideas of his father, but less capable of carrying them out: yet he showed himself liberal and sincerely desirous of improving the degraded condition into which the country had fallen.

The security of life and property became greater under his rule. Executions and confiscation of property became less frequent, and a general change for the better in the material existence of the people was decreed; but unfortunately the Sultan could not insure the carrying out of his decrees. The exchequer, impoverished by the extravagance of the palace and the corruption of the officials, was on the brink of bankruptcy, which was only postponed by the foreign loans obtained in the succeeding reign.

Had the Sultan's perseverance in seeing these changes enforced been equal to his good-will in ordaining them, Turkey might have been spared many of its present miseries.

He was beloved by his subjects, who, in the midst of their misery, forgave his weakness in remembering his gentleness and benevolence to those who appealed to his mercy. His aversion to bloodshed was so great that he was never known to decree a single execution. This was, of course, a serious hindrance to carrying on the judicial arrangements of the country. In cases of urgent necessity his signature had to be obtained by subterfuge.

A lover of pleasure and ease, Abdul-Medjid, on coming to the throne, soon plunged into that life of self-indulgence, luxury, and excess, which at once began to tell upon his delicate constitution and by degrees affected in a most fatal manner his moral and physical faculties; and he died of exhaustion on June 25th, 1861.

His successor, Abdul-Aziz, had been the first to profit by the indulgence and liberality of his brother, who from the beginning to the end of his reign showed him genuine brotherly affection, allowed him uncontrolled freedom as heir-apparent, and furnished him with a very liberal income, making a point of never getting any object of value for himself, without offering its equivalent to his brother.

Abdul-Aziz, however, did not make any good use of the liberty he enjoyed before coming to the throne.

Sensual, extravagant, and narrow-minded, his occupations and pleasures were anything but imperial: his wasteful habits were ruinous to his country, whilst his want of judgment and foresight prevented his realising the fatal effects of his conduct. This may, however, be accounted for, to a great extent, by the fact that he was subject at times to *merak* (aberration of mind). From an early age he began to give signs of that whimsical, suspicious, and morose disposition which during the latter part of his reign became the principal characteristic of his nature.

Unlike his brother, Abdul-Medjid, he was strongly built, and his personal appearance was singularly unattractive. His tastes and amusements, very much in harmony with his exterior, showed themselves in all kinds of extravagant and odd fancies. Cock-fighting was a spectacle in which he greatly delighted, by turns decorating or exiling the combatants.

In his moments of good humour he often imposed a wrestling match upon his ministers and favourites, at times taking an active part in the sport. The celebrated Nevrez Pasha, half knave, half fool, who from the lowest stage of seraglio functions had been raised to a ministerial position, was the one generally chosen by the Sultan with whom to measure his strength.

The corpulent Pasha never failed to be the beaten party, the ludicrous attitudes into which he fell; and his jokes, gave him a higher grade whenever they were called into play, and caused him to say that every kick he received from the Imperial foot was worth to him a *Nishan* (a decoration), a konak, or a vizirlik.

It would, however, be unfair not to acknowledge in this Sultan some good services rendered to his country.

One of these is the purchase of the fine fleet of ironclads the Porte now possesses; another, his untiring efforts in placing the army on the, comparatively speaking, improved and high footing on which it stood at the beginning of the war; and a third, the construction of the railways now existing in the country. Some will perhaps reckon among his merits the shrewdness he and his ministers displayed in accomplishing these undertakings with funds that were not exactly theirs.

The details of the dethronement, short captivity and death of Sultan Abdul-Aziz, though extremely curious and interesting, are as yet but little known to the public. One of the ladies of his seraglio related some of the incidents connected with these events to me, but she said, "we cannot now divulge all, for fear of prejudicing the living, but in course of time, when history reveals unknown facts, all doubts and mystery on his untimely death will be removed." Upon which she burst into tears, and repeatedly uttered the Turkish exclamation of distress, "Aman! Aman!"

She then recited to me in Arabic, the verse which the unfortunate Sultan, on entering his prison, traced

on the dust that covered the table. The following is
a translation :—

> Man's destiny is Allah's will,
> Sceptres and power are His alone,
> My fate is written on my brow,
> Lowly I bend before His Throne.

Turning towards the window the Sultan noticed that one of his much-prized ironclads had been placed in front of the *Yahli* which served as his prison, with the guns pointed towards him. But a still more appalling sight met his gaze. A sailor was seized by a few of his comrades, who, pointing him out to the Sultan, passed a crimson *kushak* or girdle round his neck and led him three times round the deck, signifying to the unfortunate captive that in three days he would undergo the same operation. Pointing this out to the Validé Sultana, he exclaimed, with emotion: "Mother! see to what use the force I have created for the preservation and aggrandisement of my empire is applied! This is evidently the death reserved for me." A belt containing some of the most valuable crown-jewels, which the Sultan had placed on his person when leaving the palace, disappeared the day he was found dead, and has never since been heard of. The Sultan had to ask for food repeatedly before he was supplied with it, and even then what he obtained was given him on the *sofra* of a common soldier. On my further questioning this lady on the cause of the Sultan's untimely end, she passed her hand over her lips, meaning they were sealed, and muttering a "*Turbé Istafourla*" said, "it is not in my power to reveal more!—the justification of the dead must be withheld so long as it endangers the living: The duty of the devoted is to keep silence until history can divulge secrets that will then harm none."

Soon after the death of Abdul-Aziz, I had occasion to discuss it with a Turkish general. Expressing his opinion of the equally unfortunate Sultan Murad, the Pasha, with smiling urbanity, said, "I cannot tell as yet; but with us, Sultans are now so numerous, that we can afford to sweep them away successively with a broom, if they do not suit us."

Every one is acquainted with the quiet and peaceable manner in which Sultan Abdul-Aziz was dethroned in 1876, to make room for his nephew Murad. This unfortunate prince was as little acquainted with the changes that were being planned as was his uncle, and his sensitive nature, unprepared for the shock that placed him on the throne, caused him to receive the messenger who came to inform him of the change in his position more as the bearer of his sentence to death than the herald of sovereignty. Taken by surprise at the moment he was about to retire, the prince hastily put on his coat and met the vizir at the door of the Mabeyn. Deathly pale, but calm and resigned, he looked in his face, and said "What is my offence, and whom have I ever harmed that I should thus be doomed to an untimely death?"

Entirely ignorant of the conspiracy that opened a path for him to the throne, and severely grieved for his uncle's misfortunes, the news of his tragical end is said to have given the first shock to the young sovereign's intellect, and, followed by the murder of the ministers, with its equally distressing details, determined the bent of his vacillating mind. One of the first symptoms of his insanity was a habit he fell into of spanning with his hand the distance between the wrist and elbow joint, striking the bend of the arm with his hand, then starting, and reflecting. I have never heard of his having broken out into acts of violence, except upon one occasion, when he raised a stick and struck his brother-in-law. On one occasion he made his escape into the garden, where he was found sitting on a marble slab, making grimaces at those who approached him. He is said to have experienced some lucid intervals; one of these chanced to be at the moment the salutes were being fired on the occasion of his brother Abdul-Hamid's ascension to the throne. Looking at his son, a promising youth of fourteen, he said, "My boy, what is the reason of this firing?" "Oh!" said the boy, wishing to spare his father's feelings, "It is the fête of a foreign monarch." "No," said the unhappy monarch, "it is the proclamation of my own dethronement, and the accession of thy uncle to the throne; God's will be done!" Heaving a deep sigh, he shed a few tears, and, happily for him, under the circumstances, relapsed into his former state.

Sultan Murad was said to possess many of the virtues of his father, a kind and gentle disposition, and intelligence and liberality of ideas. During his short reign, the affability of his manners, and the desire he showed to please all parties, irrespective of race or religion, and to abolish the burdens that weighed upon them, had gained for him the respect and affection of his subjects, which is evinced even to the present day by sorrow and sympathy for his misfortunes.

The present Sultan at first declined the imperial throne, from feelings of affection and delicacy towards his brother, and could only be prevailed upon to accept it, when all the physicians, called in for advice, pronounced Murad's case quite hopeless. Sultan Abdul-Hamid is much esteemed and highly spoken of by persons who have had the honour of conversing with his Imperial Majesty. He is, moreover, said to be qualified for his position, being liberal in his ideas, and possessed of many of the qualities of a good sovereign, and desirous of carrying out the reforms that alone can ensure the happiness of his people and restore prosperity to the country. Unfortunately, he came to the throne at a moment when the best and most gifted of sovereigns could do little single-handed. When affairs are settled, much will naturally be expected from him, which his friends and the well-wishers of Turkey feel confident he will realise.

I have not yet mentioned an important section of the Turkish community — the slaves. Slavery in Turkey is now reduced mainly to one sex. Male slaves, except in the capacity of eunuchs, are now rare, though every now and then a cargo of them is smuggled into some port and privately disposed of, since the Government professes to share the anti-slavery views of England. But female slavery is a necessary part of the seraglio and of the Turkish harem system. The seraglio is of course recruited from its numbers; and few Turks can afford to keep more than one free wife. A second wife insists upon a separate establishment, and causes endless jealousy to the first wife and trouble to the husband. But a slave is no cause of jealousy, lives in the same house as the wife, and costs much less to keep than a free woman. Female slaves, too, are generally given by fathers to their sons, to avoid the expense of a marriage; and daughters on marrying, are always supplied with a slave as lady's-maid. Moreover, slaves are in much request as servants, and do their work excellently, besides presenting many advantages and conveniences that are not found in free women.

The condition of slaves in Turkey is not a hard one. The principle is of course radically wrong, and the initial stage is full of cruelty. But the women are not often ill-treated; and when an occasional case of violence and ill-usage occurs, it excites general indignation among the Moslems. A slave is entitled to her liberty after seven years of bondage, and she generally gets it, and is dowered and married to a freeman, though sometimes a bad master will evade the law by selling her before the seven years have quite expired. But this is a rare case, and the slave system in Turkey is, as a whole, a widely different thing from American slavery.

The only class who suffer much are the negresses. When they are freed and married off it not seldom happens that from their native wildness or other causes they quarrel with their husbands and are turned off to earn their own living as best they may. Their condition then becomes very wretched, and the quarter in which they live is a dismal group of rickety houses, inhabited by a miserable and ragged set of women and children. This is by no means the case with the Abyssinians or the half-castes, who rank higher, and never have to appeal to public charity. But the negresses are hardly worse off than the disabled slaves. If a woman of this class by some accident or age becomes unfit for work, she is looked upon as a burden and very badly cared for.

Turkish slavery is not so bad as it might be: the system is softened by many humane laws, and is marked by a kindly paternal character. Yet it is a blot on the country, and so soon as the harem system and polygamy can be got rid of, it too must go.

CHAPTER V.

THE ARMENIANS AND JEWS IN TURKEY.

Historical Misfortunes of the Armenians—Refugees in Turkey, Russia, Persia—Want of Patriotism—Appearance and Character—Armenian Ladies—American Mission Work—Schools—The Jews of Turkey—Reputed Origin—Classes—Conservatives and Progressives—Jewish Trade—Prejudice against Jews—Alliance with Moslems—Wealth and Indigence—Cause of the Latter—The Jewish Quarter—Education—" L'Alliance Israélite "—Divorce among the Jews merely a Question of the Highest Bidder.

THERE are few nations that can compete with the Armenians in historical misery. Tossed about between Arsacid, Roman, and Sassanian; fought over by Persian and Byzantine; a common prey to Arabs, Mongols, and Turk, it is a matter for amazement that the nation still exists at all. Up to the fourteenth century the Armenians held persistently to their country; but after its subjection by the Mamluk Sultans of Egypt, the unfortunate inhabitants, seeing no hope of the restoration of their old independence, and despairing of relief from the oppression and spoiling to which they had been exposed for centuries, began to migrate to other countries, to try whether fortune would everywhere be so unkind to them. Some went to Anatolia, others to Egypt, or to Constantinople, where they were kindly received and allowed a Patriarch. Some wandered into Poland, whence they were soon driven out by the determined hostility of the Jesuits, and forced to take refuge in Russia, where they were joined by numbers of their compatriots and formed a colony at Grigoripol. Others went to the Crimea and Astrachan, and many of the Armenians who had first gone to Turkey followed in their steps. The Armenians in Russia were treated with great kindness by Peter the Great and Catherine, and were granted special rights and privileges. A colony of Armenians was settled at New Nakhitchevan on the Don. After more persecutions, from the Ottomans, in the sixteenth century, a large number of Armenian refugees set out for Persia. The Shah received them graciously, and settled them in Ispahan. Afterwards, during the war between the Shah and the Sultan, a depopulation of Armenia was attempted, with the view of destroying the Turkish power there. Twelve thousand families were dragged off to Persia, most of whom died on the way. The settlers at Ispahan were at first treated well, but afterwards subjected to such persecution that they were obliged to seek a home in other lands. The portion of Armenia ceded by Persia to Russia, thus acquiring for the first time the necessary conditions of peace and safety, became the refuge of the Armenians who had not already left their native land, but who now, driven beyond endurance by the oppressive rule of the Pashas, crossed the frontier and immediately found themselves possessed of the ordinary privileges of Russian subjects, and able to carry on commercial pursuits, in which the nation excels, in peace and confidence. Thus the Armenian race became scattered over the face of the earth, whilst only a remnant still lives in the land of its ancestors. The Armenians are to be met with all over the East. There are large numbers of them at Constantinople and a few other towns, such as Adrianople, Gallipoli, and Rodosto. In the towns of the interior, however, their number is small.

Ages of Asiatic oppression, varied by few glimpses of prosperity, in the traditional garden of Eden, have obliterated whatever love the Armenians formerly had for their country, which they willingly deserted to seek a home wherever they could find one. When the first cravings of their hearts for peace and security had been satisfied, they settled down in communities, forgot their country and its past history, and assimilated their external forms and customs with those of the nations among whom they lived, with the philosophic *nonchalance* of the Asiatic. In Armenia, the people who remain, remembering the terrible sufferings their country has gone through, have followed the wise policy of burying in the depths of their hearts any surviving sparks of patriotism or love of liberty; though these hidden sparks may some day be fanned into flame by the introduction of education and by the influence Russia is exerting in the country. So far the Porte may felicitate itself on the success its foreign policy has met with in Armenia. This policy, with its consequences of misery and suffering, is safe only so long as ignorance and stupid docility prevail among the masses; this cannot last for ever, and in the face of present events it will not be surprising to hear of troubles breaking out in that direction as well as everywhere else. It is only a question of time. In Turkey, political feeling among the Armenians is still in its infancy; but there must be thinking men among the educated young generation who are watchful of the present and hopeful for the future.

The Armenians as a race are strong, well-built, and hardy. With these constitutional advantages they readily take to the mechanical arts; but commerce and banking are their *forte*, and in these they show great ability and as much honesty as is possible in a country where, of all difficulties, that of following a straight line of conduct is the greatest. They are considered crafty, but at the same time exercise considerable moral influence in the countries they inhabit, especially at Constantinople, where some of the rich Armenians have been very closely connected with the high dignities of the empire. Their fancy for toad-eating is well adapted to please the Turks, who by turns show them regard and contempt.

There is an old saying, that no Turk can be happy in the evening without having cracked a few jokes with an Armenian during the day.

The physiognomy of the Armenians is generally dark. Their heads are large, with black, coarse, and abundant hair. Their eyes, overshadowed by long eyelashes and thick eyebrows, meeting over the nose, are black and almond-shaped, but lack the lustre of Greek eyes. The nose, the worst feature of the Armenian face, is large and hooked; the mouth large, with thick lips; the chin prominent. Their bearing would be dignified but for a certain want of grace. Armenians are divided into two classes denominated *Kalun* and *Injé*, or coarse and refined. The latter belong to the Roman Catholic creed, and are certainly more advanced than the former, who are far more subservient to the Turks and keep as much as possible in the background, devoting themselves to the interests of the Porte in general and to their own in particular.

In Armenia the ladies are secluded to the extent of dining and sitting apart from the men, and are said to be very backward in every respect. Their costume very nearly resembles that formerly worn by Turkish women. They display the same disregard to neatness as the latter, without possessing their redeeming point of cleanliness: their heads are specially neglected, and abound in live stock of a most migratory character. My mother once pointed out one of these creatures on the forehead of an Armenian girl, and reprimanded her for her neglect of her person: the girl answered that she did not know that any human being could exist without them!

The Armenian ladies of Constantinople are renowned for their beauty, which is supposed to lie particularly in the languid expression of their eyes. Both in Constantinople and Smyrna there are many Armenians of both sexes who are well educated, and scarcely to be distinguished from Europeans in society. I was once invited to an Armenian fancy ball, where I was the only European present. Everything was arranged as in civilised society, the stewards were equal to their duties, and the costumes were *recherchés* and varied. One slight pretty girl, in particular, dressed in the old Turkish costume, produced a great sensation, and was deservingly besieged by partners, for she waltzed to perfection. Many of the ladies and gentlemen spoke English, and nearly all French, and I certainly spent a very pleasant evening among them.

In the privacy of their homes the women, as a rule, are untidy and slatternly. They are exceedingly fond of dress, and, to the best of their ability, copy the Parisian fashions; but their natural want of taste seldom fails to make itself evident in toilettes of glaring and ill-assorted colours, while their hands, arms, and necks are overloaded with jewellery. Out of doors they are shod with boots of Parisian manufacture, on whose high heels they totter along the badly-paved streets; but they exchange them for slippers down at heel on re-entering their homes. Even those who have lived in Europe, and no longer consider themselves Orientals, sit cross-legged on their sofas in the most careless costumes.

The Armenians have advanced but a very little way on the road of education. The most enlightened are certainly those in British India, whilst those of them who are Russian subjects have of late considerably improved. Hitherto, the nation has never had a fair chance, but that it has the possibility of progress in it is shown by the fact, that no sooner are the Armenians placed under a firm and wise government than they at once begin to go forwards, in every respect. The progress of the inhabitants of Russian Armenia has begun to work a political revival among their brethren under Turkish rule. A wish for instruction is everywhere beginning to be shown, and it has received a strong and most salutary impulse from the numerous American missionaries now established throughout Armenia. The untiring efforts of these praiseworthy and accomplished workers in the cause of civilisation and humanity are beginning to bear fruit, especially since education has become one of their principal objects. They are working wonders among the uncultivated inhabitants of this hitherto unhappy country, where mission-schools, founded in all directions, are doing the double service of instructing the people by their enlightened moral and religious teaching, and of stimulating among the wealthy a spirit of rivalry, which leads them to see their own ignorance and superstitious debasement, and raises a desire to do for themselves, by the establishment of Armenian schools, what American philanthropy has so nobly begun to do for them.

The moral influence that America is now exercising in the East through the quiet but dignified and determined policy of its Legation at Constantinople, curiously free from political intrigues and rivalry, is daily increasing, and has the most salutary effect on the country. It watches with a jealous care over the rights and safety of the missionaries, who are loved and respected wherever they settle, and make their influence felt in the remotest corners of Turkey. Next to Greece, whose educational efforts are naturally greater throughout the country, it is America that will be entitled to the gratitude of the Christians for her ready aid in elevating the ignorant masses to the dignity of civilised beings.

In the Armenian schools, the Turkish, Armenian, and French languages are taught: the two former are generally well mastered by the pupils, Armenians being considered apt linguists: a very fair knowledge of French is also common among them.

Armenians do not show any taste for the arts and sciences. One seldom hears of an Armenian artist, doctor, or lawyer, and the few that do exist attain only mediocrity.

It is difficult to obtain correct statistical information of native Armenian schools, but I can affirm that of late years they have greatly increased in number, and are much improved in their organisation and mode of teaching. At Constantinople, Erzeroum, and many other towns where the Armenian communities are large, excellent schools for girls have been founded. In towns where these are wanting, many girls are sent for a few years to the boys' schools, where religion, reading, and writing are taught them. Turkish, the language with which the Armenians are most conversant, is also taught from books written in the Armenian characters. In all other respects, the education of Armenian girls is very much neglected; from an early age they fall into a listless, aimless existence, and are seldom taught to busy themselves with needlework or any useful or rational employment. Some of the wealthy families at Constantinople and Smyrna are manifesting a desire for improvement in this respect, by engaging European governesses or sending their children to European schools; but it will be long before either sex gets rid of the ignorance and indolence which circumstances, perhaps, as much as nature, have forced upon it.

The Jews of Turkey.

The Jews dwelling in Turkey are, to a great extent, descendants of those expelled from Spain by the Inquisition and the edict of 1492: their language is a corrupt Spanish dialect; but they are conversant with those of the places they inhabit. Besides these and other native Jews, there is an influential class of European Jews who are certainly in the van of progress among their co-religionists in Turkey. They are educated, liberal-minded men, and, as a rule, a prosperous class. They are untiring in their efforts to develop education among the native Jews by establishing schools, assisting the poor, and setting a good example of conduct by their own higher manner of life.

The native Jews may be divided into two classes, Conservative and Progressive. The Conservative Jews are strict, rigid, and intolerant to their brethren: they keep aloof from the rest of the world, and mix with it only in business transactions. They are cunning and avaricious, and although some possess large fortunes, they are seldom known to use them for the benefit of the community, or for any other good purpose. Strongly opposed to liberal education, the influence they exercise over their respective communities is always employed to counteract the action of the enlightened party. The Progressive Jews, who are becoming pretty numerous among the upper classes, act in direct opposition to these principles and endeavour as much as possible to shake off old customs and traditions.

The chief occupations of the Jewish community are banking and commerce. They excel in both to such a degree, that where a man belonging to another nationality can only realise a fair competence, the Israelite makes a fortune; whilst in positions in which other men would starve, the Jew will manage to keep himself and family in comfort. The secret of this well-known fact lies in the unusual finesse and ability displayed by Israelites occupying high positions in the business world, and the cunning and ingenuity of the lower orders, who with moderate exertion make the most of their trade, and extort all they can from those with whom they have dealings.

With regard to moral and personal qualifications, the Jews of Turkey are the most backward and debased of any of the races. This degenerate condition may be attributed to more than one cause. One of the chief causes, however, is the general feeling of antipathy shown towards Jews in a semi-civilised country: all kinds of real and fictitious sins are attributed to them, from the charge of kidnapping children (an absurdity still credited everywhere in Turkey) to the proverbial accusation of never transacting business with members of other creeds without infringing the laws of good faith and honesty. To apply this latter charge to the whole community would be unjust, for there are honest, liberal, and straightforward men; but there is no doubt the reputation is not altogether ill-earned among them.

The Jews in Turkey have from all times shown a greater liking for their Moslem neighbours than for the Christians. The Moslems sneer at them and treat them with disrespect as a nation, but are far more tolerant and lenient towards them than towards the Christians. The Jews, on their side, although at heart feeling no disposition to respect their Mohammedan masters, show great sympathy outwardly for them; and in case of a dispute between Christians and Mohammedans, unanimously espouse the cause of the latter. The wealthy Israelites would render every assistance in their power to remove the difficulties of the Government, while those of humbler standing tender their service for the performance of anything that may be required of them, however degrading.

In few countries is the contrast of wealth and indigence among the Jews so striking as in Turkey. On one side may be seen wealth so great as to command respect for its possessors, and give them an influence in the localities in which they spring up greater than that of all other nationalities: whilst hard by one sees poverty and wretchedness of the most sickening nature. The principal cause of this is the limited sphere of action allotted to, or rather adopted by, the Jewish communities. They evince a strong repugnance to going beyond the few trades generally practised by the labouring classes; the rest content themselves with performing the coarsest and dirtiest work of the town. From generation to generation the Jews will cling to these callings without allowing themselves to be tempted beyond them,' or raising themselves in the social scale by taking to agricultural or other pursuits that might ensure them a comfortable home and an honourable living.

In towns where the Jewish element predominates, it is packed in dingy, crowded quarters, in hovels, buried in filth. These miserable abodes contrast strongly with the fine and showy houses of the rich. Both rich and poor of the native Jews may be seen in their court-yards or at their doors, the mother rocking the cradle, the children playing in the mud, and the women and girls washing or engaged in other household occupations. The men on coming home don their *négligé* indoor costume and join the family party, lounging on a sofa smoking and chatting. This community is very noisy, the most natural conversation among them being carried on in the loud tones of lively dispute, all talking at once in such an elevated key as to be heard at a considerable distance.

They are certainly lively and cheerful, neither want nor poverty detaining them at recreation-time from listening to their discordant national music, which they accompany by a vocal performance of a deafening nature.

Some of the women are very pretty, and their beauty is heightened by their peculiar costume and gay head-dress. They are, however, cold and rather graceless in demeanour, and are not noted for intelligence.

Education among the native Jews was completely neglected until very recently, when the efforts of the European Jews and a few of the liberal natives finally produced a beneficial reaction, and schools of a superior order, principally dependencies of " L'Alliance Israelite " formed in Europe for the benefit of the Eastern Jews, have been established in all the principal towns, and are said to have greatly benefited the rising generation, which is wanting neither in intelligence nor aptitude for study. Before the establishment of these schools the Jews had to send their children to European or Greek schools, where they received an indifferent style of education, as the training, owing to the difference of religion and habits, did not include the complete course.

The director of the schools established by " L'Alliance Israelite " gave me most satisfactory accounts of the progress made by the pupils attending them, and of the increase of morality among them. The Jewish girls have not equal advantages with the boys with respect to educational establishments. This unfortunate difference will, it is hoped, be in time remedied by the schools, founded by the same society and others, in the principal towns. All these schools owe their origin to the generosity of wealthy Israelities like Baron Hirsh and others, who have endowed the establishments with the funds necessary for rendering them useful and of lasting duration. In Salonika the girls' school, established some years ago, has, thanks to the able management and munificence of the Messrs. Allatini, been placed upon an excellent footing, and, being presided over by the most intelligent and gifted European ladies of the community, is doing great and good service.

Besides these schools, there is one of older standing connected with the Missionary Society, under the direction of a missionary and three able and devoted Scottish ladies, who receive a large class of day pupils and give them the benefit of sound education for a trifling fee. This part of missionary work is in reality the best and most beneficial to the community, and far more so than the efforts made at proselytism—efforts which, so far as I can ascertain, have nowhere met with success.

Polygamy is prohibited among the Jews: but their divorce laws are very lenient; and a separation is the easiest thing in the world—for the husband. A wife cannot get a separation without her husband's consent. Practically, however, this is seldom refused if a sum of money is offered. A gentleman, aware of this Jewish weakness, and falling in love with a Syrian beauty who was married to a Jew, bought her divorce for 2,000*l*.

In some towns the morality of the community is closely watched. In Adrianople, for instance, a faithless wife is led for three successive days round the Jewish quarter, and compelled to stop before every door to be spat upon and abused. At Salonika, where the Jews are very numerous, it is quite otherwise. Among the wealthy and liberal many of the old customs have been set aside, intermarriage with European Jewish families is of frequent occurrence, and many modifications permitted which do not seem strictly conformed to the Mosaic law.

The affairs of the Jewish communities, like those of the Christians, are managed by elders. The chief Rabbi has control over all matters regarding the religious and social interests, and is in direct communication with his superior at Constantinople.

CHAPTER VI.

THE CIRCASSIANS, TATARS, AND GIPSIES OF TURKEY.

The Circassians.—Their Immigration into Turkey in 1864—Their Camp—Chiefs and Slaves—Origin of the charge of Cannibalism—Assistance of the Government and the Peasantry—Bulgarian Views of the New-comers—A Cherkess Girl—Sale of Circassian Women—Depredations—Cattle-lifting—Circassian fellow-travellers in a Steamer—Appearance and Character—Scheme of philanthropy respectfully offered to Russia.

The Tatars.—Their Arrival in the Dobrudcha with a Good Character, which they have since maintained—Their excellent qualities as Artisans—Religion—Women—Dirtiness—Tallow their Specialty—Rivalry of Jewish and Tatar Hawkers.

The Gipsies.—Legend of the origin of the name Chenguin—Abhorrence of them by the Turks—Religion and Superstitious Customs—Nomad Life—Two Classes—Physical Characteristics—Reported Witches—Indiscriminate Pilfering—A Case of Horse-stealing—Gipsy Cunning in the Market—Gipsy Avocations—Character—Gipsy-Soldiers—Town Gipsies—Agricultural Gipsies.

IN 1864, Russia, the present champion of the subject races of Turkey, was busy in her own vast dominions giving the *coup de grâce* to the unruly and only half-subjugated Circassians. These people, during a period of eighty years, resisted Russian aggression, defending their homes and liberties at the point of the sword, until the consequences of war, famine, and misery compelled them to yield to the superior power of the Czar. They were offered the choice of migrating to the lower steppes of that land, where Russian discipline alone could tame them, or of quitting the country. Some accepted the former alternative, while a large portion, consisting of about 300,000 souls, preferred to accept the hospitality of Turkey. Before leaving the shores of their beloved native land, collected on the beach like a herd of wild animals caught in a storm, they raised their voices and cried aloud against the injustice and cruelty they, with their wives and children, had received at the hands of the Muscovites. That voice reached Turkey, who, whatever her sins are, has never been known to refuse shelter and assistance to the homeless and the refugee. A proof of this may be found in the harbour offered within my recollection to the exiled Prince of Persia, Kouli Mirza, subsequently a pensioner of Great Britain; the famous Syrian chieftain, the Emir Beshir and his party; the Polish, Wallachian, and Hungarian refugees, and Abdul Kadir; the Algerine captive chief, who obtained permission from Napoleon to reside in Turkey. All these with their followers were received with hospitality, treated with kindness, and, in some cases, allowed pensions while they remained in the country.

This gift of Russia to Turkey was, as far as the female portion of it was concerned, as irresistible as the beauteous Pandora is said to have been to Epimetheus; and the Circassian ladies certainly brought with them the equivalent for Pandora's famous box, in the shape of their kith and kin, who dispersed themselves all over the country, and, from that moment, have never ceased to do mischief, and justify Russia's treatment of them. I have had opportunities of seeing these people since their arrival in Turkey, of watching them in the different stages through which they have passed, and noting the irreparable harm they have done to the country that offered them an asylum. On landing, about 2,000 were quartered in a little wood. Emaciated by the long sufferings of the journey, covered with vermin, and half famished, they encamped on the damp soil in the early spring, some sheltering themselves under the trees, others under such tattered tents as they possessed, all closely packed together, the sick lying face to face with the dead, and the living moving, gaunt and ghostlike, among them, careless of everything except getting money. As we neared the infected camp, bands of men and women came forward, holding their children by the hand and offering to sell them to any who would buy. The little wretches themselves seemed anxious to be separated from their unnatural parents, in the hope of getting food and better shelter. These Circassians were divided into two classes, the chieftains and the slaves. Each regarded the other with distrust; the one expecting from his slave the abject obedience he had been accustomed to receive in his native land; the other, aware of the change in his condition, ready to dispute this right with his former master.

Rations and clothes were distributed by the Turkish authorities, but the master took his slave's portion and sold it for profit. The slave, on his side, stole what he could, and stripped even the dead of his last covering, leaving the corpse to be devoured by dogs. The sight of these bodies by the townspeople and others originated the idea that these people were cannibals, and this reputation preceding the Circassians, on their march further into the country, caused a panic on their route. Children ran away on their approach, and even the peasants themselves, instinctively aware of the pernicious nature of the element introduced among them, did their best to avoid giving them offence in refusing assistance.

The majority of the Circassians distributed in European Turkey are settled in the Dobrudcha; the rest were allotted patches of ground in all parts of Bulgaria and in other provinces, where the peasants were called upon to supplement the Government in providing them with cattle, grain, and all other requisites necessary to start them as settlers. The Bulgarian peasants stoically made it a point of duty to render every assistance in their power to the destitute and helpless creatures so strangely brought among them, and Circassian settlements soon started up like weeds by the side of the peaceful and thriving villages.

Four years later I had again occasion to pass through these settlements, and was much surprised at the transformation in the appearance of the Circassians. The men, dressed in their picturesque costume, wearing their arms, some of which were curious and rich pieces of Eastern workmanship, were lazily lounging about the commons of their villages: while the women, arrayed in their dress of red silk braided with gold, presided over their household duties. Some well-conditioned cattle, driven by Circassian youths, were grazing in the surrounding meadows. I stopped at a Bulgarian village opposite one of these settlements. It was a *prasnik* or feast day, and the Bulgarian youth and beauty, dressed in their best, were dancing the *hora*. As our party approached, the dance stopped, and the women saluting me with a cheerful smile, regarded me with great curiosity. The headman of the village came forward, and, with a hearty welcome, offered me hospitality for the night. I had a long and interesting conversation with him and the elders of the little community upon the Circassian settlements. The Bulgarian peasants even at that early date had a long list of grievances against their new neighbours. Pointing to the opposite village, they assured me that its very foundation and prosperity was due to Bulgarian labour and money. "The Circassians," said they, "lounge about the whole day, as you see them doing now. Their industry does not extend beyond the sowing of a few bushels of millet for the use of their families. Their cattle, as well as most of their belongings, are not for work, but are stolen property that they are freely allowed to appropriate to themselves to the prejudice of the peasants." The poor men seemed much concerned at this new evil that had befallen them. "We never get redress for the wrongs done by our neighbours," said they; "and if the Government functionaries continue to disregard our complaints, and to allow the depredations of these marauders to go unpunished as they have hitherto done, not only our property but our lives will be at their mercy."

A Circassian girl from the village on seeing me came forward, and with tears in her eyes implored me to take her with me and keep her in my service. She was about eighteen years of age, a beautiful creature, dark complexioned, with sparkling eyes, which overflowed when I refused her request. "I am perishing with *ennui* here," she said, "in this dreadful outlandish place, without a hope or chance of getting away by being sold or rescued by some charitable person who might take me to Stamboul!" Surprised at her statement, I asked why she did not do as others of her nation, and insist upon being sold? With a look of hopeless despondency she replied: "None now dares to buy the *cherkess* girls belonging to the emigrants. She would give me no further information, but through subsequent inquiry I learnt that the Turkish Government, among the laws it had made relating to the Circassians, had deprived them of the right of selling their children as they formerly did in their native country, and had also decreed the liberation of the slaves held by them. But this law, like many others, was disregarded, and the chieftains continued to treat their subjects as slaves, a cause of constant quarrelling and bloodshed among them. Some broke out into open rebellion and refused to obey their master as such, while the chiefs, strong in the close alliance that existed among them, could at all times, notwithstanding the interference of the authorities, bring their subjects to terms by taking the law into their own hands.

With regard to selling their children, it was neither the law prohibiting the practice, nor the want of purchasers, that put a stop to it, but the abuse made of it by the Circassians themselves. For instance, two brothers would agree to sell a sister to some Mohammedan, who, after having paid the money and obtained possession of the girl, was suddenly called before the local courts to answer the charge brought by her father, without whose consent it was pretended the daughter had been ravished and illegally sold. The purchaser thus losing his prize without receiving back the money he had paid to the dishonest Circassians, and being condemned for the proceeding by the law, made known the undesirability of such purchases among his friends, and deprived them of any wish to participate in such troublesome business.

The depredations of the Circassians became so extensive that from one farm alone in the district of Adrianople three hundred and fifty head of cattle were stolen and never recovered.

A systematic company of cattle-stealers was established all over Bulgaria; the stolen animals taken from the villages found their way to Rodosto and Gallipoli, where they were shipped to Asia Minor and exchanged with stolen cattle from that coast. The dexterity with which a Circassian, introducing himself into a stud, takes possession of the best horse, is the terror and wonder of the farmer. He uses a kind of lasso, which, cast over the head of the animal, enables him to mount it and stick to it as if horse and rider were one. The wildest animal is soon cowed under the iron sway of the rider, and disappears, to be seen no more.

A gentleman wishing to procure a good horse from a Circassian, asked the owner if the animal was a good trotter? The Circassian with a malicious smile answered, "Sir, he will take you to the world's end, so long as you are careful not to turn his head in the direction of Philippopolis, but in that case I do not guarantee him!"

Another incident, illustrative of the thievish propensities of these people, was related to me of a carter who, driving his waggon from town, fell asleep in it, and was met by a band of Circassians, who thought the prize too tempting to be allowed to escape. Some of the party, therefore, took to unharnessing the oxen, and two of them, taking the place of the captured animals, kept the cart going while the others went off with the oxen. When these were at a fair distance, their substitutes gave the cart a strong jerk to arouse the poor unsuspecting driver, and heartily saluting him, disappeared across country.

So long as Circassian marauding was limited to incidents of this nature the peasants put up with it, and in many cases abstained even from complaining to the authorities; but gradually the proceedings of this dangerous race assumed a character the gravity of which only escaped public notice because of the general disorganisation that followed.

Becoming prosperous and wealthy through their continual depredations and robberies, the youthful portion of the community that had escaped sickness on first landing formed a lawless hostile faction in the land, having as little respect for the authority of the Porte as for the life and property of the natives. When the Government tried some years ago to bring a portion of them under military discipline, they rebelled and gave much trouble to the authorities in the capital itself, where it was found necessary to seize, exile, and otherwise punish some of the chiefs for insubordination.

I happened to be travelling in a Turkish steamer with thirty of these rebellious subjects. Their chief was said to have been an influential person, holding the rank of aide-de-camp to a member of the Imperial family, perhaps the famous Cherkess Hasan, who nearly two years ago murdered the Ministers. The Turkish officer who had charge of these troublesome prisoners told me that for two months he and his men had given chase to this band, who had escaped into Asia Minor, where they had continued their depredations, and were only secured at last by being surrounded in a forest. They appeared a dreadful set of cut-throats—not at all pleasant fellow-passengers—and their guards had to keep good watch over them. This officer further stated that the Sultan, out of kindness, had invited them into his dominions, giving them land, and every opportunity of settling down and becoming useful members of society; but it was a sad mistake, for they would neither work nor yield to discipline, neither would they make any efforts to requite the Government for the benefit they had received, but in every instance proved their reputation for lawlessness and depredation. It is an important fact that before the Bulgarian troubles the peasants of the districts where the Circassians were in force dared no longer circulate except in companies of fifty or sixty, and that murderous attacks had become every day occurrences.

Although protected in some high quarters in consequence of their close connection through family ties, the Circassians are generally disliked and distrusted, especially by the people, who have no such strong reasons for protecting them. In physical features they often present splendid specimens of the famed Circassian type, though not unfrequently bearing a great resemblance to the Mongolian. In manner they are haughty and even insulting, with an air of disdain and braggadocio such as no really brave man assumes. In character the Cherkess is undoubtedly cowardly, cruel, and false. Education he has none, so that all the evil passions of his nature, unchecked by any notion of moral, religious, or civil obligation, have developed themselves with irresistible force, and prompted him to acts that during the last two years have placed the name of the Circassian below that of the gipsy.

It is said that they are to be expelled from European Turkey. If this is the case, the unfortunate population of Asia Minor, both Mohammedan and Christian, among whom they will be quartered, are most deeply to be pitied, as well as the Government, whose duty it will be to re-establish and discipline these ruffians now rendered desperate and doubly hardened by the crimes and horrors of every description into which they have lately plunged with impunity.

The best and wisest plan would be to request Russia, if she really and earnestly desires the welfare of the Christians in Turkey, to take the Circassians back and reinstate them in their native land. Should this be impracticable, the Turkish Government would do well to send them to colonise some of the fertile but waste lands in the heart of Asia Minor, in the vicinity of half-savage tribes like themselves, in whom they might find their match, and cease to become a perpetual source of trouble and injury both to the Government and its peaceful subjects.

The migration of the Tatars into Turkey preceded that of the Circassians by half a century. When their country passed into the hands of Russia, the Tatars, unwilling to remain under her dominion, removed, at a great sacrifice of life and property, into Bessarabia, where, scarcely had they begun to feel settled and to forget their wrongs and sufferings, than the Muscovite eagle again clouded the horizon, and the emigrants, fluttering at its approach like a flock of frightened birds, collected their families and belongings, and took to flight. Weary and exhausted, they alighted on the Ottoman soil, and settled in the Dobrudcha. They were a quiet and industrious people, and before long, through toil and exertion, they made themselves homes, and peopled the Dobrudcha with their increasing numbers. Some of the Tatar princes migrated with their subjects, and took up their abode in the vicinity of Zaghra, where they retained their title of *Sultanlar*, or "the princes." They became in time wealthy landowners, but, unlike their less exalted brethren, they were hard, unjust, and oppressive masters to the Bulgarian peasants, and by their cruel treatment of these people, were among the causes of their being cited as rebels before the authorities.

A second emigration of Tatars took place after the Crimean war, when these unfortunate people, in a similar plight to the Circassians, came to join their kinsmen in the Dobrudcha and other parts of European Turkey. They were poor, and for the most part destitute of every requisite of life. The Turkish Government did its best to help them by giving grants of land, etc., but those who settled as agriculturists were unfortunate, for a series of bad seasons crushed their first efforts, and, unassisted by further relief, they remained in a stationary condition of poverty, notwithstanding many praiseworthy efforts to better their condition. Those who settled in towns fared better; all who were acquainted with some handicraft at once set to work and executed their different branches of industry with so much activity, neatness, and honesty, that they soon reached prosperity and comfort.

Their religion is Mohammedan, but they are by no means strict or fanatical. Their women do not cover their faces when among their own community, but when abroad are veiled like the Turkish women. They are very thrifty in their habits, and some are pretty and sweet-looking, but as a rule they are the dirtiest subjects in the Sultan's dominions. Their uncleanliness with regard to dress, dwellings, and food is so great as to shock and horrify the Turks, who certainly have that virtue which is said to come next to godliness.

The principal ingredient in their cookery seems to be tallow: as candlemakers they are greatly superior to the natives, and the preference given to this article of their manufacture has induced them to take the principal portion of this branch of industry into their hands.

When a colony settled in the town of A――, one of my friends took a great interest in the efforts made by these estimable artisans to earn a livelihood as shoemakers, tailors, tallow-chandlers, etc. Some opened small shops for the sale of different articles, while those who had no distinct calling or possessed no capital became wood-cutters, or hawkers of vegetables, fruits, etc. In this business, however, they met with shrewd and knowing professionals—the Jews, who were far more able and practised hands at it, and at first gave very little chance to the poor Tatars. It became a race between Jew and Tatar who should get up earliest in the morning and go furthest to meet the peasants bringing their produce to market. In this the Tatar was most successful, as he was the better walker of the two, and less afraid than the Jew of venturing some distance from the town; but the latter contented himself with the reflection that there are many roads that lead to the same goal, and many ways of making profit which are not dreamt of in Tatar philosophy.

The Gipsies in Turkey, numbering about 200,000 souls, profess outwardly Mohammedanism, but keep so few of its tenets that the true believers, holding them in execration, deny their right to worship in the mosques or bury their dead in the same cemetery. Although not persecuted, the antipathy and disdain felt for them evinces itself in many ways, and appears to be founded upon a strange legend current in the country. This legend says that when the gipsy nation were driven out of their country and arrived at Mekran, they constructed a wonderful machine, to which a wheel was attached. Nobody appeared able to turn this wheel till in the midst of their vain efforts some evil spirit presented himself under the disguise of a sage and informed the chief (whose name was Chen) that the wheel would be made to turn only when he had married his sister Guin. The chief accepted the advice, the wheel turned round, and the name of the tribe after this incident became that of the combined names of the brother and sister, *Chenguin*, the appellation of all the gipsies of Turkey at the present day.

This unnatural marriage, coming to the knowledge of one of the Moslem saints, was forthwith, together with the whole tribe, soundly cursed; they were placed beyond the pale of mankind, and sent out of the country under the following malediction:—" May you never more enter or belong to the seventy-seven and a half races that people the earth, but as outcasts be scattered to the four corners of the earth, homeless, wretched, and poor; ever wandering and toiling, never realising wealth, enjoying the fruits of your labour, or acquiring the esteem of mankind!" *

I have related this legend because it represents in a very striking manner the condition of the gipsies of Turkey as well as the belief placed in it by people of all creeds, who not only put them beyond the pale of humankind, but also deny to them what would be granted to animals—their alms. Last year during the Ramazan, a popular Hodja, preaching on charity to a large congregation of Mohammedans, thus addressed them—" O true believers, open your purses every one of you, and give largely to the poor

---

* Turkish ethnology divides the human race into seventy-seven-and-a-half nations, the Jews representing the half, and the Gipsies being entirely excluded. This is clearly an improvement upon Mohammed's estimate of the number of different sects in Islam, etc.

and needy! Refuse not charity either to Mohammedans or Christians, for they are separated from us only by the thickness of the skin of an onion, but give none to the Chenguins, lest part of the curse that rests upon their heads should fall upon yours!"

Mohammedanism and the Christian rites also practised by a few of the gipsies can only be a mask to hide the heathen superstition handed down among them from generation to generation, together with their native language, and some other observances, such as keeping a fire continually burning in their camp. On the first of May all go in a body to the seacoast or the banks of a river, where they throw water three times on their temples, invoking the invisible *genii loci* to grant their special wishes.

Another custom, observed with equal constancy, is that of annually drinking some potion, the secret of whose preparation is known only to the oldest and wisest of the tribe. This draught is partaken of by the whole community as a charm or preventive against snake bites. It is certain that, owing to some agency, the gipsies can catch snakes and handle them with the greatest impunity, but are never known to kill or hurt these animals.

The habits of these people are essentially nomadic. Sultan Murad IV. tried to check their roving disposition by ordering that they should be permanently settled in the vicinity of the Balkans, and obliged to live a regular life; but disregarding the imperial decree, they dispersed all over the country, now pitching their tents in one place and now in another, like evil spirits bent on mischief, or birds of prey ready to pounce upon any game that offers itself. Their pilfering propensities are entirely directed to supplying the common wants of nature; they never grow rich on their plunder.

The tribe is divided into two classes—those who live in the towns for short periods, and those, the wildest and vilest, who wander about all the year round; during the summer pitching their tents in the open country or on the road side, men, women, and children all huddled together under the tattered rags that form their only shelter. The men and women are miserably clad, and the children walk about in their original nakedness. The Chenguins are muscular, thin, and of middle size; with dark skins, bright sparkling eyes, low undeveloped brows, and well defined nose, wide at the nostril; the lower part of the face is ill-formed and sensual. When quite young, some of the women are very pretty and much appreciated by the Turkish community as dancing girls, in which calling their utter want of decency and morality makes them adepts. When the gipsy woman is advanced in years she becomes perfectly hideous; her brown skin shrivels up through privation and exposure, her body gets thin and emaciated, and her uncombed elf locks, half concealing her features, give her the appearance of a witch. The cunning creature, aware of the effect she produces, makes capital out of it, by impressing the credulous with a belief in her uncanny powers of predicting the future, casting or removing the evil eye, or other magic spells, invoking benefits or bringing evil upon those who refuse charity or provoke her anger; thus extorting from fear the alms that pity refused.

In winter they quarter themselves in the vicinity of towns or villages, where they have a better chance of carrying on their trade of petty thieving. The nuisance they become to a neighbourhood is increased by the hopelessness of obtaining any recovery of property stolen by them. The gipsy is by no means particular as to the nature of the object he covets, but will condescendingly possess himself of an old horse found conveniently in his neighbourhood, or venture further and lay hands on anything from a useful article of dress to a stray ox.

The following incidents that came under my personal observation were attributed to an encampment of gipsies in the vicinity of the town of M——, and will give an idea how these people, called by the peasants *Taoukjis,* set about business, and the precautions they take to avoid detection and escape punishment.

In our stable were three fine and valuable horses,

much admired in the town, which had evidently awakened the cupidity of some gipsies encamped opposite the house on the other side of the river. On one occasion, when the two best were away from home together with the groom, the third horse disappeared during the night. In the morning I sent to give notice of the occurrence to the sub-governor and request his aid in discovering the thief or thieves. This functionary, a kind and civil man, at once called upon me and gave me the assurance that the horse would be recovered, as none but the gipsies encamped opposite could have stolen it. The police were sent to the camp to request about a dozen to come to the Konak to answer for the robbery.

On arriving, the gipsies were placed under close examination by the Kaimakam and Medjliss; they naturally denied all knowledge of the robbery and protested against the accusation. Finding them obstinate, the Kaimakam ordered them to be placed under the pressure of the whip, but this appearing to produce no effect, made the governor suspect that some trick had been resorted to, in order to prevent the culprits feeling the smart of the punishment they had anticipated. They were ordered to undress, upon which, looking very crestfallen, they began to pray for mercy, but their prayers were soon drowned in the sounds of general hilarity that followed the discovery of the successive layers of sheepskin in which they had taken the precaution of enveloping their bodies. The first few blows that fell upon their now unprotected backs, drew forth screams of "Aman, Effendi!" followed by sundry revelations on the disappearance of the horse. "Last night," said one, "it came quite unexpectedly into our camp; we tried to secure it but it escaped again, we will endeavour to find and bring it back, but, oh, Aman! Effendi! beat us no more! we will pay the value of the horse for the honour of the Chenguin tribe!" When these proceedings came to my knowledge, I begged the Kaimakam not to be too hard on the poor rogues, but set them free after the severe punishment they had received. I may add that the horse was never found.

On the shapeless, ill-paved, mud-pooled space which usually occupies the centre of small Turkish towns, the peasants collect from all parts of the surrounding country with their carts and beasts of burden, laden with goods for sale or barter. On one occasion an industrious Bulgarian cloth-weaver took up his habitual post at the corner of a narrow street, where he exhibited his stock of goods and invited purchasers. Shortly afterwards, a ragged, thievish-looking Chenguin, with a couple of sieves of his own manufacture, came and seated himself opposite, apparently with the object of selling his stock in trade. No customer appeared, and the gipsy began to show signs of weariness and sleepiness; he yawned desperately, stretched his limbs, looked at his neighbour, yawned again and again, until he succeeded in infecting him with a sympathetic drowsiness. Gradually passing into the second stage of somnolence, he closed his eyes and nodded. The Bulgarian following his example, was soon fast asleep, and the gipsy, quickly springing to his feet, seized a fine piece of *shayak*, and walked away with it. The Bulgarian unsuspectingly slept on until roused by his head coming in contact with the wall, against which he was leaning; his bewildered gaze instinctively turned to the spot which the other slumberer had occupied, and, finding that it was empty, he looked at his merchandise and discovered that his best piece of cloth had disappeared also. Much troubled, he packed up the rest of his goods and proceeded to the house of the Chorbadji, who advised him to find the gipsy and point him out to the police, who might succeed in recovering his property. To this he responded, "All the gipsies have the same wild, tattered, and cunning appearance, and follow the trade of *taoukjis;* if I call the attention of the police to my case, I shall be made responsible for the imprisonment of the whole band, and incur expenses greater than the value of my cloth. I must therefore forego it; but never again shall this stupid 'Bulgarski glava' be outdone by gipsy cunning!"

The other callings followed by the Chenguins are

those of tinkers, blacksmiths, leaders of bears and monkeys, and musicians of a primitive kind. The women keep up the *Nautch* dance of the East with an excruciating kind of accompaniment, consisting of a drum, bagpipe, tambourine, and pipe, with which they make the round of the towns and villages on feast days, when they are hired by the people, and dance and shout to their hearts' content.

The gipsies are idle, false, and treacherous. They have none of the manly virtues; and on account of their known cowardice, they were never pressed into military service by the Turks until last year, when a certain number of those settled in towns and villages were sent off as recruits. It was a picture worth seeing, when a band of these wild creatures was embarked at the town of S——. Guarded by a detachment of soldiers headed by a drum and clarionet, and followed by the whole tribe of old men, women, and children, screaming, crying, and dragging their rags after them, these doubtful warriors marched through the town. I asked an old crone how it was that the Chenguins had to go to war? "God knows," was her reply; "it is the Sultan's command and must be obeyed."

The hatred shown by the Turks to the invaders of their country was so great, and their patriotism and bravery in defending her so conspicuous, that even this degenerate race became infected with a certain degree of the same devotion, and evinced a desire to go and fight for Allah and the Sultan, although at the last moment their natural cowardice proved too strong for them. Some mutilated their hands, others feigned sickness or insanity as an excuse for remaining behind, whilst those who actually reached the seat of war gave great trouble to their officers, did no service whatever, and deserted whenever a chance presented itself.

The class of gipsies living in towns is slightly better and more respectable as a community. They generally occupy hovels built round a court, in which they take shelter during the night; but during the day, in winter or summer, they live out of doors. A great part of their time is spent lounging about the court, hammering at their forges, smoking or quarrelling, while the girls listlessly parade the streets, and the children beg or fall into any mischief that presents itself. They are never sent to school, and I do not think there is a single person of either sex who is able to write a word of any language.

The gipsies settled in the villages take to field work as far as their roving habits and thievish propensities allow them. These are either *chiftjis*, who work regularly, or *ailikjis*, who do odd jobs. They present a strong contrast to the rest of the rural population in their thriftlessness and want of care for the morrow. They are so careless of health that an aged gipsy is rarely met with. As labourers they are very unsatisfactory, and require much supervision from their employers. No gipsy ever becomes wealthy or respectable: as a class they are always in debt.

The whole tribe is a curious mixture of the human and the animal: it is endowed with the scent of the dog, the cunning of the monkey, and the form and vices, but none of the virtues apparently, of mankind.

PART II.

LANDS AND DWELLINGS.

PART II.

LANDS AND DWELLINGS.

CHAPTER VII.

TENURE OF LAND.

Three Classes of Lands in Turkey—*Vakouf* Lands, their Origin and Growth—Turkish Equivalent of Mortmain—Privileges of Tenants on *Vakouf* Land—Maladministration—Corruption of Charity Agents and Government Inspectors—General System of Embezzlement—Sultan Mahmoud's Attempted Reform—Insufficiency of *Vakouf* Revenues as administered; Supplemented by State—General Decay of *Vakouf* Property, Mosques, Medressés, and Imarets—Misapplication of *Vakouf* Funds intended for the Support of the Public Water-Supply—*Mirié* Lands, Government Grants, Military Proprietors, Growth of a Feudal System—Miserable Condition of the Rayahs—Anxiety of the Porte—Destruction of the Feudal System by Mahmoud and Abdul-Medjid—Reduction of the Bosnian and Albanian Beys—Present Condition of the Country Beys—*Mirié* Lands reclaimed from the Waste—Title-Inspectors—A Waste-Land Abuse—Similar Difficulties in Connection with Ordinary *Mirié* Tenure—*Mulk* or Freehold Lands—Their Small Extent—Difficulty of Establishing Safe Titles—Descent and Transfer of Land—Tenure of Land by Christians and by Foreign Subjects—Commons and Forests—The Inspectors of the Forest Department.

REGARDED from a conveyancer's point of view, land in Turkey is of three kinds: *merkoufé* (or *vakouf*), "church" property; *mirié*, crown property; and *mulk* or *memlouké*, freehold.

1. *Vakouf* lands are those set aside for the support of the religious establishments, the mosques, *medressés* (or mosque-colleges) and other religious schools, and the *imarets* or institutions for public almsgiving. The appropriation of a just part of a man's wealth for purposes of religion and charity is one of the most constantly reiterated principles of Islam, and, to the credit of Moslems be it said, it is a principle very regularly reduced to practice. It is not surprising, therefore, that on the conquest of European Turkey a large share of land was set apart "for God." But this original grant was not the only source of the present large extent of vakouf lands. Private munificence has constantly added to the original foundation. The piety of some Moslems, and the vain-glory of others, has ever been displayed in the erection and endowment of mosques, with their attendant medressés and imarets. In the one case it was a sure key to heaven; in the other, it was the best way to get the praises of men of one's own generation and the admiration of posterity. Formerly ordinary people used frequently to indulge in this architectural luxury; but, during the present century, only Sultans and Grand Vizirs have found the practice convenient.

Besides the original grant and the private additions which each century contributed, vakouf lands have been greatly increased from a third source. The people of Turkey seem to have duly appreciated those privileges against which our own Mortmain laws were directed. The parallel is not indeed strictly accurate, but there are strong points of resemblance. A Moslem (or, for that matter, a Christian) sells his land to a mosque for about one-tenth of its real value. The land is now the property of the mosque, but the seller has the right of lease, and may retain his tenancy on payment of a fixed rent. During his life he may sell the lease, or at his death it passes on to his heirs; but in default of direct descendants the lease reverts absolutely to the mosque.* By this transaction both parties are the gainers, and only the Government and its corrupt officials the losers.

The mosque receives a large interest for a comparatively trifling expenditure of capital; and has besides the reversion in the event of default of heirs. The tenant, though he has to pay a rent where formerly he paid none, is not burdened by this slight charge, and sets against it the immense privileges he has acquired: for, as a tenant on vakouf land—that is, holding direct of Allah—he pays no taxes; he is safe from confiscation by the Government, extortion from its officials, and persecution from private creditors. It is the most profitable and secure tenure to be met with in Turkey, and it is a matter of congratulation that the mosque authorities place so high a value upon

---

* In August, 1875, the law of inheritance on vakouf lands was modified and improved.

money, that they are willing to accept it even from dogs of Christians who wish to avail themselves of the protection afforded by vakouf leasehold.

No official report of the extent of the vakouf lands has, so far as I can learn, been published; but it is easy to understand that their extent and value must be very great. It is even estimated at two-thirds of the whole land of Turkey. It is therefore remarkable that the revenues derived from them do not nearly suffice for the purposes for which they were intended. The expense of maintaining the services of the mosques and of keeping up the extremely economical system of religious education would not seem to be excessive, though the charitable imarets would of course require considerable support. But these are not the real reasons why these rich revenues are not sufficient. One reason is, that they are expected to maintain a large class of Ulema, whose numbers are altogether disproportionate to the educational results they produce. The other and far more disastrous cause is that the revenues are corruptly administered.

At first the management of the funds lay in the hands of agents appointed by the pious founders. When an agent died, his successor was named by the Roumeli Kadisi (or Anadoli Kadisi if in Asiatic Turkey). The agents were under the supervision of inspectors, whose business it was to verify the mosque accounts. These inspectorships were generally given to high functionaries of the Porte, and so lucrative were they, that they excited keen competition (in the Turkish sense), and eventually came to be regarded as the fixed appendages of certain offices. It may easily be imagined that between the agents and the inspectors there was not much of the vakouf revenues left for the right purposes. As a matter of fact, most of the money found its way into the pockets of the inspectors of the Sublime Porte.

Among the many schemes that engaged the attention of the Reformer-Sultan Mahmoud there was of course a place for vakouf reform. He wished to amalgamate the vakouf lands with the mirié or crown lands, but had not the boldness necessary to the carrying out of so revolutionary a measure. He contented himself with clearing away some of the more obvious abuses of the administration of vakoufs, and appointed a director with the rank of Minister, to see to the proper management of the property. Still, however, the revenues did not prove sufficient. The annual budget of vakouf returns reached a total of 20,000,000 piastres; yet in 1863 it had to be supplemented by another 20,000,000 piastres from the Treasury, and is ever in need of similar assistance. The funds are still misapplied; and, as the result, the mosques and medressés have fallen more and more into ruin and decay; the imarets are become instruments of a merely nominal almsgiving; and every charitable or religious intention of the pious founders is daily trodden under foot.

Among the minor objects of vakouf endowments are the construction and maintenance in repair of aqueducts and road fountains. I have often witnessed with regret the manner in which the trust is abused by its holders. In most towns the principal water supply is endowed by vakoufs, the revenues of which were intended to defray all expenses connected with keeping the channels and fountains in repair. In three cases out of four these funds are misapplied. At Salonika, for instance, the water supply is richly endowed, and the town ought clearly to be well furnished with water. Instead of this, a great number of the fountains are dried up, and a serious waste of water is caused by the neglect of the water pipes. It is painful to see the crowd of miserable Jewish children waiting for hours round the dribbling fountain under a burning summer sun, or pierced with the biting winter winds, till they get a chance of filling their pitchers—too often only to get them broken in the battle that immediately ensues. In summer, when the want of water is most severely felt, many people do not scruple to dig down to the water pipes in some deserted street, stop the current that leads to the fountain, and thus obtain the supply they need. In former times fountains were erected on all the main roads and in every town and village; but most of them are now dried up or fallen to ruin.

Some of those that remain are of solid marble, with a carved frontage inscribed with the name of the donor, the date of erection, and some verses from the Koran. Some are in the form of basins, with jets playing in them, sheltered sometimes by little kiosks, and always shaded by fine old trees. The thirsty traveller and his beast are all the more grateful when they do find a fountain with water running, because the chances are so overwhelmingly against such good luck—thanks to the vakouf administrators, who from this point of view deserve credit for intensifying the virtue of gratitude.

2. The *Mirié* or crown-lands include the private demesnes of the Sultan and the royal family, the lands reserved for the partial support of the administration, the waste lands, together with an enormous extent of land originally granted on condition of military service to the most zealous supporters of the Sultan, with a view to retaining their fidelity and assuring the supremacy of the Government over the native princes. The country was thus given over to the power and licence of an army of occupation. It was divided into sandjaks governed by Pashas, Beys, and Beglerbeys. Those last-named were the administrators of the sandjaks. Their duty it was to collect the taxes and furnish the contingents of troops to the Imperial army. The favoured officers of the Porte received immense grants of land in return for their

zeal: they were exempt from taxation, and only required to find soldiers for the wars of the Porte. Excluding vakouf lands, the greater part of Turkey was thus placed on a sort of feudal tenure, the proprietor holding of the crown by military service. All the evil effects of the system soon developed themselves.

The lands of these military proprietors were of course chiefly tilled by the rayahs, who had formerly held them in freehold. Although these underholdings were supposed, like all mirié lands, to be registered, and thus to enjoy the advantage of a legally fixed rent, they were yet subject to the endless extortions invariably associated with the notion of Turkish officials. Especially heavily did this system press upon the Christian tenants of the military landowners. In principle the conduct of the Turks to their Christian subjects was not greatly blameable; it was in practice, as usual, that the grievances arose. The Christian communities were managed by their Kodja-Bashi, or headman, who had to collect the tribute, proportioning it to the means of each individual; and to gather the kharadj or poll-tax, and other impositions. A community was allowed to compound for each or all its taxes by a fixed sum. Thus far all appears surprisingly satisfactory. But when the actual condition of the Christian tenants is looked into, a very different impression is produced. Their landlords were ever devising some new extortion: the taxes were levied with ruinous irregularity; fresh impositions were constantly being added; and, in fine, their state became so intolerable that large numbers of them deserted their faith (of which they are generally highly tenacious in spite of ignorance and persecution), and became Moslems, and were at once placed in possession of the privileges of the dominant race. A curious instance of this conversion by necessity was that of the Krichovalis, a lawless race of mountaineers about Vodena. About the beginning of this century they found themselves unable longer to endure the disabilities of their condition. They met in solemn assembly in their old church on a great feast day, and swore the sacred oath upon the Bible that they became Mohammedans under protest, being compelled to abandon their faith in order to escape the intolerable trammels of their bondage. The Bible on which they swore, containing the signatures of the chief men, still exists, I am told, in the keeping of the Greek priest.

The evils of military tenure bore upon the Porte as well as upon the rayahs. The Sultans were not slow to note with alarm the growing power of the great feudatories. They endeavoured to curtail their privileges and to strengthen the hands of the rayahs and attach this class to themselves. But for a long time the efforts of the central government were unavailing.

The military landowners made common cause with the Beglerbeys, who had by degrees acquired the supreme control of their sandjaks; and these two united in defying the authority of the sovereign. A great landed aristocracy had grown up, like the baronage of England in Angevin times, and threatened the very extinction of the supremacy of the Porte over its subjects. A great blow must be struck at the country Beys: and Mahmoud II. resolved to strike. He was completely successful, and left to his successor Abdul-Medjid only the task of bringing some of the rebellious chieftains to punishment. Some were beheaded, others banished, and all had their property confiscated. Inoffensive tenants by military service received compensation: but the system was rooted out, and has now ceased to exist.

How the great feudal landowners were crushed will be understood from a few examples. A short time ago I made the acquaintance of one of the dervish sheikhs who followed Ali Pasha when he was despatched by Abdul-Medjid to reduce the Bosnian rebels. I asked how the reduction was effected: and this was his account.—Ali Pasha, with a small but well-organised army of Nizams, on approaching the country, asked permission of the Bosnians to cross into the Austrian territory. The Bosnians unsuspectingly granted leave, and we marched into the country and pitched our camp in its very heart. After a few days the Pasha produced the Iradé of the Sultan, containing a demand for 60,000 recruits from the Bosnians. They refused to furnish them, and began to assemble and arm. The Pasha did not insist upon the enforcement of the Imperial order, but opened negotiations. He was a wily man and knew his business. He managed with soft words and fair promises to entice all the Bosnian grandees into the camp, under the pretext of holding a general council. Having thus collected all the influential persons of the country he put them under arrest and proceeded to try them. Some were beheaded, and Ali Pasha with his own hand struck down the leading chief. The rest after some further parley were brought to terms, and were then exiled and their goods confiscated. The 60,000 recruits were soon raised, and the general marched triumphantly back to Constantinople at their head.

The Albanian chieftains were dealt with in the same way: when force failed, treachery prevailed. Their two leaders, Veli-bey and Arslan-bey, were enticed by a friendly invitation to Monastir, where they were received with every mark of consideration and kindness. A few days afterwards they and their friends were invited to a great feast by Reshid Mehemet Pasha. This was to take place in a kiosk outside the town near the head-quarters of the regular troops.

On the appointed day Veli-bey and Arslan-bey proceeded to the rendezvous accompanied by nearly all their beys and retinue; in all about 400 men. The kiosk was hidden from view by a turn in the road till they had almost reached it, and it was only on entering the space in front that they perceived the troops ranged in order of battle. A suspicion crossed the mind of Arslan-bey, who said to his companion in Eastern phrase, "We have eaten dirt!" Veli-bey replied, "It is the regular way of paying honour." "At all events," said Arslan-bey, with doubtful friendship, "let us change sides." This was done, and Arslan-bey found himself screened from view by the imposing figure of Veli-bey and his horse. They had reached the centre of the line when an order issued from the window of the kiosk, the soldiers raised their pieces, and a murderous fire was opened on the ranks of the Albanians, followed by a bayonet charge. Veli-bey and his horse fell pierced with nineteen balls, but Arslan-bey was unhurt. Followed by those who had escaped the first discharge he turned his horse and took to flight; but a second fire reached their flank. Arslan-bey again miraculously escaped, and owing to the speed of his horse soon left the place of carnage at a distance. But his flight had been observed from the kiosk from which the Grand Vizir had directed the massacre, and he was pursued: but putting spurs to his horse he urged it up the precipitous side of the hill, making for the summit with furious speed. The top was almost reached when a shower of balls brought down man and horse; and they rolled down the steep hill-side to join the bodies of their fellow-victims below. Such were the last fatal blows aimed at the expiring feudal system,— exile and confiscation did the rest.

The once powerful Beys, when thoroughly crushed and impoverished, were allowed a small income, and after many years of expatriation were finally permitted to return to their native districts. Their power is completely gone, although their personal influence is still considerable over the populations among whom they live, and in the local courts in which they sit. It is however of a mutinous nature, and seldom employed either in facilitating the introduction of the new measures attempted by the Government for the improvement of the administration, or in promoting the general welfare of the country.

Some beys in the interior still possess considerable landed property, but with few exceptions their estates are dilapidated and heavily mortgaged; while their owners are so deeply in debt to the Government, that if called to a reckoning under a well-regulated administration they would be ruined men. A few, however, whose estates are in better condition, are more enlightened, and take a real interest in the welfare of their country.

The country contains extensive areas of mirié lands

reclaimed from the waste, for which of late years there has been a great demand made by the peasants, who reclaim portions of them by paying a small fee of about 1s. an acre. They cultivate or build upon them, and after paying tithes for the space of twenty years get the *Tapou* or title deed from the Porte constituting them legal owners. But although subjected to special laws and restrictions and under government supervision, it is a dangerous speculation, often involving litigation, and liable to usurpation.

Great abuses are occasioned by the corruption of the *Tapou Memours* or inspectors, who within the last seven years have been entrusted with the supervision and legislation of such lands, and regulate them (irrespective of the rights of Christian or Turkish landholders) in favour of the highest bidder. The consequences are that many persons have been dispossessed of their property, others have had to pay high prices to retain it by obtaining *Tapous*, whilst many are daily being driven out of their lands. An example of this kind presented itself the other day in the local court of the town of L——. The claimant was a Turkish *Hanoum*; the disputants Turkish and Christian peasants. The lady, a widow, had inherited an estate bordering on some waste land upon which these peasants had built a village. The *Hanoum* in the meantime married an influential person at Constantinople, through whose authority and assistance she managed to obtain a *Tapou*, including the village of the settlers on the waste land within her own property. The villagers indignantly protested against this act of usurpation, and refused to acknowledge the authority of the lady, who, however, returned, furnished with powerful *Emirnamés* from the Porte to the town of L—— to enforce her claims. The complaints of the peasants were disregarded, and they themselves were seized as criminals and brought to the Konak, driven into it by blows that fractured the skull of one and occasioned severe injuries to others, and then imprisoned.

Disputed claims like this on commons, forests, etc., are innumerable. The estates sold by the crown also labour under the same disadvantages. Among many cases I may relate one in which the purchaser was an English gentleman, who bought a large estate in Upper Macedonia, comprising one of the most beautiful lakes in the country. It was an ancient fief, sold for the sum of 2,000*l*. The speculation promised to be a splendid one, and a fortune was expected to be realised. One day, however, as the owner was walking over his grounds, an old Turkish peasant presented himself, and with much natural eloquence, and perhaps some truth, explained to the English bey that the former owner had usurped part of his fields which were comprised in the estate. The proprietor, either convinced of the man's rights, or out of kindness, ordered that the contested lands should be restored; but the one individual thus righted soon developed into a legion, all presenting equal claims. Subsequently the legion became a band of armed and menacing Albanians, who by their hostile attitude stopped all attempts at culture, and threatened to shoot the tenants and the steward, burn the crops, etc. A long litigation followed, and the affair terminated, after much loss of time and damages amounting to several thousand pounds, in the gentleman re-selling the estate for the amount he had paid for it.

Besides the above-mentioned drawbacks, the holders of mirié lands cannot sell, transfer, or mortgage them without a licence from the authorities, nor can they make them *Vakouf* property without a special *Firman* from the Sultan.

3. The *Memlouké* or *Mulk* lands are the freehold property of their owner, who can do with them whatsoever pleaseth him well. They do not form a large proportion of the lands of Turkey, and a reason for this is the prejudice entertained against this form of tenure on account of the difficulties encountered in establishing titles. It is unfortunately no unusual thing in Turkey for title-deeds to be forged, substituted, destroyed, and otherwise interfered with.

The descent and division of Mirié and Vakouf lands are regulated by imperial firmans and the special ordinances of the Vakouf laws; but Memlouké land comes under the regulation of the *Mehkemé* or court of the town Kadi. The laws of Moslem inheritance are too complicated to be recorded here, and their complexity is aggravated by the mixture of Christians and the different ways of holding land. In the absence of heirs, mirié and memlouké lands revert to the state; vakouf, as already mentioned, to the administration of pious foundations.

Memlouké land is transferred legally by conveyance; vakouf and mirié by conveyance together with registration. The duty on the sale of memlouké land is five per cent., and the succession duty, two and a half per cent.; on mirié, five per cent. on sale, and the same on succession; on vakouf land, five per cent. on sale, and the same on succession. A difference, however, is made if the land is built over.

The division of property among all the children and the reduction of its value by these duties tend constantly to the diminution and deterioration of Turkish estates and lead generally to mortgage. Mortgage on landed property is at an average interest of eighteen per cent. The result is easily imagined. Freehold lands may be legally mortgaged before two witnesses without any further precaution; but crown and "church" lands to be mortgaged must be registered by the registrar of title-deeds, or the directors of vakouf property, for the fee of (nominally) one per cent.

A great number of large estates can be purchased

in all parts of Turkey for very small sums. The wealthy native Christians would gladly purchase these, but for the complications that surround the possession of landed property that is not vakouf, and the difficulties and opposition to which a Christian landholder is exposed. Turks seldom look favourably upon the passing of such estates into Christian hands. Those who purchase them are generally foreign subjects; the rayahs who venture to do so can never enjoy their acquisitions in the same peace and security. Among many instances of encroachment on such estates by hostile beys, Circassians, and other neighbours, I may mention two that have come under my personal observation. The first refers to a wealthy Bulgarian gentleman, whose acquaintance I made ten years ago at R——. He was a man of great influence, and a member of the Medjliss, or town council. A large estate owned by him, not far from the town, was twice set on fire by his Mohammedan neighbours, and a large mill he had constructed was pulled down. Neither his influence in the district, nor his wealth, nor his position as member of the council, could protect his estate, which he was finally obliged to abandon.

The second case was that of a wealthy Greek at Baba Eski, a pretty village between Constantinople and Adrianople. Some years ago I passed a night in the house of this Chorbadji. When I talked to him about his property he complained bitterly of the hostility he experienced from his Turkish neighbours, and of the encroachments of the Circassians. The former had attempted to set fire to his mill, and the latter had stolen in the course of one year three hundred and fifty head of cattle from him. "Wealth and prosperity," said he, "are the sure recompense of every man's labour in a fine country like this, but it is hard work to keep them when acquired." Last year I met the unfortunate man at C——; he was a complete beggar in appearance, and, with tears in his eyes, told me how the Circassians and other enemies, profiting by the troubles in Bulgaria, had completely destroyed his property. He had come to the town to obtain redress, but I thought that his efforts would be fruitless.

Many gentlemen in Macedonia are owners of large estates. Some of them are Greeks by birth, and all foreign subjects; for foreign subjects are now permitted to hold land in Turkey on the same conditions as the subjects of the Porte. Having capital at their command, and being more intelligent than the Turks, they improve their property, and realise from seven to ten per cent. profit; but even their estates are not quite free from the attacks and depredations of brigands, who often prevent them from visiting their farms freely, or introducing all the improvements they are desirous of making. Out of four of these, three sent their sons to Europe, where they were educated for the profession of agriculturists, a proceeding quite unknown among the Turkish proprietors. *Bonâ fide* Europeans are more respected and feared, and consequently are not exposed to the hostilities to which native Christians are subjected. Some English gentlemen possessing farms in Macedonia have had no occasion to complain, even in these disordered times, when perfect anarchy prevails; their property has been respected, and every assistance is afforded them by the local authorities.

Estates can also be rented for a mere trifle, and when restored to good condition are said to yield lucrative returns. Here again, however, great care has to be taken to ascertain that they are not disputed property, and, in the case of their belonging to several individuals of one family, that all are of age, and sign the title-deeds. A case was related to me by a member of the civil court of A—— of a rayah who had rented an estate from a Turkish family, consisting of a widow and her three sons, all of whom were of age and had signed the contract together with their mother. The tenant, who was a man of moderate means, set to work to improve the property, and spent £1000 upon it; but just as he was beginning to realise the profits of his toil and outlay, a fourth son of the widow came of age and disputed the validity of the contract. The case was tried before the local civil court, and the rayah was declared to have justice on his side; but as the case was one of heritage, the Turk had the right to transfer it to the Mehkemé, or religious court of the Kadi, which decided it in his favour. The result was that the tenant was driven out of his estate, and lost all the money he had spent upon it.

Almost every village in Roumelia and Macedonia, and in fact all over Turkey, had once its own common and forest, in which the peasant proprietors, under certain laws and regulations, had the right to burn charcoal, cut wood, and let the pasturage in spring to the herdsmen, who brought down their sheep and cattle and kept them there the greater part of summer. This was a great resource for the rural population, who, in bad years, could always make some profit out of it.

After the organisation of the vilayet system, this privilege was curtailed, and the forests and grazing grounds were placed under government supervision. A Forest Department was established at Constantinople, and a chief inspector appointed in every district, together with agents to superintend the pasturages. The laws that were to regulate these were said to be excellent, and, whilst equitable towards the peasants, promised at the same time to yield considerable revenues to the state. One of these regulations set forth that a portion of forest and pasturage land should be left to the use of each village, securing its provision of fuel and pasturage for its cattle. None of these laws were, however, observed in the interior, and nothing definite was decided with respect to either of these rights.

The beys, through bribery and favouritism, continued to enjoy their ancient privileges over the forests and grazing lands, while the forest inspectors are said to have realised such immense profits that every official was desirous of becoming connected with the Forest Department. The Government at the beginning, no doubt, derived some good receipts from this new source, but the great expense inseparable from it, the robberies that took place, and the destruction of property allowed, could not fail, in the long run, to be injurious to its interests. The abuses, partiality, and waste that mark the proceedings of this branch of the administration are most prejudicial to the rural population.

But the agents of pasture lands and the forest keepers are still more tyrannical.

The extent of these grounds in the government possession was never defined nor has a limit ever been drawn. The beys rented the commons to the herdmasters; the contracts were made with the cognisance of the local authorities, and on stamped paper. Some of the villages that possessed pasturage let it to the Wallachian sheep owners, who, in the early part of spring, migrate annually into Macedonia to pasture their flocks on the commons.

Some herdsmen had made contracts for bringing down 300,000 sheep into the plains, paid the fees for the contract, and the stipulated sum to the peasants. All the arrangements seemed in perfect order until the arrival of the flocks upon the different grazing grounds, when they were driven off with violence and brutality by the forest keepers and their subordinates, who declared that they had no right to the pasturage unless they paid the rent. The poor people produced their contract to show that they had paid the money, and refused to do so a second time; justly observing that, if any illegal action existed in the renting of the pasturage, it regarded the Government and the villagers, and not them, and that the Government should reclaim the money from the peasants. This dispute lasted a week; some of the Wallachians referred it to the local authorities, while others in their distress applied to any person from whom assistance could be expected. Day after day these men, women, and children, might be seen in the streets of the town with desponding, careworn faces, anxiously looking out for some of their people who might tell them how the case was prospering. When I saw them no more about the town, I asked one of the principal officials how the affair had terminated; he replied, "Madame, malheureusement le gouvernement n'a pas su encore mettre toutes ces choses en ordre, et il nous arrive souvent de ces cas tristes: mais ça vient d'être arrangé." He would not enlighten me further on the subject, but I subsequently learnt that a great amount of bakhshish had settled the matter in favour of the Wallachians.

CHAPTER VIII.

PEASANT HOLDINGS.

Small proprietors *South of the Balkans*—Flourishing State of the Country a few Years ago—A Rose-Harvest at Kezanlik—Bulgarian Villages—Oppressive and Corrupt System of Taxation and of Petty Government—The Disadvantages counterbalanced by the Industry and Perseverance of the Bulgarian Peasant—The Lending Fund in Bulgaria—Its Short Duration—Bulgarian Peasant often unavoidably in Debt—Bulgarian Cottages—Food and Clothing—Excellent Reports of German and Italian Engineers on the Conduct and Working Power of Bulgarian Labourers—Turkish Peasants—Turkish Villages—Comparative Merits of Turkish and Bulgarian Peasants—Land *in Macedonia*—Chiefly Large Estates—*Chiftliks*—The *Konak* or Residence of the Owner—Country Life of the Bey and his Family—His Tenants (*Yeradjis*)—Character of the *Yeradji*—His Wretched Condition—The Metayer System Unfairly Worked—The *Yeradji* generally in Debt—Virtually a Serf bound to the Soil—Difficulty of getting Peasants to become *Yeradjis*—Statute Labour—Cultivation and Crops.

THE land South of the Balkans, from the Black Sea to the frontier of Macedonia, is divided into small holdings, which belong to and are farmed by a peasant population of an essentially agricultural nature. Before the late destruction of property in Bulgaria, almost every peasant in those districts was a proprietor of from five to forty acres, which he farmed himself. The larger estates, of which there were a considerable number, were superintended by the proprietors themselves, but farmed by hired labourers. The following figures will give an idea of the average extent of the holdings in those districts:—Out of a thousand farms, three had five hundred acres; thirty had between one hundred and five hundred; three hundred between fifty and a hundred; four hundred between ten and fifty; and two hundred and sixty-seven under ten acres. All these lands were well cultivated and yielded rich returns. I was astonished at the beauty and flourishing condition of the country during a journey I made some years ago from Adrianople to Servia. It appeared like a vast and fruitful garden. The peace-loving and toiling Bulgarian was seen everywhere steadily going through his daily work, while his equally active and industrious wife and daughters were cheerfully working by his side. *En route*, I stopped a few days in the lovely town of Kezanlik, and was most kindly received by its well-to-do and intelligent inhabitants, who pressed their hospitality upon me with a genuine kindness never to be forgotten. I visited the schools, in which the people prided themselves as much as in the astonishing progress the pupils were making in their studies. I was also taken on a round of visits into well-built clean houses where European furniture was beginning to find a place, and contrasted pleasantly with the well-made native tissues that covered sofas and floors. At dawn next morning a tap at my door announced that it was time to rise and witness the rose-gathering, which I wished to see. The roses begin to be collected before sunrise, in order to keep in them all the richness of their perfume. It requires expedition and many hands; so large bands of young men and maidens, adding pleasure to toil, whilst gathering the roses amuse themselves by carrying on their innocent little flirtations and love-makings.

The large garden to which I was conducted belonged to the wealthy Chorbadji in whose house I was staying. It was at some distance from the town, and by the time we reached it the bright rays of a lovely spring morning were fast spreading over the horizon. The field was thickly planted with rose bushes, with their rich harvest of half-open dew-laden buds. The nightingales, in flights, hovered over them, disputing their possession with the light-hearted Bulgarian harvesters, and chorusing with their rich notes the gay songs of the scattered company, who, dressed in their *Prasnik* (feast-day) clothes—the youths in snow-white shirts and gaudy sleeveless vests, the girls in their picturesque costume, the coloured kerchiefs on their heads floating in the breeze,—had the appearance of a host of butterflies flitting over the flowers. The girls were actively and cheerfully employed in stripping off the buds, and throwing them into the baskets slung on their arms. The youths helped them in the task, and were rewarded each with a bud from his sweetheart, which he placed in his cap. The children ran to and fro emptying the baskets into larger receptacles presided over by the matrons, who sat under the shade of the trees and sorted the roses. The whole picture was so bright, and happy, in such harmony with the luxuriant beauty surrounding it, that I was perfectly fascinated by it, and felt almost envious of those happy beings (as I then thought them), the careless simple children of nature. Their happiness was not for long.

It is not a week since my attention was attracted by an article in one of our papers describing the destruction of Kezanlik and the horrors the writer had witnessed. The once smiling and fruitful district was become the valley of the shadow of death.

The general appearance of the villages in Bulgaria was very pleasing. Those in the plains were not so well built or so picturesque as those nestled among the hills, where the abundance and cheapness of the material needed for building afforded greater facilities for more solid and more artistic construction. Some of these villages had increased to such an extent as to look like small towns. This was owing to the more equal division of land among the people and the large number of landed proprietors that cultivated it. In the midst of the difficulties that surrounded them, such as an irregular and unequal system of taxation and the encroachment and tyrannies of petty government officials, Zaptiehs, Circassians, and sometimes native beys—the Bulgarian peasant, by his steady and persevering habits of industry, managed to get on, and in some places, when favoured by circumstances, even to become wealthy. A species of lending fund was organised (since the introduction of the vilayet system) by the provincial government, chiefly for the benefit of the peasant class of proprietors. The capital of this fund was derived from an annual tax of two bushels of wheat (or their equivalent in money) levied on every yoke of oxen owned by the farmers, and of money contributed by those not engaged in agriculture, to the value of one-tenth of their income-tax. The agricultural interest of the country derived great advantage from this institution. It helped the small farmers to borrow the sum needed for the cultivation of their crops and the purchase of stock at a reasonable rate of interest, and enabled those who had large estates to improve them without mortgaging; while others were enabled to free their estates from the mortgages which already burdened them. I believe that this excellent institution did not long continue in working order, and that latterly it was beyond the reach of those who really needed the money and might have benefited both their farms and the State by its use.

As a general rule the Bulgarian peasant is not wealthy. There are many villages that were so deeply in debt that for years they had not been able to pay their taxes. A rising was occasioned in one of the villages of the district of Sofia on this account. The Pasha of Sofia had been pressed by the Porte to send some money to Constantinople; he, on his part, had to collect it from the people. Calling up a Chaoush of Zaptiehs, he told him to make the round of the villages, and, under pain of instant dismissal, not to return empty-handed. The Zaptieh was a bandit, like many of his brethren who have represented the police corps since the diminution of pay and abolition of the excellent body that had been organised by the wise policy of Fuad Pasha and Ali Pasha. He marched with his band into one of the villages and demanded that £400 should at once be paid to him. The men were absent from the village, and the women, not authorised to act in such matters, could not accede to his demand. The Zaptiehs then seized some and locked them up in a barn, and, after subjecting them to gross ill-treatment, left the village. The unfortunate peasants, thus pressed by the authorities for taxes they could not pay, and subjected to foul and violent treatment, revolted.

A Bulgarian cottage is neither neat nor regular in construction. A number of poles are stuck in the ground, secured to each other by wattles, plastered within and without with clay and cow-dung mixed with straw. The walls are generally white-washed, and the roof raised to a dome covered with tiles or thatch. The interior, divided into three rooms, is neat and clean. One of the apartments is used as the living-room of the family, another as sleeping-room, while the third is reserved for storing provisions and such like domestic purposes. These rooms are of tolerable height, and from fifteen to twenty feet long and ten to fifteen wide. The earthen floor is hardened and covered with coarse matting and woollen rugs, the handiwork of the inmates. The furniture consists principally of the thick woven tissues used for bedding and carpeting.

Pictures of the saints and relics from Mount Athos adorn the walls; a night lamp may be seen suspended before the most venerated of these objects, serving the double purpose of *veilleuse* and mark of regard to the saint. The shelves round the walls contain the crockery and shining copper pans, a pair of pistols, and various other articles. The bedding, neatly rolled up, is piled in one corner, while near the door stand the jars of fresh water. Attached to these cottages are sheds for the farm stock; and a cowhouse, pigsty and poultry house, an oven, and sometimes a well, are enclosed in the yard, which is surrounded by walls or fences, and guarded by dogs.

In the hilly districts, the cottages of both Mohammedans and Christians are constructed with considerable solidity. The peasants throughout European

Turkey are economical and frugal; their wants are few, and they are content with very little. They seldom taste fresh meat, and generally live on rye bread and maize porridge, or beans seasoned with vinegar and pepper. The dairy produce is consumed at home, and on great occasions a young pig or lamb serves as a *pièce de résistance*, washed down by home-made wine. For pastry, they have a cake called *Banitza*, much relished by all.

The clothing of the peasants is warm and comfortable. It is chiefly composed of woollen stuffs, coarse linen, or cotton cloth. Every single article of wearing apparel is woven, embroidered, and made up by the hands of the women, who are at the same time spinners, weavers, and tailors. When coming to town, and on *Prasnik* days, coarse socks and sandals are worn; these are also home-made, and their use on other occasions is dispensed with.

The Bulgarian peasant is strong and healthy in appearance. Both in Bulgaria and Macedonia he is a diligent worker. He may not have the smartness and activity of the English labourer, but I have often been assured that, notwithstanding the numerous feast-days he keeps, at the end of the year he is found to have completed almost as much work, for the simple reason that he makes his working-day much longer, and his whole family turn out to assist him: for the women of these districts are as industrious as the men; no sooner are their household tasks accomplished than they join the paterfamilias in the field.

The German and Italian engineers who undertook the construction of the railways in Macedonia repeatedly asserted that the labours of the natives was equal to that of Europeans. In Macedonia, the Italian company, on commencing operations, brought out five hundred Italian navvies to work on the line; but on discovering that the natives, when well paid, well treated, and shown how to set about it, did the work better than the Italians, the latter were sent away. These gentlemen were most warm in their praises of the steadiness of the men and of the excellence of their work; but I must add that they did not omit to study the character of the people and treat them with the kindness and consideration that, in the long run, never fail to improve and elevate even the most debased.

The Turkish peasants, who are in the minority both in Bulgaria and Macedonia, have also a healthy appearance, added in the former place to a look of audacity and in the latter to a look of ferocity. The Greek peasant is tall and rather slim, with an intelligent look and a hardy and self-reliant expression.

All the rural population is sober. Greek and Bulgarian peasants have, it is true, every now and then, an orgie; but there is no systematic drunkenness. All the well-to-do farmers and peasants keep a provision of wine and *raki*, or spirit, but their daily portion is moderate, and excesses are only indulged in on feast days, and even these are not of a very serious nature.

All the villages, both Greek and Bulgarian, have their *Kodja-Bashis*, who see to the administration of the village, proportion the taxes, settle petty disputes, attend to the arrival and reception of guests, Zaptiehs and troops, and other wants or necessities of the community.

The Turkish villages bear a more impoverished appearance and look more neglected and decaying than the Christian. This is partly owing to the seclusion of the women, who are little seen about, and, unlike the Christian, never sit working at their doors. They are helpless; do no field work, and very little weaving; and occupy themselves solely about their indoor duties, and as these are not very heavy, they consequently spend much of their time idly. The men are laborious, but not so active and energetic as the Christians. They spend a good deal of time smoking in the coffee-houses of the village, and are much poorer than the Christians. This is due, partly to their character and to the absence of all help from their wives; but also in great part to the conscription, which takes many valuable years of labour from the working-man. Drunkenness is rare among Turks of this class, but when chance cases occur they are of the most vicious and incurable kind.

In Macedonia landed property is more unequally divided than in Bulgaria. Great portions of it are united in large estates held by native beys, or by pashas and officials at Constantinople. Some of these estates comprise an immense area, of which only a part is cultivated. They are called *Chiftliks*; the house, or *Konak*, on the estate, is the residence of the owner when he visits it, for he seldom resides on his property, but is represented by a *Soubashi*, or agent. The elegance, dimensions, and comfort of the Konak depend, of course, upon the means and habits of the owner. Some of the more ancient of these edifices are large and spacious, built in the style of the old Konaks at Stamboul; but they present a still more dilapidated and neglected appearance. Others of more recent erection are smaller, but neither more comfortable nor more tidy in appearance. Some, again, are in the form of turrets, which, if not elegant, have at least the merit of being as strong as small fortresses. A large courtyard contains, beside the house, the usual farm buildings. On entering the yard of the best regulated *Chiftlik*, the first thing that attracts the attention is the air of complete disorder and dirt that pervades the premises. In one or two corners may be seen heaps of refuse, in others, broken carts and farm implements standing in the midst of mud pools and filth of every description, including a collection of old brooms that could never have been worn out in sweeping the place. Among these, children, fowls, geese, ducks, and dogs roam in freedom. The interior of the Konak is usually divided into Haremlik and Selamlik, if sufficiently large. One or two rooms in each department may be furnished with a few hard sofas and dingy calico curtains. The room reserved for the master sometimes presents a somewhat better appearance, its walls decorated with fire-arms, sometimes of beautiful workmanship, and its furniture boasting a deal table and a few chairs. When the Bey intends paying a long visit to his estate and is accompanied by his family, the bedding and other household necessaries are brought from town. It is astonishing to see how little luggage a Turkish family travels with on such an occasion. Each person will have a *boghcha*,* containing his or her wearing apparel ; the articles for general use comprise a few candlesticks, petroleum lamps, perhaps two *Leyen* † and *Ibrik* ‡ for ablutions, which in the morning and at meal times make the round of the house; kitchen utensils and a few tumblers, plates, etc., are all that is needed for the *Villeggiatura* of a Turkish family.

The way in which the Bey spends his time on his estate is also regulated by the means and tastes of the individual. If he be a sportsman, he will have a battue on his lands and enjoy the pleasures of the

* Boghcha, bundle.
† Leyen, basin.
‡ Ibrik, jug.

chase. Should he be addicted to drinking and debauchery, he has every means of indulging his taste. His duties as landlord consist in regulating accounts with his agent, hearing the cases that need his interference, giving general instructions for future operations, and, above all, realizing the profits. As to improving his estate, ameliorating the condition of the tenants, beautifying the property by planting trees and laying out gardens, such things are never thought of or known to have been practised by any large landowner in Macedonia.

The harem, on their side, bring friends to stay with them; and the days are spent in roaming out barefooted in the most *négligés* costumes, eating fruit, and helping to make the winter provisions, such as *Tarhana Kouskous, Youfka,* Petmaiz,† Rechel,‡ and Nichesteh*.§ No needlework is brought to fill up the leisure hours of country life; the only amusements are the indecent conversation and the practical jokes of the parasites who never fail to accompany such parties.

The villages owned by the bey are made up of the dwellings of the tenants. These for the most part present a pitiable appearance of poverty and misery, though their interiors are as clean as circumstances will allow. They are constructed of mud and wattle, and

---

* Pastes for soup and pilaf.
† Molasses made from grapes.
‡ Preserves made with molasses from fresh or dried fruits.
§ Starch made from wheat, much used for making sweets.

divided into two or three rooms, with small openings for windows, and open chimneys. A fence encloses the house, together with the granary and cattle shed. The tenants are, with few exceptions, Christians, and are called *Yeradjis*. They are poor, and look dejected and depressed, a demeanour I have often heard superficial observers attribute to laziness and natural worthlessness. This judgment may be just in some instances, but can by no means be taken as generally correct; the people are as willing to work and gain an honest living as those of any other land, but they labour under certain disadvantages which merit attention, and which, when carefully examined, will go far to justify their failings.

A Yeradji's house costs from £30 to £50; sometimes it is built by the landlord, sometimes by the tenant himself. This may happen for instance when the Yeradji has a son to marry and the landlord refuses to build a house for him, in which case he has to build it at his own expense, and should he leave the estate, receives no compensation for it. These *Chiftliks* are cultivated on the Metayer system as it is understood and practised in Macedonia: the landlord provides the seed in the first instance, the Yeradji finds his own yoke of oxen or buffaloes and implements, tills the ground, sows the grain, reaps it, threshes and winnows it, and when the seed for the next year and the tithes have been deducted, shares the produce with the landlord. The Metayer system on a luxuriant soil like that of Macedonia would not only pay, but would also contribute to increase the wealth of the estate and improve the wretched condition of the Yeradji if it were only properly and equitably administered. But it is not difficult to point out capital failings in the working of the system. When the grain is cut, a certain number of sheaves, forty for instance, of the finest and heaviest, are set aside as samples. These are threshed separately, and the seed for the next year, the tithes and the landlord's share, deducted according to this standard, which leaves the Yeradji an iniquitously small proportion of the produce. Under this unfair arrangement the Yeradji has to give for every head of cattle he possesses six Constantinople kilés of barley and six of wheat to the *Soubashi* of his bey.

In addition to these the Yeradji has to defray the heavy burden of his own taxes, and the quartering of troops and Zaptiehs upon him, besides other burdens, among which must be reckoned the wasted time of the numerous feast days, that deprive him of so much work in the year. Toil as hard as he may, he can never become an independent and prosperous man.

When these estates are transferred by sale or other causes, the Yeradji, should he be in debt to the estate, goes with it into a sort of bondage terminable under certain conditions, viz.: his industry and activity and the honesty of the landlord and his agent. If on one hand the superabundance of feast days is to be looked upon as a hindrance to the Yeradji freeing himself from debt, the unscrupulous manner in which his master or the Soubashi reckons accounts opposes fresh obstacles to the breaking of the chain that binds him to the soil. Farm accounts are generally kept by means of *chetolas*, or notched sticks, a very primitive mode, leading to many errors being committed, wittingly or unwittingly. The consequence is, that all tenants are more or less in debt to their landlords in the same manner as all Turkish landlords are in debt to the Government or to private individuals.

The scarcity of Yeradjis and their disqualifications as tenants are now a general complaint throughout Macedonia. It is not, however, surprising that the better class of peasants should refuse to become Yeradjis, and that the inferior classes, employed in their absence, should be found fault with and be always in debt.

Of late years some of these estates have passed into the hands of Christians, by purchase or mortgage. These proprietors, as a rule, do not reside on their estates, which are left in the charge of an agent, but content themselves with an occasional visit. When this property is well situated, and (as seldom happens) free from litigation, it is said to be a good investment.

Besides these Yeradji villages, there are the

Kephalochoria, or head-villages, composed of petty landholders, some of whom were formerly wealthy and might have continued so but for the injury done to them by the forest regulations and the heavy impositions laid upon them by the Government since the commencement of the war.

One of the principal grievances peasants labour under is the *angaria*, or statute-labour, into which man, beast, and cart are impressed at the command of a mere Zaptich, causing a loss of time, and injury to property and cattle, which is often fatal to an otherwise well-to-do village. A village on a main road is never free from all kinds of vexatious impositions and the quartering of Zaptichs and troops, who, whether they pay or not for what they have consumed, extort sums of money from their hosts, and are always careful to take away with them a declaration from the *Kodja-Bashi* that all accounts have been settled.

The Angaria work lately exacted from the inhabitants of Cavalla for the transport of flour for the use of the army was very nearly occasioning troubles of a nature likely to prove fatal to the whole town. The affair originated in the townspeople being required to carry on Sunday loads which they willingly carried on Saturday. They refused, and shut themselves up in their houses; whereupon an excess of zeal was displayed by the police in trying to force them out by breaking into some of the dwellings. This led to a slight disturbance which encouraged some noted bad characters belonging to the Moslem population to take a menacing attitude, and conspire to break into the offices of some of the principal merchants of the town, ransack them, and then proceed to follow the precedent with the rest of the town, threatening the Christians with massacre. Panic soon spread, and the people shut themselves in their churches. Men-of-war were telegraphed for, but luckily the local authorities were able to put down the tumult, and order was restored without loss of life. The incident is instructive in showing the difficulties and dangers under which the Macedonian peasant carries on his work. It is no wonder that the land is ill-cultivated.

Among the peasant farmers of Roumelia there is no regular system of rotation of crops observed; but with the occupants of large estates the ordinary rule for rich lands is two wheat crops and one of oats, then fallow one or more years, wheat, and then sesame. In Macedonia, where arable land is more abundant, one year's rest is allowed to some lands. The only manure some of these lands obtain is from the treading of the sheep on the land in early spring and after the harvest is reaped, and yet the soil is naturally so rich that a generally bad harvest is of rare occurrence. The mode of cultivation is very primitive, employing much hand labour and involving much waste. Tillage is performed with the native plough, on an average depth of four inches to the furrow. The instrument used for the purpose is very rude and has only one handle. The number of buffaloes used varies from two to five. In Roumelia some large estate owners attempted introducing agricultural implements from Europe, but threshing machines alone met with any success. In Macedonia even these proved a failure, as their management is not understood, and fuel is diffi cult to procure in the interior. In some parts the grain is scattered over the stubble and then ploughed in. Much of the harvest is done by young women and girls in Roumelia and Macedonia. They and the male harvesters hire themselves for the June harvest. On the 21st August the harvest-home is celebrated. Decked in their holiday costumes, crowned with garlands, and carrying bouquets composed of ears of corn, the reapers proceed to the nearest town to dance and sing before the doors of the principal houses and in the market-place.

Threshing is performed in the most antique manner imaginable. The instrument used for the purpose consists of two pieces of wood curved at one end, fastened together, and studded with a number of flints. This is attached at the curved end to a team of three or four horses. A girl stands on this sledge and drives the team rapidly over the corn thrown in bundles on the ground, which has been hardened and prepared for the purpose. This process breaks the straw into very small lengths, making it very palatable food for the cattle. The corn is winnowed by being thrown up in the air with wooden shovels, the breeze carrying away the chaff. In some parts of Macedonia the process is even more simple. A team of horses is driven over the bundles of corn, treading out the grain. The women and children also sit on the ground and help in the operation by beating it with sticks.

The principal crops raised in Roumelia are wheat, barley, maize, rye, oats, sesame, and canary-seed. A considerable quantity of rice is grown in some parts. In the south, towards Adrianople, the vine reaches some degree of perfection, and excellent wine is made, which, when kept for some years, resembles sherry in taste and colour. The mulberry grows abundantly, and before the silkworm disease appeared in those districts formed a very profitable branch of industry. The mulberry gardens sometimes comprise several acres of land; when they are near towns or large villages, the silkworm nurseries are placed in them. The rearing process begins in early spring, with the budding of the leaves, and lasts over two months. It is a very tedious and laborious work, requiring great neatness and attention, and is generally undertaken by the women. When the crop succeeds and is free from disease, it is an interesting process to watch. In Macedonia the same crops are grown, with the addition of a large supply of excellent tobacco. The best comes from Drama and Cavalla.

The cattle in Turkey, though small, are hardy and very serviceable. Little attention has hitherto been paid by the Government towards improving the breed. The sheep, too, are small, and their wool is of an inferior quality. Those in Asiatic Turkey are mostly of the Karamanian, or broad-tailed, breed. Their fat is much used by the natives for cookery, and their milk made into cheese. Sheep-farming is carried on to a great extent both in European and Asiatic Turkey. Buffaloes for draft purposes and ploughing, and camels as beasts of burden, are very numerous, especially in Asia Minor. Great numbers of goats are also kept; their milk is much used for making cheese. The Angora goats are (I need hardly say) much prized for their fleece. Their introduction into other parts of the country has been attempted several times, but has invariably failed. They do not thrive away from their native mountains.

CHAPTER IX.

TURKISH HOUSES.

The Turkish Quarter—A Konak—Haremlik and Selamlik—Arrangement of Rooms—Furniture—The Tandour—Turkish Clemency towards Vermin—Bordofska—An Albanian Konak—The Pasha and his Harem—A Turkish Bas-blev—Ruins of Konaks outside Uskup—The Last of the Albanian Deri-Beys—A Konak at Bazardjik—The Widow of the Deri-Bey—Kiosks—Koulas—A Koula near Salonika—Christian Quarters—Khans—Furniture—Turkish Baths, Public and Private—Cafés.

BRIGHT sunshine, fresh air, ample space, and pure water are indispensable to the felicity of a Turk. Both in the capital and in provincial towns the Turkish quarter is invariably situated in the most healthy and elevated parts, and occupies, on account of the gardens belonging to almost every Turkish house, double the ground of the Christian and Jewish quarters. These gardens are all more or less cultivated, but, except in the capital, where horticulture has obtained some degree of perfection, they seldom display either taste or order. A few fine mulberry or other fruit-trees may be seen here and there overshadowing patches of ground bordered with box or tiles, and planted with roses, lettuces, and garlic; and in the gardens of the better class of houses, one may often see pretty fountains.

The streets of the Turkish quarter are narrow and irregular, and, except in the principal thoroughfares, look solitary and deserted; they are, however, cleaner than those of the Christian and Jewish quarters, and this for three good reasons:—they are little frequented; they are not encumbered with rubbish, owing to the space the Turks possess in their courtyards and gardens, where they can heap up most of the refuse that the Christians have to throw into the streets; and they are better patrolled by the street dogs, for these famous scavengers, being under the special protection of the Mussulman, are more numerous in the Turkish than in the other quarters, and eat up all the animal and vegetable refuse.

A Turkish *konak* or mansion, is a large building, very irregular in construction and without the slightest approach to European ideas of comfort or convenience. This building is divided into two parts, the *haremlik* and the *selamlik*; the former and larger part is allotted to the women, the latter is occupied by the men and is used for the transaction of business, the purposes of hospitality, and formal receptions. The stables are attached to it, forming part of the ground floor, and rendering some of the upper rooms rather unpleasant quarters. A narrow passage leading from the *mabeyn* (or neutral ground) to the *haremlik*, joins the two establishments. The materials used for building are wood, lime, mud and stone for the foundations. A Konak generally consists of two stories, one as nearly as possible resembling the other, with abundant provision for the entrance of light and air. A large hall called the *devankhané*, forms the entrance into the Haremlik; it is surrounded by a number of rooms of various sizes. To the right, the largest serves as a sort of ante-chamber, the rest are sleeping apartments for the slaves, with the exception of one called *kahvé-agak*, where an old woman is always found sitting over a charcoal brazier, ready to boil coffee for every visitor. A large double staircase leads to the upper story, on one side of which is the *kiler*, or storeroom, and on the other the lavatories. The floors are of deal, kept scrupulously clean and white, and in the rooms generally covered with mats and rugs. The furniture is exceedingly poor and scanty; a hard uncomfortable sofa runs along two and sometimes three sides of the room; a *shelté*, or small square mattress, occupies each corner, surmounted by a number of cushions piled one upon the other in regular order. The corner of the sofa is the seat of the Hanoum, and by the side of the cushions are placed her mirror and *chekmegé*.

A small European sofa, a few chairs placed stiffly against the wall, a console supporting a mirror and decorated with two lamps or candlesticks, together with a few goblets and a small table standing in the centre with cigarettes and tiny ash-trays, complete the furniture of the grandest provincial *Buyuk-oda*. Though some Turks possess many rare and curious objects, such as ancient armour and china, which, if displayed, would greatly add to the elegance and cheerfulness of their apartments. These are always kept packed away in boxes.

Windows are the great inconvenience in Turkish houses; they pierce the walls on every side, with hardly the space of a foot between them. The curtains are usually of coarse printed calico, short and scanty, with the edges pinked out, so that when washed they present a miserably ragged appearance. The innumerable windows render the houses ill-adapted either for hot or cold weather; the burning rays of the sun pour in all day in summer, and the frames are so badly constructed that the cold wind enters in all directions in winter.

Bedsteads are not used by the Turks; mattresses are nightly spread on the floor, and removed in the morning into large cupboards, built into the walls of every room. These walls being whitewashed and roughly furnished, increase the uncomfortable appearance of the rooms, which at night are dimly lighted by one or two sperm candles or a petroleum lamp, the successors of the ancient tallow candle. The halls and passages are left in obscurity, and the servants find their way about as well as they can.

The *mangals* or braziers are the warming apparatus generally used by the Turks in their houses. These are made of different metals; some fixed in wooden frames, others in frames of wrought brass of very elegant and costly workmanship. The fuel consists of a quantity of wood ashes in which burning charcoal is half buried.

The *tandour*, now nearly fallen into disuse, is also worthy of notice. It consists of a square deal table with a foot-board covered with tin, on which a brazier stands; the whole is covered with a thick quilted counterpane which falls in heavy folds on a sofa running round it, covering the loungers up to the chin, and giving one the idea of a company of people huddled together in bed. The tandour is still very much used in Smyrna, and round it the Levantine ladies love to sit during the winter months. More than one English traveller, newly arrived in the country, when ushered into a drawing-room, is said to have rushed frantically out again under the impression that he had surprised the family in bed.

The furniture of the *selamlik* is similar to that of the Haremlik. A family often removes from one set of apartments to another; this propensity is doubtless stimulated by the desire to escape from the assaults of the fleas and other vermin that swarm in the rooms. When once these insects obtain a footing in a house, it is difficult to get rid of them, partly on account of the unwillingness of the Turks to destroy animal life of any description, and partly because these insects take up their abode between the badly joined planks under the mats and rugs.

I was once visiting at the house of a Pasha lately arrived at Adrianople. The Hanoum, a charming woman, was complaining bitterly to me of her rest having been much disturbed the previous night by the abundance of these creatures in her apartment. One of the slaves modestly remarked that she had occupied herself all the morning in scalding the floor of the room her mistress had slept in, and expressed a hope that she would not be longer troubled in that respect. A general outcry against this slave's want of humanity was raised by all the women present, and a chorus of "Yuzuk! Gunah!" (Pity! Sin!) was heard. It is curious that they raised no such outcry when they heard of the frightful destruction of human life that took place a few years later among their Christian neighbours in Bulgaria, but a few miles from their own secure homes!

When in the interior I had the opportunity of visiting some Konaks worthy of note; one of these called Bordofska, situated in the heart of Albania, some leagues from Uskup, had been built as a country residence by the famous Hevni Pasha. It was an immense building, solidly constructed of stone at the expense and with the forced labour of the people, who were pressed into the work. It occupied the middle of a large garden that must have been beautiful in its time, and being surrounded by high walls bore a strong resemblance to a feudal castle. This fine old building had become the property of Osman Pasha, a venerable Turk of the old school; all the furniture was European and of a very rich and elegant description, but looked worn and neglected. The aged Pasha received me with the politeness and hospitality his nation knows so well how to show when it pleases.

After an interchange of civilities and having partaken of coffee, I was invited to visit the harem. A hideous black monster, the chief of the eunuchs, led the way through a long dark passage lined with forty of his brethren, not more pleasant-looking than himself, who salaamed to me as I passed.

My then limited experiences of the customs of harems made me regard this gloomy passage and its black occupants with feelings of curiosity, not unmingled with dread. The chief wife of Osman Pasha (for I believe he had six others, besides slaves) was a very fat, elderly person, who showed little disposition to give me the hearty and civil reception I had just received from her husband, and I soon discoverved that she belonged to that peculiar class of Turkish women called *Soffous*—the *bas-bleus* of Mohammedanism, bigoted zealots of the straightest sect of the Moslem Pharisees.

On entering the room I found the Hanoum seated

in her sofa corner, from which she did not rise but merely gave a bend of the head, with a cold "Né yaparsen?"* in response to my deep Oriental obeisance. She spoke very little, and the few words she was obliged to utter were intermingled with *Duras* she muttered; perhaps asking forgiveness for the sin she was committing in holding direct intercourse with a *Giaour*. The other wives, who were all pretty and gay, tried to make amends for the ill-humour of their *doyenne*, and were as kind and amiable as etiquette would allow in her presence.

Four other Konaks of the same description may still be seen outside the town of Uskup, standing alongside in melancholy decay. The first and largest was intended for the residence of the once powerful Hevni Pasha himself; the second for his son, and the two others for his daughters. I was deeply impressed by the sight of these imposing ruins, and visited them with the double object of satisfying my curiosity and ascertaining the possibility of lodging myself in some habitable corner of one of them during my stay in the neighbourhood. The interior was well worth seeing, and comprised splendid apartments, the walls and ceilings being decorated with gildings and elaborate carvings in walnut wood. The baths of sculptured marble could still be taken as models of that luxurious and indispensable appendage to a Turkish house. A

* "How do you do?"

wing of one of these buildings was habitable; but when I proposed to instal myself in it, some natives who had accompanied our party, objected, saying the houses were *hursous* and *nahletli*, having been cursed by the people at whose expense, and by whose unrequited labour, they had been erected. Even the beasts, they said, that had carried the heavy loads of building-materials, were seen to look up to heaven and groan under the pressure of their burdens; and a prophet of the place had foretold the downfall of the owner on the day of the completion of the work. This prophecy was fulfilled to the letter, for on the day the Pasha was to have entered his new abode, the Turkish government, suspicious of his growing power and wealth, managed to lay hands upon him.

This Deri-Bey * is said to have been a wonderfully intelligent man, counterbalancing many of his tyrannical actions by the zealous care he showed in promoting the individual safety of his people and in increasing their prosperity. Though entirely uneducated, his natural talents were great enough to enable him to comprehend the advantages of modern civilisation, and to lead him to introduce some recent inventions into the country; he also attempted to render the river Vardar (the ancient Axius) navigable.

Hevni Pasha and his *voïvodes*, or captains, twenty-five or thirty years ago, may be looked upon as the

---

* "Valley-lord," or feudal chief.

last representatives of the chiefs of the wild Albanian clans, who at that time still refused to recognise the authority of the Porte, and when pressed to do so broke out into open rebellion. Badjnksis Ahmet Pasha, then a mere colonel, marched with his regiment upon Uskup, one of the principal strongholds of the Albanians, and partly by stratagem and partly by threats, managed to penetrate into the town and take possession of the fortress. In the meantime, Frank Omar Pasha, the field marshal, came with some regular troops to his assistance, having previously defeated the Albanians in battle at Kaplan, and dispersed them into the plains. He surrounded the town, and invited Hevni Pasha with his captains and the principal beys of the town into the fortress to hear the Imperial Firman read. This ceremony being concluded without disturbance, Hevni Pasha and such of his party as were likely to continue their resistance to the orders of the Porte were requested by the military authorities to mount at once the horses that had been surreptitiously prepared for them, and were conveyed under escort to Constantinople, whence they were sent into exile, their families being sent after them, and their goods confiscated. Notice was next given to the rest of the native beys, that, should any of them be found in direct or indirect communication with the scattered bands of Albanians, or sending provisions to them, the guns of the fortress would be turned upon the town, which would be razed to the ground. This was a master-stroke on the part of the Government; the Albanians, after a few vain attempts at Monastir, Vrania, Philippopolis, and other places, to resist the authority of the Sultan, partially submitted and returned to their impregnable mountain fastnesses; not, however, without having committed some barbarities similar to those recently enacted in Bulgaria.

During my trip to Bazardjik, I visited another konak: it belonged to Kavanos Oglou, another of the too famous Deri-Beys, who had acquired complete control over his part of the country, and who was similarly seized by the Porte, despoiled of his possessions, and sent into exile. This konak was an immense quadrangular building, enclosing a courtyard with a verandah running round it supported on massive wooden pillars. Upon this verandah a hundred rooms opened. The house was low and clumsy in appearance, but timber of remarkable size and solidity had been used in its construction.

At the time of my visit it was abandoned; the doors and windows had disappeared, giving to the edifice an appearance of solitude and emptiness, rendered still more dismal by the presence of innumerable bats and owls, its only occupants. The old dungeon with its cruel associations could still be traced in a low building, about thirty feet long and twenty wide, surrounded by a wall of immense thickness and strongly roofed. For windows nothing was seen but a few slits. The interior on one side was occupied by a double wall, with just enough space between to admit a person in a standing position; in this the offenders against the laws, and the victims of vendetta, were squeezed, secured by heavy chains that hung at equal distances from iron rings. A well, now filled up, occupied the centre, into which the heads of decapitated prisoners were thrown to disappear in the dismal darkness of its depths.

I was not sorry to leave this cheerless scene of former despotism and present decay, and to turn my steps towards a gate on the opposite side of the garden leading into a kiosk more modern in appearance than the house, though bearing traces of decay. This last refuge of a once powerful family was occupied by Azizić Hanoum Effendi, the much respected widow of the tyrant. Her two sons, who occupied inferior positions under Government, were absent. The descendants of Kavanos Oglou continue to be much respected in the country in spite of their downfall and the confiscation of their property. The venerable lady into whose presence I was ushered bore, notwithstanding her advanced age, traces of a beauty that must have been perfect in its bloom. She was a fine tall blonde of the Circassian type, of a commanding appearance, softened by the sweet dignity of fallen sovereignty, before whom I felt I could bow the knee and kiss the hand she graciously extended to me. I had a long and interesting conversation with her on the state of the country, which she described as having been more flourishing under the rule of her husband than at this time. " But," said she, with a sigh, " God ordains all things, casting some into misfortunes and raising others into prosperity, according as Kismet has prepared for all. *Allah Kerim!* "

Everyone has heard or read of a *kiosk*, the indispensable pleasure-seat of a Turk. The imperial and other kiosks on the Bosphorus are miniature palaces, luxuriously furnished, whose elegance and beauty are only equalled by the incomparable advantages of their situation on the richest of soils, and beneath the sunniest of skies. Kiosks may be situated anywhere, and may comprise a suite of apartments or be limited to one; they are light and airy in style, generally commanding a fine prospect, often floored with marble, and containing a *shadravan* or sculptured fountain playing in the midst; a range of sofas runs all round the walls, on which the Turk loves to sit for hours together lost in meditation, and in the fumes of his inseparable companion the *nargilé*.

The interiors of old kiosks and konaks used to be ornamented with a peculiar open woodwork of arabesque design decorating the walls and ceilings, but this is now completely out of fashion. The ceiling of a house I formerly inhabited was decorated with this work, and attracted the attention of all travellers. One, an Englishman, was so much struck with it on entering the room, that hardly had he bowed to the company before he asked permission to make a sketch of it. We were so accustomed to similar displays of originality in British tourists that the request was at once granted.

A *koula* is a high turret found on every large *chiftlik*, or farm, and used as a refuge in case of assault by brigands; it is a quadrangular edifice, from three to four stories high; the lowest is used as a granary and for storing seeds and other valuable property belonging to the farm; the others, light and airy, are reserved for the habitation of the owner of the chiftliks during his occasional visits to his property.

The last stronghold of this description I visited was the property of a British subject in the district of Salonika. It was solidly constructed, with massive iron doors and shutters, and some years ago resisted the assault of a band of brigands who besieged it for three days, till the arrival of a corps of Zaptiehs occasioned their hasty disappearance. The marks of their bullets may still be seen on the doors and shutters, but no further damage was done.

There is no very marked difference between the quarters of the town occupied by Christians and those occupied by Turks. The Christians' houses are built very much in the same style, though they are not so large, and open directly on the street, with shops in their lower stories in the principal thoroughfares. The windows are free from the lattices invariably seen in a Turkish *haremlik*. There is much more life and animation in a Christian or Jewish quarter, partly in consequence of one house being occupied by several families. This is especially the case among the lower orders of Jews, where one may count as many families as there are rooms in a house.

In most Eastern towns the Jewish quarters, containing the fish, meat, and vegetable markets, are the most unclean, and consequently the most unhealthy. Few sanitary regulations exist, and little attention is paid to them or to the laws of hygiene. The streets are frequently nearly impassable, and some of the dwellings of the poor are pestilential, the hotbeds of every epidemic that visits the country.

Most of the ancient khans, warehouses, and bazars at Stamboul, and in large provincial towns, are fine solidly constructed edifices. The bazars are of a peculiarly Oriental style of architecture, and appear well adapted to the use for which they were designed —the display and sale of goods. In the interior, however, many of these bazars are neglected, and some left to decay have been by degrees abandoned by the tenants of the innumerable shops they once contained.

The *charshi*, or market-place, consists of an incongruous assemblage of shops, huddled together without any attempt at architecture or regard to appearances; for the most part protected only by large shutters that are raised in the morning and lowered at night. A low platform of boards occupies the greater part of the interior, in the front corner of which the shopkeeper sits on a little carpet, cross-legged, with a wooden safe by his side and his account-book and pipe within easy reach, ever ready to attend to the wants of his customers. Rows of shelves, constructed in recesses in the walls, serve as receptacles for his goods.

The *khans*, or warehouses, in towns are used as deposits for merchandise and for the transaction of business by merchants and bankers who have offices in them. A series of hostelries of all descriptions and dimensions, also called khans, some built of stone and others of timber, exist in large numbers in all parts of the country, serving as hotels to travellers and store-rooms for merchandise during transit. The ruins of the most ancient of these, built by the Turks at the time of the conquest and used by them as blockhouses, still exist on the main roads and in some of the principal towns. By the side of these substantial stone buildings have arisen a number of miserable edifices dignified with the name of khan, with whose discomforts the weary traveller too often makes sad acquaintance.

The furniture of wealthy Greek houses in Constantinople is European; in those of Jews and Armenians of high position it is a compromise between European and Turkish. All Orientals are fond of display; they like to build large houses and ornament their reception rooms in a gaudy manner; but the *ensemble* lacks finish and comfort. At A—— I had fixed upon an old Turkish konak as my residence; but on coming to inhabit it I discovered that extensive alterations and improvements must be made before it approached in the remotest degree to my idea of an English home. Some officious person, at a loss to understand the object of these changes, gave notice to the proprietor that his tenant was fast demolishing his house, upon which the good old Turk asked if she were building it up again, and being answered in the affirmative, quietly said, "*Brak yupsen! (laissez faire!)*"

The furniture found in the dwellings of all the lower classes is much the same throughout the country; a Turkish sofa, a few deal chairs, and a table serving for every purpose. The bedding is placed on the floor at night and removed in the morning. But if furniture is scanty, there is no lack of carpets and copper kitchen utensils, both being considered good investments by the poor.

Before concluding this chapter I must not forget to describe one of the most necessary adjuncts to a Turkish house—the bath. In a large house or konak, this is by far the best fitted and most useful part of the whole establishment. A Turkish bath comprises a suite of three rooms; the first—the *hammam*—is a square apartment chiefly constructed of marble, and terminating in a kind of cupola studded with a number of glass bells, through which the light enters. A deep reservoir, attached to the outer wall, with an opening into the bath, contains the water, half of which is heated by a furnace built under it. A number of pipes, attached to the furnace, circulate through the walls of the bath and throw great heat into it. One or two graceful fountains conduct the water from the reservoir, and on each side of the fountain is a low wooden platform which serves as a seat for the bather, who sits cross-legged, and undergoes a long and complicated process of washing and scrubbing, with a variety of other toilet arrangements too numerous to mention.

The second room, called the *saouklouk*, is constructed very much in the same style as the first, but is smaller, and has no furniture but a marble platform upon which mattresses and cushions are placed for the use of those who wish to repose between intervals of bathing, or do not wish to face the cooler temperature of the *hammam oda*. This room is furnished with sofas, on which the bathers rest and dress after quitting the bath.

Turkish women are very fond of their bath, and are capable of remaining for hours together in that hot and depressing atmosphere. They smoke cigarettes, eat fruits and sweets, and drink sherbet, and finally, after all the blood has rushed to their heads, and their faces are crimson, they wrap themselves in soft burnouses, and pass into the third or outer chamber, where they repose on a luxurious couch until their system shakes off part of the heat and languor that the abuse of these baths invariably produces. A bath being an indispensable appendage to every house, one is to be found in even the poorest Turkish dwelling. Some more or less resemble a regular *hammam*, others are of a very simple form—often a tiny cabinet attached to one of the rooms, containing a bottomless jar buried in the ground, through which the water runs. I consider these little baths, which are neither expensive nor require much space, excellent institutions in the houses of the poor as instruments of cleanliness. The constant and careful ablutions of the Turk are the principal preventives to many diseases, from which they are, comparatively speaking, freer than most nations.

The public baths, resorted to by all classes, are to

be found in numbers in every town. They are fine buildings, exact copies of the old Roman baths, many of which are still in existence, defying the march of centuries and the work of decay. Like the home baths, they consist of three spacious apartments. The outer bath-room is a large stone building lighted by a cupola, with wooden platforms running all round, upon which small mattresses and couches are spread for the men; but the women not having the same privilege, are obliged to bring their own rugs, upon which they deposit their clothes, tied up in bundles, when they enter, and repose and dress upon them on coming out of the bath. A fountain of cold water is considered indispensable in this apartment, and in the basin surrounding it may be seen water-melons floating about, placed there to cool while their owners are in the inner bath.

The bath itself contains a number of small rooms, each of which can be separately engaged by a party, or used in common with the other bathers. It is needless to say that the baths used by men are either separate or are open at different hours.

Turkish women, independently of their home baths, must resort at least once a month to the public *hammam*. They like it for many reasons, but principally because it is the only place where they can meet to chat over the news of the day and their family affairs.

Some of these baths, especially the mineral ones at Broussa, are of the finest description. Gurgutly, containing the sulphureous springs, is renowned for the remarkable efficacy of its waters, its immense size, and the elegant and curious style of its architecture. It comprises two very large apartments, one for the use of the bathers previous to their entering the bath, the other the bath itself. This is an immense room with niches all round containing fountains in the form of shells, which receive part of the running stream; in front of these are wooden platforms, on which the bathers collect for the purpose of washing their heads and scrubbing their bodies. On the left as you enter stands an immense marble basin, seven feet in length and three in width, into which the mother stream gushes with impetuous force. From this it runs into a large round basin about ten feet in depth, in which dozens of women and children may be seen swimming, an exhausting process, owing to the high temperature of the water and its sulphureous qualities. This wonderful basin is in the shape of a reversed dome, sunk into the marble floor, which is supported underneath by massive columns.

Coffee-houses are to be met with everywhere, and are very numerous in the towns. The Turks resort to them when they leave their homes early in the morning, to take a cup of coffee and smoke a nargilé before going to business. In the evening, too, they step in to have a chat with their neighbours and hear the news of the day. Turkish newspapers have become pretty common of late in these quiet rendezvous, and are to be found in the most unpretending ones. Few of these establishments possess an inviting exterior or can boast any arrangements with regard to comfort or accommodation; a few mats placed upon benches, and a number of common osier-seated chairs and stools are the seats afforded in them. Small gardens may be found attached to some, while others atone for the deficiencies of their interiors by the lovely situations they occupy in this picturesque and luxurious land.

CHAPTER X.

THE SERAGLIO.

The Chain of Palaces along the Bosphorus—*Eski Serai*, the Oldest of the Seraglios—Its Site and Appearance—Beauty of its Gardens—Contrasts—Its Destruction—*Dolma-Bagché* and *Begler-Bey*—Enormous Expenditure of Abdul-Medjid and Abdul-Aziz on Seraglios—*Yahlis* or Villas—*Begler-Bey* Furnished for Illustrious Guests—Delicate Attentions of the Sultan—Furniture of Seraglios—Mania of Abdul-Aziz—Everything Inflammable thrown into the Bosphorus—Pleasure Grounds—Interior Divisions of the Seraglio—The *Mabeyn*—The Padishah *en négligé*—Imperial Expenditure—Servants, &c.—Food—Wages—Stables—Fine Art—Origin of the Inmates of the Seraglio—Their Training—Adjemis—A Training-School for the Seraglio—Ranks in the Seraglio—The *Bash Kadin Effendi* and other Wives—*Hanoums* or Odalisks—Favourites—Equal Chances of Good Fortune—Ceremonies Attending the Sultan's Selection of an Odalisk—A Slave seldom sees the Sultan more than Once—Consequent Loss of Dignity and Misery for the rest of her Life—Precarious Position of Imperial Favourites—Intrigues and Cabals in the Seraglio—Good Fortune of the Odalisk who bears a Child—Fashions in Beauty—Golden Hair—The *Validé Sultana*—The *Husnadar Ousta*—Ignorance and Vice of the Seraglio Women—The Better Class—The Consumptive Class—The " Wild Serailis "—Amusements of the Seraglio—Theatre—Ballet—Shopping—Garden Parties in Abdul-Medjid's Time—Imperial Children—Foster-Brothers—Bad Training and Deficient Education of Turkish Princes and Princesses.

THERE are more than twenty Imperial Palaces, variously named, according to their size and character, seraglios, yahlis, and kiosks, scattered about Constantinople, some on the Bosphorus, others inland, but all equally to be admired as striking spectacles of

Eastern magnificence. Dolma-Bagché and Beshiktash, linked with other mansions and kiosks, mingling European architecture with Oriental decoration, form a chain of splendid palaces such as can be seen nowhere but on the historic shores of the Bosphorus.

The most renowned of the Ottoman palaces was Eski Serai, on the point of land where the Bosphorus enters the Sea of Marmora. Built on the site of old Byzantium by Mehemet II., this celebrated palace was enlarged and beautified according to the wants and caprices of each successive sultan. It presented to the eye a crowded pile of vast irregular buildings, crowned by gilded cupolas and girt with shaded gardens. Beautiful mosques, varied with hospitals and other charitable foundations, were scattered about in detached groups, amid clusters of stately cypresses and the burial-grounds of kings. Here might be seen a gorgeous pavilion, there a cool jet, here again a mysterious building with high impenetrable walls and latticed windows, the monotonous dwelling-place of bright young creatures who, once engaged, were rarely permitted to regain their freedom. And there, dwarfing all else, rose the tall white minarets, accenting their clear outlines against the tender sky of the East. In this irregular confusion the artist saw one of the choicest sights of the capital; and a closer view offered to the curious a clear and minute conception of the palace of an Eastern despot.

All was there: the gorgeous and the squalid, the refined and the loathsome, the splendid state rooms of the Vicar of God, beside the gloomy cages of those unhappy princes, who, cursed by their royal blood, were left to pine in solitude, until death came to settle accounts between them and the tyrants who had doomed them to their chains. There were the charitable establishments whence the poor never turned away unrefreshed,—and there the dungeon where the powerful were left to starve and die. There was the gilded kiosk where the Padishah smoked his chibouk and issued his decrees,—whose terrible ordinances were carried out in the adjoining chamber-of-blood. Beyond were the mausoleums of his race, lifting up their rich adornment in the chill beauty of the city of the dead—severed by a little space from the scarcely more splendid dwellings of the living. There lay those doomed princes to whom a life without liberty and ofttimes a cruel death were ill balanced by the useless splendour of their tombs. " What is the use of thy getting children," once with a mother's bitterness said a Circassian slave who had borne a son to one of the sultans, " when they are only destined to people the tombs?"

In later times Eski Serai was abandoned to the use of the harems of deceased sultans, who were sometimes shut up there for life. Its last occupants, the multitudes of wives, slaves, and odalisks belonging once to Sultan Abdul-Medjid, unable any longer to endure its dismal solitude, are reported to have set it on fire in the hope of obtaining a dwelling more congenial to the habits of comparative liberty they had acquired. At all events the palace was destroyed, and a vast number of valuable and rare objects perished with it. The site is now occupied by gardens, and a railroad runs across it: the gem of the Golden Horn has vanished.

Dolma-Bagché, built by Sultan Mahmoud II., was a large wooden edifice. This and Begler-Bey became the usual winter and summer residences of the imperial family. Sultan Abdul-Medjid, on coming to power, rebuilt Dolma-Bagché and several other kiosks and seraglios. Gentle, sensitive, refined, and loth to shed blood, he is said to have evinced a superstitious aversion to the old imperial palaces whose splendour was tainted by the memory of the crimes of his ancestors. He, and still more his brother Abdul-Aziz, spent incalculable sums in the erection and decoration of seraglios. The latter's yearly expenses on this alone were reckoned to have exceeded £580,000 : —one of the items which ran away with the money which trusting or speculative capitalists of Europe had been foolish enough to supply for the future benefit and improvement of Turkey (not, of course, forgetting a slice in the pie for themselves), but which has fallen somewhat short of the end for which it was designed: Turkish bondholders do not seem to consider themselves of all men the most fortunate, and Turkey itself has not gained by loading its exchequer with a mountain of debt for the sake of the reckless extravagance of imperial luxury.

Holding a middle place between the great palaces and the kiosks, the sultans of Turkey possess *yahlis* or villas not less beautiful than the mansions of greater pretensions. These villas often rise on the shores of the Bosphorus from a bed of verdure. Generally they are closed and silent, with a solitary guard standing sentinel at the gate: but every now and then one of them may be seen lighted up, as by magic, and teeming with life, with the rumbling of carriages to and fro, and the clashing of arms. At the sound of the trumpet a strain of sweet music strikes up, and the approach of a water-procession of caïques swiftly gliding towards the gates announces the arrival of the august master.

Sometimes the sultan goes alone to spend a few hours of *dolce far niente;* at others he makes an appointment with some special favourite to meet him there. Abdul-Medjid's known partiality for Bessimé Sultana, the most worthless but most beloved of his wives, induced him on one occasion, while on a visit to his Yahli at the sweet waters of Asia, to send his own yacht for her in the dead of night, alarming the whole seraglio by its unexpected appearance at so unusual an hour.

One of the three palaces most renowned for beauty of architecture and magnificence of furniture is Begler-Bey. It is worthy of the use for which it has been selected, of being the palace offered for the occupation of illustrious foreign visitors. The arrangements made in it for one imperial guest were presided over by Sultan Abdul-Aziz in person, and the private apartments of the illustrious lady were perfect copies of those in her own palace. The fastidiousness of the host on this occasion was so great, that on discovering that the tints on the walls and furniture slightly differed from those he had seen when on his European tour, he ordered that everything should be removed and new ones brought from Paris. The fair visitor is said to have been equally surprised and flattered by the delicate attention that had not omitted even the smallest object of her toilet table. The Sultan, in truly Oriental fashion, caused a new pair of magnificent slippers, embroidered with pearls and precious stones, to be placed before her bed every morning.

Since the time of Sultan Abdul-Medjid, the furniture of the imperial palaces and kiosks has been made to order in Europe. It is of so costly a description as to be equal in value to the edifices themselves. On entering Tcheragan, and some of the other serails, the eye is dazzled by the gilt decorations, gold and silver brocades, splendid mirrors and chandeliers, and carved and inlaid furniture they contain. In Abdul-Medjid's time, clocks and china vases were the only ornaments of the apartments. The absence of pictures, books, and the thousand different objects with which Europeans fill their houses, gave the rooms, even when inhabited, a comfortless and unused appearance.

Some years ago, when visiting the private apartments of this Sultan, I noticed a splendid antique vase. Lately, on speaking of this priceless object to a seraglio lady, I was informed that it had been thrown into the Bosphorus by order of its owner. This act of imperial extravagance was caused by the supposition that the vase had been handled by some person afflicted with consumption.

Sultan Abdul-Aziz, a year or two before his dethronement, possessed with a nervous terror of fire, caused all inflammable articles to be taken out of the palaces, and replaced them by articles manufactured of iron. The stores of fuel were cast into the Bosphorus, and the lights of the Sultan's apartments were placed in basins of water. The houses in the neighbourhood of the Seraglio were purchased by the Sultan, their occupants forced to quit at a very short notice, their furniture turned out, and the buildings pulled down at once. These tyrannical precautions served to heighten the general discontent of the capital against the Padishah, especially among the poor, who justly complained that they might have benefited by what had been wasted; while some of the wealthy, though not more contented, profited by the freak, and carried off many of the rich objects taken out of the palace.

The vast pleasure grounds attached to the seraglios are laid out with a tasteful care, which, added to the beauty of the position and the fertility of the soil, goes far to justify the renown of the gardens of the Bosphorus. The hills, valleys, and gorges that surround them are covered with woods; here orchards and vineyards, weighed down with their rich burdens, lend colour to the scene; there the slopes are laid out in terraces, whose perpendicular sides are clothed with the contrasted shades of the sombre ivy-leaf and the bright foliage of the Virginian creeper. Banks of flowers carry the thoughts back to the hanging gardens of Babylon. Nature and art have ornamented these delightful spots with lakes, fountains, cascades, aviaries, menageries, and pavilions. "Here in cool grot" every opportunity is offered for love-making, and if this one is already engaged, there are highly romantic nooks, concealed by overhanging boughs, that will answer the purpose as well. Trees and plants seem to rejoice in the bright sunshine; the birds' songs mingle strangely with the roar of the wild beasts from which the Sultan is perhaps trying to learn a lesson of humanity; and gorgeous butterflies hover round, kissing the sweet blossoms that fill the air with their fragrance. Here the ladies of the harem, when permitted to escape for a time from their cages, roam at liberty like a troop of school-girls during recreation hours, some making for the orchards, others dispersing in the vineyards, with screams of laughter and wild frolic that would astonish considerably any European garden party. The conservatories and flower beds suffer terribly during these incursions, and great is the despair of the head-gardener.*

A Seraglio, like all Moslem dwellings, is divided into Haremlik and Selamlik. The former is reserved for the family life of the Sultan and his women; the latter is accessible to officials who come to transact state business with his Highness. The Mabeyn consists of a number of rooms between the two great divisions, and may be considered the private home of the Sultan. It is here that the Padishah resorts between nine and ten in the morning, attired in his *gedjlik* or morning négligé; consisting of a *takké*, or white skull-cap; a bright-coloured *intari* (dressing-gown) and *cichdon* (trousers) of similar material; a pair of roomy *terliks* (slippers), a *kirka* (quilted jacket), or a *kirk* (pelisse lined with fur), according to the season.

---

* Generally a European, who often attains to high rank and fortune.

Thus attired, he resorts to his study and gives his attention to state affairs, or to any other occupations that suit his tastes and inclinations. Close by are the apartments where the gentlemen of the household, the private secretaries, and other functionaries, await their Imperial Master from sunrise.

An account I recently saw of the Imperial expenditure estimated the annual outlay of Sultan Abdul-Aziz at £2,000,000. The Palace contained 5500 servants of both sexes. The kitchens alone required 300 functionaries, and the stables 400. There were also about 400 caïkjis or boatmen, 400 musicians, and 200 attendants who had the charge of the menageries and aviaries. Three hundred guards were employed for the various palaces and kiosks, and about 100 porters. The harem, besides this, contained 1200 female slaves.

In the Selamlik might be counted from 1000 to 1500 servants of different kinds. The Sultan had twenty-five "aides de camp," seven chamberlains, six secretaries, and at least 150 other functionaries, divided into classes, each having its special employment.

One is entrusted with the care of the Imperial wardrobe, another with the pantry, a third with the making and serving of the coffee, and a fourth with the pipes and cigarettes.

There were also numberless attendants who carried either a torch, or a jug of perfumed water for ablutions after a repast. There is a chief barber, a superior attendant who has special charge of the games of backgammon and draughts, another superintends the braziers, and there are at least fifty kavasses, and one hundred eunuchs; and the harem has also at its service a hundred servants for going on errands and doing commissions in Stamboul and Pera.

Altogether, the total number of the employés of the Palace is about 5500. But this is not all; these servants employ also other persons beneath them, so that every day 7000 persons are fed at the expense of the Palace. So great is the disorder in the organisation that the contractors claim five francs per diem for the food of each of these 7000 persons, which amounts to £511,000 per annum for the employés only.

The various items comprise £1120 for wood, £1040 for rice, and £16,000 for sugar.

The wages of employés included in the civil list, amounted to a total of £200,000, exclusive of the salaries of aides de camp, doctors, musicians, etc., which were paid by the minister of war.

The stables of the Palace contained 600 horses, whose provender, according to the estimates of the most reasonable contractors, cost three Turkish liras per month, making a total of about £20,000.

More than 200 carriages of every description were

kept in the palace. These were for the most part presents from the Viceroy of Egypt, but the expenses of the 150 coachmen and footmen with their rich liveries are paid by a civil list, also the harness-maker's accounts, and other items of this department.

The annual expenditure for pictures, porcelain, etc., was never less than £140,000, and in one year Sultan Abdul-Aziz spent £120,000 for pictures only. As for jewels, the purchases attained the annual sum of £100,000, and the expenses of the harem for presents, dresses, etc., absorbed £160,000 per annum.

Besides these items, the allowances to the mother and sisters of the Sultan, to his nephews and nieces, and to the heir apparent, amounted to £181,760. This gives a total of at least £1,300,000 annually. To this must be added £80,000 for keeping in repair the existing Imperial kiosks and palaces, and £580,000 for the construction of new ones. The Imperial revenue in the civil list was £1,280,000. The expenditure was really over £2,000,000.

I am unable to give an estimate of the expenses of the seraglio of the present Sultan, but I have been informed on good authority that his Majesty personally superintends the management of the palace, and regulates its expenditure with great wisdom and economy; it will take some time however to put an end to the disorder, corruption, and irregularity that have become so rooted in the whole system, and caused the extravagance and waste that prevailed in the households of former sultans. A Turkish proverb says, "Baluk bashtan kokar," "The fish begins to decompose at the head:" accordingly, if the head be sound there is every hope that the body will also keep fresh.

The haremlik of the Seraglio contains from 1000 to 1500 women, divided among the Sultan's household; that of his mother, the Validé Sultana; and those of the princes.

This vast host of women of all ranks, ages and conditions are, without exception, of slave extraction, originating from the cargoes of slaves that yearly find their way to Turkey from Circassia, Georgia, Abyssinia, and Arabia, in spite of the prohibition of the slave trade. These slaves are sold in their native land by unnatural relations, or torn from their homes by hostile tribes to be subsequently handed over to the slave dealers, and brought by them into the capital and other large towns. All these women are the offspring of semi-barbarous parents, who seldom scruple to sell their own flesh and blood. Born in the hovel of the peasant, or the hut of the fierce chieftain, their first condition is one of extreme ignorance and barbarism. Possessed with the knowledge of no written language, with a confused idea of religion mixed up with the superstitious practices that ignorance engenders; poorly-clad, portionless, and unprotected, they are drawn into the seraglio by chains of bondage, and go under the denomination of *Adjemis* (rustics). No matter how low had been their starting point, their future career depends solely upon their own good fortune. Their training in the seraglio is regulated by the vocations for which they are destined; those chosen to fulfil domestic positions, such as negresses and others not highly favoured by nature, are put under the direction of *kalfas*, or head-servants, and taught their respective duties.

The training they receive depends upon the career to which their age, personal attractions, and colour, entitle them. The young and beautiful, whose lot has a great chance of being connected with that of his Imperial Majesty, or some high dignitary to whom she may be presented by the Validé or the Sultan as odalisk or wife, receives a veneer composed of the formalities of Turkish etiquette, elegance of deportment, the art of beautifying the person, dancing, singing, or playing on some musical instrument. To the young and willing, instruction in the rudiments of the Turkish language are given; they are also initiated in the simpler forms of Mohammedanism taught to women, such as the *Namaz* and other prayers and the observance of the fasts and feasts. Most of them are, however, left to pick up the language as best they can, and for this they display great aptitude, and often succeed in speaking Turkish with a certain amount of eloquence, although their native accent is never lost, and the extraction of a seraili can always be discovered by her particular accent. Many of these women possess great natural talent, and if favoured with some education, and endowed with a natural elegance, become very tolerable specimens of the fair sex.

All the seraglio inmates, on their entrance to the imperial abode, do not belong to this class of *Adjemis*; many of them have been previously purchased by Turkish hanoums of high station, who from speculative or other motives, give them the training described, and when sufficiently polished sell them at high prices, or present them to the seraglio with the view to some object.

An ex-seraili of my acquaintance had herself undertaken this task and had offered as many as fourteen young girls to the seraglio of Abdul-Aziz, after having reared each for the duties that would probably devolve upon her. This lady said to me, "What other gift from a humble creature like myself could be acceptable to so great a personage as his Imperial Majesty?" At the time this conversation took place she had a fresh batch of young slaves in hand. They were all smart-looking girls, designated by fancy names such as Amore, Fidèle, Rossignole, Beauté, etc. Their dress was rich, but ludicrous in the extreme, being composed of cast-off seraglio finery of all the colours of the rainbow; some children were even dressed in the Turkish military uniform, which contrasted strangely with the plaits of their long thick hair tied up with cotton rags. Their politeness, half saucy, half obsequious, was very amusing; on entering the room they all stood in a row at the lower end, and when some jocose observations were made to them by their mistress, a ready and half impudent reply was never wanting. The youngest, about eight years of age, was dressed in a miniature colonel's full uniform; on being addressed by her owner by the name of "*Pich*,"* and asked, "Will you have this lady's little son for your husband? I mean to marry him to you when you grow up!" the little miss laughed, and seemed perfectly well acquainted with the meaning of the proposal, and by no means abashed at it.

The treatment these girls received seemed to be very kind, but sadly wanting in decency, morality, and good principle.

On the accession of a new Sultan to the throne, it was customary to make a clearance of most of the inmates of the seraglio, and replenish it with fresh ones, such as those that already belonged to the household of the new sovereign, and others further to augment the number. Ottoman sultans, with two exceptions, have never been known to marry; the mates of the Sultan, chosen from among the

---

* In polite language, "child of unknown paternity."

ranks of slaves already mentioned, or from among those that are presented to him, can only be admitted to the honourable title of wife when they have borne children. The first wife is called Bash Kadin Effendi, the second Ikinji Kadin Effendi, and so on in numerical order up to the seventh wife (should there be so many), who would be called Yedinji Kadin Effendi.*

The slaves that have borne children beyond this number bear the title of Hanoums, and rank after the Kadin Effendis; their children are considered legitimate, and rank with the other princes and princesses. To these two classes must be added a third, that of favourites, who having no right to the title of Kadin Effendi or Hanoum, are dependent solely upon the caprice of their master or the influence they may have acquired over him for the position they hold in the imperial household.

Under this system every slave in the seraglio, from the scullery maid to the fair and delicate beauty purchased for her personal charms, may aspire to attaining the rank of wife, *odalisk*, or favourite. The mother of the late Sultan Abdul-Aziz is said to have performed the most menial offices in the establishment.

---

* A few years ago the mother of Sultan Abdul-Aziz, desirous of further reducing this number, brought forward an old palace regulation, that every seraglio woman found *enceinte* should be subjected to the operation of artificial abortion, with the exception of the first four wives.

When thus engaged one day she happened to attract the attention of her imperial master, Sultan Mahmoud II., who distinguished her with every mark of attention, and raised her to the rank of Bash Kadin. Generally speaking, however, the wives of sultans are select beauties who are offered to him yearly by the nation on the feast of Kandil Ghedjessi, others are gifts of the Validé and other persons wishing to make an offering to the Sultan.

When one of these odalisks has succeeded in gaining the good graces of the Sultan, and attracted his attention, he calls up the Ikinji Hasnadar Ousta,* and notifies to her his desire of receiving the favoured beauty into his apartment. The slave being informed of this, is bathed, dressed with great care and elegance, and introduced in the evening to the imperial presence. Should she be so fortunate as to find favour in the eyes of her lord and master, she is on the next morning admitted into a separate room reserved for slaves of this category, which she occupies during the time needful for ascertaining what rank she is in future to take in the seraglio. Should the arrival of a child raise her to that of Kadin Effendi or hanoum, a *Dairé* or special apartment is set apart for her. Those who are admitted to the Sultan's presence, and have no claims to the rights of maternity, do not

---

* Under-superintendent of the harem.

present themselves a second time, unless requested to do so, nor can they lay claim to any further attention, although their persons, like those of the Kadin Effendi and hanoums, become sacred, and the contraction of marriage with another person is unlawful. The distinction between the favoured and the discarded favourite is made known by her abstaining from going to the *hammam*. The lot of these discarded favourites is naturally not an enviable one. Accidentally noticed by the Sultan, or entertained by him as the object of a mere passing caprice, they seldom have the good fortune to occupy a sufficient ascendancy over the mind or heart of the sovereign to enable them to prolong or consolidate their influence.

A seraglio inmate, who had herself enjoyed Imperial favour of this description, told me that it was very seldom that a slave enjoyed more than once the passing notice of the Sultan, a disappointment naturally very deeply felt by those who after being suddenly raised to the height of favour find themselves quickly consigned again to oblivion, in which their future is passed. There are many among the rejected favourites who have sensitive natures and are capable of a serious attachment, and in consequence of the sarcasms the more favoured fail not to heap upon them, the disappointment they have experienced, or the devouring jealousy that unrequited love occasions, are said to become broken-hearted or die of consumption. "Nor," continued my informant, "was the condition of those more closely connected with the Sultan such as insured to them perfect happiness, mental unconcern, or security."

They are obliged to have recourse to every art to preserve their beauty, fight hard against the attacks and intrigues of rivals, and carefully to watch over themselves and their offspring.

Bessimé Sultana, one of the few who obtained a right to that title by marriage, was an emancipated slave adopted by the lady who had brought her up, and consequently could not be possessed by Sultan Abdul-Medjid unless through *Nekyah* or legal marriage.

In relating her strange and adventurous life, as one of the Kadin Effendis, to a personal friend of mine, she said, Nothing can give a clear idea of the intrigues and cabals perpetually carried on within the walls of the seraglio. The power and happiness of some contrast strangely with the trials and sufferings of those who are in the power of the influential and malicious. Every crime that has a chance of being silently passed over can be committed by these.

The slave who, by her interesting position, becomes entitled to the use of separate apartments, receives a pension, has her own slaves, her eunuchs, her doctors, banker, carriages, and caïques, and is supplied with apparel, jewels, and all other requisites suited to her rank. She dines in her own rooms, receives her friends, and goes out when allowed to do so. On attaining this rank a new world dazzling with gold, luxury, and every refinement belonging to the favoured and elevated is opened to her, raising her far above her former companions in toil and frolic, who in future, setting aside all familiarity, stand before her with folded arms, kiss the hem of her garment, and obey her orders with profound respect.

The favoured beauty fulfils the duties of her new position, with the elegance, dignity, and *savoir faire* of an enchanted being, who accustomed to the distant perspective of the fairy-land which has been the one object of her dreams, suddenly attains it, and feels at home. Her single aim in life is now to preserve those charms which have caused her elevation.

In Sultan Abdul-Medjid's time, blue-eyed, delicate beauties with golden hair were the most admired by the Sultan; fair beauties consequently became extremely *recherchées*, and the grand ladies of the capital vied with each other in their assiduity in finding out and educating them, in order to present them to the seraglio. By degrees the taste for *Laypisca*, or goldenlocks, became so general in Turkish society as to make the fortune of many a Pera perruquier, who sold for a guinea the tiny bottle of fluid that changed the dusky hair into golden tresses, whilst the ladies paid the penalty of its abuse in the injury done to their eyes and the nervous maladies contracted by its use. Besides this, all the seraglio ladies indulge to a great extent in paint, rouge, and *rastuk* (antimony) for the eyes and eyebrows.

A French proverb says, "La femme est un animal qui s'habille, babille et se barbouille." If this can be applied to any particular class of womankind, it is surely to the inhabitants of the fairy-land I have attempted to describe.

The Validé Sultana, or mother of the Sultan, ranks first in the seraglio; one of the wings of the palace nearest to that occupied by her son is set apart for her use. She possesses state apartments, has an innumerable train of slaves, and every mark of attention is paid her not only by the Sultan, but also by all the high functionaries of the Porte, who at times have more to dread from her influence and interference than from the Sultan himself. The other members of the Imperial family rank next by courtesy, but these are all under the direct control of the Hasnadar Ousta, or superintendent, who, with her assistant, the second Hasnadar Ousta, attends to all the wants of each department, regulates their internal administration, and acts as go-between of the Sultan and his wives when they have any request to make to him or when he has orders to give respecting them; she also regulates the receptions and ceremonies as well as the expenses.

Some of her duties are of the most delicate, difficult, and responsible nature, and require a great amount of judgment and experience. The person appointed to this important post is generally the favourite slave of the Validé.

Very few of the seraglio inmates, except young princesses and other children that are brought up from their infancy in it, possess any knowledge of writing, or have had the advantage of regular training. All started in life from the same condition: chance alone settles the difference between the wife, odalisk, favourite, and Imperial mother, and draws a line between them and their luckless sisters left to the exercise of menial functions.

Education, much neglected as yet among Turkish women, has made very little progress in the seraglio, where it would prove an invaluable aid to those destined to hold the responsible positions of wives and mothers of Sultans. If the former, instead of being chosen as they are from a host of human beings chained to the service of a single individual with the sole object of amusing his leisure hours, attending to his wants, and giving him the progeny that is to succeed him on the throne, were selected, as in other countries, from among educated ladies, and their number fixed (or reduced to one) by the laws of religion and civilization, how different would seraglio life be! Dignity and esteem would replace humiliation; woman elevated to her true sphere would exercise her influence for high and noble objects, instead of the unworthy purposes which she effects through the only channel left open to her.

Under such a system it will not be surprising to hear of vice and corruption prevailing in a centre where virtue is crushed, and the benefits of sound education are neither acquired nor appreciated. The correctness of this statement, which may appear severe, can only be understood and appreciated by those who have come in contact with inmates of the seraglio, and are well acquainted with the language, manners, and customs of the Turks. Such persons would have no hesitation in admitting that exceptions are to be found in the seraglio, as well as in the rest of Turkish society. The class which is in the minority consists of those naturally gifted natures, to be met with in this country as elsewhere, who possess virtues that yield not to the influences of temptation and vice, and become ladies in the true sense of the word. The real Turkish Hanoum, or lady, is a dignified, quiet person, elegant, sensible, and often naturally eloquent, condescending and kind to those who gain her goodwill, proud and reserved to those who do not merit her esteem. Her conversational resources are certainly limited, but the sweetness and poetry of the language she uses, the pretty manner in which her expressions are worded, and the spirited repartee that she can command, have a charm that atones for her limited knowledge. Her manners, principles, and choice of language offer a pleasant contrast to those prevalent among the generality, and render her society extremely agreeable.

There is another class of serailis who present a not less interesting study. Sensitive and refined, fragile and dreamy in appearance, gifted, perhaps, with virtues they have no occasion to exercise, or with strong and passionate feelings that in a seraglio can never find vent in a solid and healthy affection, they become languid and spiritless, verging towards decline, to which they fall victims, unless released (as occasionally happens) by being set free and married.

Another class of serailis is the independent set, who are denominated Deli Serailis, or wild serailis, famous for their extravagant ideas, disorderly conduct, and unruly disposition; endowed with the bump of cunning and mischief, joined to a fair amount of energy and vivacity, they carry out, in spite of high walls and the watchful surveillance of more than a hundred eunuchs, all the wicked plans and mad freaks their disorderly minds and impulsive natures suggest to them; their language, manners, and actions, are such as no pen can describe. In the reign of Sultan Abdul-Medjid, the misconduct and extravagance of this set had reached its climax, and attracted the attention even of that indulgent sovereign, who was induced to order the expulsion of the most notorious. A few of them were exiled, others given in marriage, by Imperial order, to some dependant of the palace, who received an official appointment or was sent into the interior. These unfortunate men, burdened with their uncongenial helpmates, were but inadequately compensated by the rich gifts they received at the same time. During a long residence in the interior of Turkey, I became personally acquainted with a number of these ladies. One of them, a stout, coarse-looking woman, would not even deign to show that outward appearance of respect required from every Turkish woman towards her husband. She was the wife of a sub-governor, in whose house I passed a day and night; she was gay, and of a sociable disposition, but evidently not much attached to her husband, whom she designated as *Bezim Kambour* (my hen-pecked one), and to whom she addressed invectives of a very violent nature, accompanied, as I was subsequently informed, by corporal chastisement.

A second seraili, worthy of mention, was a thin Circassian brunette, married to a governor-general of high rank. She had a propensity, rather unusual amongst Turkish women, to an abuse of strong drinks, and she and her boon companions indulged in this excess to such a degree as to shock and scandalise the Mohammedan portion of the inhabitants wherever she went.

The other serailis of this class were so strange and extravagant in their manners, and their actions had made them so notorious, that details of their freaks would be as unedifying to the public as painful to me to describe.

Generally speaking, I frequented this class of serailis as little as the *convenances* of society permitted, but, on the other hand, experienced great pleasure in associating with the serailis that belonged to the respectable class, in whose society, conversing upon seraglio life, I have spent many a pleasant hour.

The amusements in the Imperial palace depend very much upon the tastes and disposition of the reigning sovereign, whose pleasure, in such matters, is naturally first consulted. In the days of Sultan Abdul-Medjid these amusements daily received some increase in the shape of European innovations. A theatre of great beauty was built in one of the palaces, by order of the Sultan, and a European company of actors played pieces, which the ladies were allowed to witness from behind lattices. Ballet-dancing, for which the Sultan evinced great partiality; conjurors of European celebrity; the Turkish Kara Guez or Marionettes; *al fresco* entertainments, etc., were among the entertainments. Shopping in the streets of Pera was not the least appreciated of their amusements. The French shop-keeper himself played as prominent a part in the matter as the perfumes and finery he displayed and sold. There were also delightful garden-parties, when the seraglio grounds would be lighted up with variegated lanterns and fireworks, and all that the Palace contained of youth and beauty turned out; some, dressed as young pages, would act the part of Lovelace, and make love to their equally fair companions, dressed in light fancy costumes; others, grouped together, would perform on musical instruments, or execute different dances; others, again, seated in light caïques, with costumes so transparent and airy as to show every muscle of the bodies, and with flowing hair to preserve their white necks from the evening dew, would race on the still waters of the lakes.

The Sultanas and hanoums, seated on carpets, beguiling the time by drinking sherbets, eating fruits and ices, and smoking cigarettes, would gaze on the scene, while strains of music and the notes of the Shaiki (songs) would be heard in all directions. All, however, both slaves and ladies, were similarly occupied with one sole object—that of rendering the scene pleasant and beauteous to the lord and master for whom it was designed. All would redouble their life and animation as the Sultan listlessly approached each group, acknowledging its presence with a sweet smile, a gentle word, or a passing caress, which he never withheld even when all the faculties of enjoyment were destroyed, and his earthly paradise of houris had become an object of indifference.

During the reign of his successor the tone of the seraglio became more serious and the life of its inmates more constrained; there was less European amusement and more Turkish; such as a Turkish theatre, whose actors and actresses, Turkish and Armenian, performed Turkish pieces, with a certain amount of success, such as the *Meydan Oyoun*, a coarse kind of comedy, and other representations of a similar character.

A child born in the seraglio is allowed to remain under the care of its mother, who, with the assistance of a wet-nurse and several under-nurses, has charge of its infantile wants up to the age of seven. The wet-nurse is generally sent for from Circassia. On entering upon her duties as foster-mother she is entitled to special attention, and exercises great influence over her charge. Her own child is received as *Sut Kardash*, or foster-brother, of the Imperial offspring, and enjoys the privilege of becoming his playmate and companion. The two children, as they grow up together, never lose sight of one another, the fortune of the one being assured in right of the privilege of having drawn its nourishment from the same source as the other.

I obtained these details from a Pasha of high rank, who had himself the honour of being foster-brother to one of the Sultans: he said,—"Before I saw the light, my mother was sent for from Circassia, and my birth, which took place in the seraglio, preceded that of his Imperial Majesty by a few weeks. As I grew up, the prosperity of my family, due to Imperial bounty, was not limited to my mother and myself, but extended to my father and the rest of my relatives, who were brought to Constantinople, and enriched with grants of wealth, rank, and position." The results, however, of these ties are not always so favourable to the Imperial prince as to those who owe their all to his generosity. These persons, being of humble origin, on finding themselves suddenly raised to a higher sphere, do not possess the necessary qualification for making a good and judicious use of the influence they thus acquire. The foster-mother of Sultan Abdul-Aziz was notorious for her rapacity and spirit of intrigue; she had, by degrees, acquired such ascendancy in the seraglio as to have it in her power to appoint or dismiss, at her will, governors-general and other important personages. One of her special protégés, on being informed that he was about to be transferred from his post as Governor-General of a vilayet of R——, smiled calmly, and said to me, "So long as the Sultan's foster-mother is there to protect my interests, I am in no danger of that! The attempt made to remove me will cost a little money, that is all!"

The training of the Imperial child is not free from

the many drawbacks that attend other Turkish children. From its earliest infancy, left in the hands of fond but weak and uneducated women, the child becomes wayward, capricious, and difficult to please.

This lenient treatment of the infant is continued in the more advanced stages of its life, and seriously retards its education. At this period Imperial princes and princesses command absolute attention, obedience, and respect from the legion of menials that surround them, who, anxious to lay the foundations of future favouritism, refuse nothing in their power, and pamper their vanity and precocious ideas to such an extent, as to destroy in great part the effects of the teaching they receive, often rendering profitless the instruction given them in morality and good principle.

The knowledge generally acquired by Turkish princes was formerly limited to the study of Arabic, and the Persian, Turkish, and French languages, with other branches of the general Turkish education, but the harem indolence, and the maternal and paternal indulgence, sadly interrupt the course of their lessons, which are gone through in a most negligent manner, and fail to have their due effect upon the young mind that pursues them with little assiduity.

The education of the young princesses is still more deficient, both in the substance of the teaching, and in the manner and time in which it is undertaken. An elementary knowledge of their native language, of music, and needlework, given at leisure and received at pleasure, is considered quite sufficient. These girls, on attaining the age of fifteen or sixteen, are richly portioned, receive the gift of a splendid trousseau, jewellery, and a palace, and are married to some court favourite. In consequence of their high birth, and the precedence they have over their husbands, these princesses are very independent, and absolute mistresses in their households.

Few of the married princesses in the reigns of the more recent Sultans enjoyed good reputations or acquired public esteem or even the affection of their husbands. Wayward and extravagant in their habits, tyrannical, and often cruel, their treatment of their little-to-be-envied spouses furnished cause for endless gossip to the society of Stamboul. The few princesses who formed exceptions to this rule are still remembered with affection by the numerous dependants of their establishments.

CHAPTER XI.

MUNICIPALITY, POLICE, AND BRIGANDAGE.

Municipality.—Improvement at Constantinople—No improvement in Country Towns—Sanitary Negligence.—*Police.*—The Corruption of the old Police—Formation of the new Corps—Its various Classes—Economical Reductions—The Corruption of the new Police—Voluntary Guards the connecting link between Police and Brigandage.—*Brigandage.*—Ancient and Modern Brigands—Great Diminution of Numbers—Constant Outrages however—Albanians the born Brigands—Systematic Attacks—Uselessness of the Police—My Brigand Guides—Usual Manner of Attack—Danger to *Kheradjis*—Brigands at Vodena repulsed by a Chorbadji and his Wife—Impotence of the Authorities—Outrage at Caterina—Modern Greek Klephts.

The sanitary and protective laws of Turkey are in their application still very primitive, although of late years they have been revised and reorganized, and a municipality and district police corps have been formed. The carrying out of these new laws was entrusted to a regular administration, having its chief seat at Constantinople, with branches in all the provincial towns, and it has done good service in the capital itself, for many of the improvements that have been made there are due to the efforts of the municipality.

In other towns, however, its good influence, though

well paid for by the inhabitants, has hitherto been little felt. The streets continue to be ill-paved and but dimly lighted with petroleum; sanitary measures are neglected; immense heaps of refuse are piled up on pieces of waste ground and stray spots, and are left to decompose by the action of the air, be devoured by unclean animals, or float away on some small stream of water. Enough, however, remains in the streets and in the vicinity of towns and villages to pollute the air and cause intermittent fever. Fortunately the climate is naturally salubrious, and the public health, taken on an average, is good. Some districts are considered very unhealthy, but the fault lies with the municipality of the place, who, when they become more intelligent and active, may perhaps attend less to their own interests and more to those of the public. Besides the above-mentioned innovations of the *Beledié* or municipality, small portions of pavement two or three feet in length are now and then constructed, professing to be the commencement of a magnificent pavement that is to traverse the town; but alas! after a few weeks the work is abandoned, and these short lengths of footpath are left isolated in the midst of pools of mud and water, which can only be crossed by using the boulders scattered here and there as stepping stones.

Sometimes a number of scavengers may be seen doing duty in the streets, or carting away the rubbish collected in the town, but they only convey it to the quay, where it is left for the ragged Jews and other beggars to explore.

The defects of the police were far more serious and more deeply felt throughout Turkey than those of the municipality. The police were insufficient as a protective force. They were badly organized, and they showed an utter want of principle, honesty, and morality. The deplorable condition of this corps, and the oppressive and illegal influence it exerted over the people, gave rise to great public indignation, and induced the people to complain loudly against it.

Ali and Fuad Pashas, well aware of the grievance, were the first to attempt a thorough police reform. By their united efforts a regular corps was formed, more numerous, better conditioned, better paid, clad in uniform, and classified as follows :—

(1.) The *Kavasses*, doing duty in the capital and attached to embassies and other foreign offices.

(2.) The *Seymen*, doing police duty at Constantinople.

(3.) The *Zaptichs*, foot police for the service of the district administration.

(4.) The *Soubaris*, mounted police, charged with the superintendence of public safety; with the office of receiving the taxes from the villages and transmitting them to the authorities; and with the duty of accompanying overland mails, travellers, etc.

(5.) The *Bekchis*, or rural police, placed at the Beklemés or guard-houses on all the main roads.

(6.) The *Teftish*, or detectives.

The uniform worn by the Kavasses consists of a black cloth coat and trousers, braided with gold, a belt, and a formidable-looking Turkish sword and pistol. That of the detectives is similar, but they carry no arms. The rest of the police wear a uniform similar to that of the Zouaves, of dark blue *shayak*, braided and turned up with red, a black leather belt and a cutlass. The Soubaris have long guns, and all wear the fez. The officers' uniform is similar to that of the officers in the army. The arms are supplied by the Government, and a new suit of clothes allowed every year.

When this body was first organised, some attention was paid to enrolling in it men of respectable character. The increase of pay and the regularity of the pay-days gave it for some time a better name than the old force; but unfortunately, hardly had the people begun to feel the benefit of the changes created during the reform fever, than these were set aside to make room for the economical mania that took possession of the administration on the formation of a new ministry. This latest epidemic, of the many that have attacked Turkey, was fatal to the provincial administration in general, and affected the police in particular. Their numbers were reduced, and pay diminished and irregularly distributed. The guard-houses on the highways, which had been established at the distance of four miles from each other, and entrusted to *Bekchis* who were held responsible for the security of their districts, were abandoned and fell into ruin, or were occupied by worthless fellows who undertook the duty for a small recompense, which proving difficult to obtain, these so-called "guards" were compelled to make up their financial deficits as best they could.

I heard of a fellow of this kind who had taken the post of Bekchi in a mountain pass, as a chiplak or tattered Albanian, but who, after a year had passed, was the owner of 700 goats and a fine house, and was dressed in all the glory of his national costume.

How did he obtain it? is a question not easily answered, if put to a great many of his class. I do not, myself, find the problem difficult of solution. These amateur guards would seem to be the connecting link between the police and the brigands; if, indeed, any such link were needed.

Conversing, some time ago, with some highly educated Bulgarians well versed in the affairs of their country, I was told that the chief causes of the discontent of their nation were the increase of the taxes, the harshness with which the payment was enforced upon them by the district officials, the extortion of the police, and the robberies and crimes committed by the Circassians. The people complained most bitterly of the insolent arrogance of the police, which they declared drove them to desperation, and made them ready to listen to any one who promised release, rather than continue to submit longer to such evils. There are, of course, some honest men in the police force who are ready to do their duty, but the generality are unquestionably immoral and unscrupulous, and, even if they were honest, their number is too small for the protection of the millions who depend upon them for their safety.

From time immemorial, brigandage has played so prominent a part in both the political and social condition of Turkey, that a description of life in this country would be incomplete without a few words about this lucrative profession.

I shall pass over the time, which may still be remembered by some of the oldest inhabitants, when brigands, mustering in overwhelming forces, composed of degenerate janissaries and malcontents from all the provinces of European Turkey, gathered under chieftains like Passvan Oglou and Ali Pasha of Joannina, defied the authority of the Porte, ravaged and devastated whole provinces, besieged towns, spread terror and bloodshed on every side, and left behind them nothing but misery and tears. The Greek Klephts were not more renowned for their bravery and patriotism than for the ravages and crimes they committed during and after the war of Greek independence.

Since that time great changes have taken place in Turkey, and brigandage lost its ancient power. The thousands that filled its ranks have, in our day, been reduced to tens. But the evil, though deprived of its force, and even entirely eradicated in some parts of the country, has not been wholly suppressed.

Of late years in Turkey, brigandage has ceased to clothe itself in the garb of politics; it is now represented merely by bands of cut-throats belonging to all creeds and nationalities. The chiefs, however, and the backbone of these bands, are Albanians. The number is made up by Greeks, Turks, and Bulgarians. The Mussulman Albanian takes to brigandage because he likes it and willingly makes a profession of it: the others join in order to evade justice, or to avoid want and misery, or simply to respond to the dictates of a vicious and criminal disposition. It is generally in early spring, when the trees have lost their nakedness and the hedges are covered with green leaves and sweet-smelling blossoms, that this element of infamy and destruction makes its appearance, taking to the highway or lurking for its prey among the hills and valleys, and polluting with its blood-stained feet the freshness and purity of resurgent nature. Its victims may often be found lying dead on a bed of violets or lilies, gazed upon by the wild rose that hangs its head and seems to blush for man's outrage. Such sights are of everyday occurrence.

The brigands have associates living in the towns with every appearance of respectability, who furnish them with timely notice when and where a good piece of business can be done. They have spies who give them warning when danger is at hand, and they often find protectors in high places to help them to escape the arm of the law. As for food, the flocks of the terror-stricken Christian shepherds are at their mercy, and the peasant, trembling for the safety of his home, dares not refuse to satisfy them with bread and wine. He dares not give notice to the authorities of the presence of these marauders, as that would expose him to their vengeance, and he would pay for his temerity with his life. But should the authorities suspect a countryman of having furnished provision or other necessaries to the brigands, he is forthwith prosecuted and cast into prison as their associate and a participator in their spoils. These are the causes that breed and rear brigandage in Turkey in defiance of laws and of the power of the authorities. The police regulations, theoretically excellent, are practically useless, and may be looked upon as one of the principal reasons of the continuance of brigandage, a scourge on the inhabitants and a disgrace to the administration.

When a band of brigands has taken up its quarters in a district, the country round is continually kept on the *qui vive* by its repeated crimes and depredations. A force of *Soubaris* (mounted police) is sent in chase, but the laxity with which their duty is generally discharged, the neglect of proper precautions to ensure success, and the usual futile termination of such expeditions, are often caused by unwillingness to risk a dangerous encounter, or by interested motives for letting off the brigands.

The inhabitants, on the other hand, suffer in any case by the pursuit, for, when it proves fruitless, it does not save them from danger, and only aggravates the enemy; and when the chase is successful, the expenses of having these armed men and their horses quartered upon them, besides the suspicions and injuries to which they are often exposed under the pretence of having direct or indirect communication with the brigands, are so great as to render the remedy almost worse than the evil, and induce them to petition the authorities to withdraw the Soubaris sent for their protection.

If these policemen are headed by an honest and courageous chief, as occasionally happens, and he sets to work earnestly to do his duty, success is almost certain, and the brigands are either captured, destroyed, or dispersed. Those who are caught are disarmed, handcuffed, and, if numerous and of a desperate character, chained in couples and marched off to prison. Still the hardy freebooters are not dispirited, for if they are wealthy, or the proofs of their crime are not transparently clear, their chances of escape, especially in the interior, are not small, and bribery affords them a ready means of regaining their liberty.

When brigands disperse or retire in winter from the field of action, they find shelter in a well-protected refuge. Such places are easily found in the country *chiftliks* of influential beys, who, from motives of self-preservation or ignorance of their guests' antecedents, allow their Albanian guards to harbour the malefactors who venture to seek shelter under their roof.

The severe laws formerly existing in Turkey for the punishment of crime, whereby mutilation was ordained in certain cases, are no longer in use. Crime, according to its extent and the circumstances that surround it, is punishable by imprisonment for a certain period, or condemnation to death; the sentence, however, is seldom put into execution except in very bad cases, or when the authorities are desirous of making an example of severity in the town. When a long and careful procedure has taken place before both the civil and religious courts, the Kadi decrees the sentence, which must be presented to the Sultan for his sanction before it can be carried out. The culprit is strung up to some shop front in the most frequented part of the bazar, or decapitated, and his head exposed, sometimes for three days, in the market place.

I have heard many stories of the outrages of brigands during my long residence in remote and semi-barbarous parts of the country. I have even been in close contact with some and on a friendly footing, and once escaped from their pursuit only thanks to the swiftness of a powerful horse. On two other occasions, yielding to necessity and in the interest of self-preservation, I accepted the services of two or three Albanians who were suspected of being cut-throats, instead of the Government escort.

They were fine, hardy fellows, with deep scars on their faces, that attested the lease upon which they held their life and the manner in which they had disputed it with others. They were reputed to be as venturesome in crime as they were ready to sacrifice their lives, if need were, for the preservation of those entrusted to their care. I penetrated into deep gorges with these men, and stopped in isolated and ill-reputed khans, and throughout the night slept as securely as if I had been in my own home. The worst of men, like the wildest of beasts, has his good side; the secret of finding this out lies in striking the right chord; put the Albanian on his honour, and he will never desert you or betray your trust.

The attacks made by brigands vary according to the locality, the nature of the enterprise, and the result desired. Should the attack be upon a caravan of peasants returning home from market or elsewhere, they are waylaid, stripped of all they possess, cruelly beaten, wounded, and sometimes killed. When the assault is directed against a person that has been singled out for them either for his wealth or other purposes, the assault made upon him and his escort is always of a murderous nature, terminating in the infliction of cruel wounds or death.

The long gun of the Albanian, or the yataghans of his equally dreaded companions, are ever suspended over the heads of the wealthy Chorbadjis: when the slightest opportunity is afforded they assault the villages, rob, murder, and carry off hostages in the persons of young men or boys—the sons of people who are sufficiently wealthy to redeem them by the payment of large ransoms.

Such attacks are of not unfrequent occurrence, especially in troubled times, when the ends of justice are rarely attained in the punishment of the criminals or the recovery of lost property.

Kheradjis, the brave and trustworthy fellows who

undertake to convey the goods of the merchants from town to town on the backs of their horses and mules, and the Tatar couriers, who are entrusted with the transport of sums of money, are great temptations to brigands. The last attack on a Kheradji I heard of took place last summer when he and his companion, an Albanian Mohammedan, had quitted one of the smaller towns in the Vilayet of Salonika, conveying a considerable sum of money concealed in the sacks of corn with which his animals were laden. While on the road, and a short distance from their destination, they were suddenly attacked by two brigands, who wounded the Christian Kheradji, and, after a struggle, succeeded in disarming the Mohammedan. They then searched the persons of the two men, and not finding the expected booty proceeded to cut open the sacks and abstract the money, after which they made off, leaving the unfortunate Kheradjis to find their way back to the town they had left, and to which both were strangers.

Next morning the Albanian presented himself before the Medjliss, or local court, to deposit his complaint; on looking round he started, and pointing to one of the members of the Bench exclaimed, " By Allah and Mohammed I swear that here is one of the two brigands that attacked us yesterday! If any one doubts my word let this man's house be searched, and a jacket with a torn sleeve will be found, to attest the truth of my accusation!" The culprit, in the midst of the general surprise and confusion, made his escape. Search was made in his house, and the jacket described by the Kheradji found, but the owner has not since been heard of.

Another robbery of a far more daring and serious nature was attempted by a gang of Albanians in the autumn of 1876 in the town of Vodena. The assailants, seven in number, had been frequently noticed lurking in the woods and gardens that lie in the beautiful plain by which this picturesque town is surrounded. The brigands had marked out the house of one of the wealthy Chorbadjis as the object of their attack. This man possessed a certain amount of education, and had taken the precaution of building a house sufficiently solid to protect himself and family and to secure his treasure. The building was not large but well protected, and surrounded by a large courtyard with high walls and a strong gate. The house door was very solid and furnished with triple bolts; and the windows, opening on a verandah, were well-barred. The robbers having planned their attack and posted a sentinel at the only open end of the street, proceeded to attack the gate. Finding it impossible to break it open, they undermined it, and entered the yard. The first barrier thus passed, and persuaded that an attempt on the house-door would prove fruitless, they placed a ladder which they found against the verandah, supposing that where the Chorbadji and his wife slumbered there would their treasure be. They set to work at the window of this chamber, attempting to demolish the iron bars.

The night was dark and stormy and the rain fell heavily, but the unconscious slumberers were not awakened for some time. At length the wife of the Chorbadji, startled by the unaccustomed noise at the window, aroused her husband and acquainted him with what was going on. His coolness and courage were quite equal to the occasion, and after a short consultation with his wife, he decided upon using the firearms that hung against the wall. It was a terrible moment for both. Standing a little on one side, and protected by the darkness of the room, they could see several men trying to force the bars. To face these men openly was certain death, and it was hard to get a good aim at them. He decided finally to attempt a shot, first calling out in a determined voice, "Who goes there? Let him leave the spot, or he is a dead man!"

This appeal, however, instead of having the desired effect stimulated the energy of the brigands, who, forming into two bands, now attacked the door of the house as well, and were making strenuous efforts to open it. The Chorbadji, cautiously advancing towards the side of the window and screened by the projecting walls, fired his pistol and shot one of the

Albanians dead who stood on the ladder; another mounted, and a second shot stretched him wounded on the floor of the verandah. The rest, whose shots into the room proved ineffective, abandoned the window and went to the door, at which they continued pounding with the fury of fiends, but as yet to no effect.

In the meantime the brave couple, freed from the immediate vicinity of their enemies, struck a light, and while the husband was pouring his fire upon them the wife loaded his pistols. A girl who slept in the next room opened her window and called loudly for help, but was nearly paying for her rashness with her life, as one of the brigands in the yard fired at her, and the ball struck the iron bar against which her head was pressed, but glanced off.

The Albanians, after some further efforts, began to fear the consequences of the alarm the affray was beginning to excite in the neighbourhood, and bethought themselves of making good their retreat. But previously to doing so they cut off the head of their dead comrade to avoid detection, and carried it away with them, together with their wounded. A few weeks subsequently, the assault was renewed, but the owner was well prepared to receive and repel it, without, however, being able to obtain definite peace and security for his home.

The Albanians, doubly incensed against him for the

loss of their comrade and their disappointment at not having been able to effect their purpose, sent threatening messages to the Chorbadji, and claimed 160*l.* for the widow and children of the slain brigand, or in lieu thereof himself to pay the debt with his life. The poor man, being hard pressed, appealed to the Kaimakam, or sub-governor of the town, for protection; but this dignitary, being an Albanian, old and void of energy, and incapable of bringing the culprits to justice, offered his services as peace-maker between the two parties, and proposed a compromise for half that sum. The Chorbadji refused to pay anything, and the Albanians renewed their threats. The persecuted man in the meantime had to remain indoors on the pretext of ill-health, and only expects to be able to regain his liberty when affairs settle and better times come.

Among the many sad cases of children and youths being carried off from the villages, which have become so prevalent during these disordered times, I may relate one which happened last year, in the district of Caterina, at the foot of Mount Olympus. The victim was a fine promising young Greek of two and twenty, an only son, doated upon by a grief-stricken mother, whose husband had been killed by brigands. This youth was suddenly attacked as he was returning home, carried off, and never more heard of. The unfortunate mother, distracted with grief, and prompted by mingled hope and despair, wandered up to the mountains, and for days was seen by the shepherds roaming about and calling for her son. It was thought that he had been put to death in consequence of his father having killed one of the brigands that had attacked him.

I have not included the Circassians as members of this general fraternity of brigands, because they form a distinct set, who, ever since their arrival in this country, have been notorious for theft and crime and outrage.

Although political brigandage has ceased to exercise its former influence in the country, it has in a small degree again made its appearance as an inseparable incident of war and internal trouble. A few bands, mustering from thirty to fifty men, have lately made their appearance in different parts of European Turkey. They are composed of Greek desperadoes, supposed to be the agents of an Ἐταιρεία or secret society of violent Greek patriots holding extreme views. Their object in maintaining these *Klephts* in different localities is that of having them in readiness in case of an insurrection among the discontented peasantry. One or two of these bands have been stationed since last spring in the district of Caterina. They have not been known to molest any one; but their presence somewhat kept in check the Albanian brigands and prevented them devastating the Greek villages. The

Klephts obtained their provisions from the peasants, for which they regularly and scrupulously paid. The *Eteria* that supports these individuals is disapproved of by the Greek authorities, who consider it an element of disorder and trouble.

END OF VOL. I.

BRADBURY, AGNEW & CO., PRINTERS, WHITEFRIARS.

50, Albemarle Street, London,
May, 1878.

MR. MURRAY'S
GENERAL LIST OF WORKS.

ABINGER'S (LORD Chief Baron) Life. By the Hon. P. CAMPBELL SCARLETT. Portrait. 8vo. 15s.

ALBERT MEMORIAL. A Descriptive and Illustrated Account of the National Monument erected to the PRINCE CONSORT at Kensington. Illustrated by Engravings of its Architecture, Decorations, Sculptured Groups, Statues, Mosaics, Metalwork, &c. With Descriptive Text. By DOYNE C. BELL. With 24 Plates. Folio. 12*l*. 12s.

—————— HANDBOOK TO. Post 8vo. 1s.; or Illustrated Edition, 2s. 6d.

—————— (PRINCE) SPEECHES AND ADDRESSES, with an Introduction, giving some outline of his Character. With Portrait. 8vo. 6d.; or *Popular Edition*, fcap. 8vo. 1s.

ALBERT DÜRER; his Life, with a History of his Art. By DR. THAUSING, Keeper of Archduke Albert's Art Collection at Vienna. Translated from the German. With Portrait and Illustrations. 2 vols. 8vo. [*In the Press*.

ABBOTT (REV. J.). Memoirs of a Church of England Missionary in the North American Colonies. Post 8vo. 2s.

ABERCROMBIE (JOHN). Enquiries concerning the Intellectual Powers and the Investigation of Truth. Fcap. 8vo. 3s. 6d.

—————————— Philosophy of the Moral Feelings. Fcap. 8vo. 2s. 6d.

ACLAND (REV. CHARLES). Popular Account of the Manners and Customs of India. Post 8vo. 2s.

ÆSOP'S FABLES. A New Version. With Historical Preface. By Rev. THOMAS JAMES. With 100 Woodcuts, by TENNIEL and WOLF. Post 8vo. 2s. 6d.

AGRICULTURAL (ROYAL) JOURNAL. (*Published half-yearly*.)

AIDS TO FAITH: a Series of Essays on Miracles; Evidences of Christianity; Prophecy & Mosaic Record of Creation; Ideology and Subscription; The Pentateuch; Inspiration; Death of Christ; Scripture and its Interpretation. By various Authors. 8vo. 9s.

AMBER-WITCH (THE). A most interesting Trial for Witchcraft. Translated by LADY DUFF GORDON. Post 8vo. 2s.

ARMY LIST (THE). *Published Monthly by Authority*.

ARTHUR'S (LITTLE) History of England. By LADY CALLCOTT. *New Edition, continued to* 1872. With 36 Woodcuts. Fcap. 8vo. 1s. 6d.

ATKINSON (DR. R.) Vie de Seint Auban. A Poem in Norman-French. Ascribed to MATTHEW PARIS. With Concordance, Glossary and Notes. Small 4to, 10s. 6d.

AUSTIN (JOHN). LECTURES ON GENERAL JURISPRUDENCE; or, the Philosophy of Positive Law. Edited by ROBERT CAMPBELL. 2 Vols. 8vo. 32s.

—————— STUDENT'S EDITION, compiled from the above work, by ROBERT CAMPBELL. Post 8vo. 12s.

—————— Analysis of. By GORDON CAMPBELL. Post 8vo. 6s.

ADMIRALTY PUBLICATIONS; Issued by direction of the Lords Commissioners of the Admiralty:—

A MANUAL OF SCIENTIFIC ENQUIRY, for the Use of Travellers. Fourth Edition. Edited by ROBERT MAIN, M.A. Woodcuts. Post 8vo. 3s. 6d.

GREENWICH ASTRONOMICAL OBSERVATIONS, 1841 to 1847, and 1847 to 1871. Royal 4to. 20s. each.

REENWICH OBSERVATIONS. 1848 to 1855. 20s. each.

MAGNETICAL AND METEOROLOGICAL OBSERVATIONS, 1841 to 1847. Royal 4to. 20s. each.

APPENDICES TO OBSERVATIONS.
- 1837. Logarithms of Sines and Cosines in Time. 3s.
- 1842. Catalogue of 1439 Stars, from Observations made in 1836 to 1841. 4s.
- 1845. Longitude of Valentia (Chronometrical). 3s.
- 1847. Description of Altazimuth. 3s.
  - Twelve Years' Catalogue of Stars, from Observations made in 1836 to 1847. 4s.
  - Description of Photographic Apparatus. 2s.
- 1851. Maskelyne's Ledger of Stars. 3s.
- 1852. 1. Description of the Transit Circle. 3s.
- 1853. Refraction Tables. 3s.
- 1854. Description of the Zenith Tube. 3s.
  - Six Years' Catalogue of Stars, from Observations. 1848 to 1853. 4s.
  - Plan of Ground Buildings. 3s.
  - Longitude of Valentia (Galvanic). 2s.
- 1864. Moon's Semid. from Occultations. 2s.
  - Planetary Observations, 1831 to 1835. 2s.
- 1868. Corrections of Elements of Jupiter and Saturn. 2s.
  - Second Seven Years' Catalogue of 2760 Stars for 1861 to 1867. 4s.
  - Description of the Great Equatorial. 3s.
- 1856. Descriptive Chronograph. 3s.
- 1860. Reduction of Deep Thermometer Observations. 2s.
- 1871. History and Description of Water Telescope. 3s.
- 1873. Regulations of the Royal Observatory. 2s.

Cape of Good Hope Observations (Star Ledgers): 1856 to 1863. 2s.
—————— 1856. 5s.
—————— Astronomical Results. 1857 to 1858. 5s.
Cape Catalogue of 1159 Stars, reduced to the Epoch 1860. 3s.
Cape of Good Hope Astronomical Results. 1859 to 1860. 5s.
—————— 1871 to 1873. 5s.
—————— 1874. 5s.

Report on Teneriffe Astronomical Experiment. 1856. 5s.
Paramatta Catalogue of 7385 Stars. 1822 to 1826. 4s.

ASTRONOMICAL RESULTS. 1847 to 1875. 4to. 3s. each.
MAGNETICAL AND METEOROLOGICAL RESULTS. 1848 to 1875. 4to. 3s. each.
REDUCTION OF THE OBSERVATIONS OF PLANETS. 1750 to 1830. Royal 4to. 20s. each.
—————— LUNAR OBSERVATIONS. 1750 to 1830. 2 Vols. Royal 4to. 20s. each.
—————— 1831 to 1851. 4to. 10s. each.
BERNOULLI'S SEXCENTENARY TABLE. 1779. 4to. 5s.
BESSEL'S AUXILIARY TABLES FOR HIS METHOD OF CLEARING LUNAR DISTANCES. 8vo. 2s.
ENCKE'S BERLINER JAHRBUCH, for 830. Berlin, 1828. 8vo. 9s.
HANSEN'S TABLES DE LA LUNE. 4to. 20s.
LAX'S TABLES FOR FINDING THE LATITUDE AND LONGITUDE. 1821. 8vo. 10s.
LUNAR OBSERVATIONS at GREENWICH. 1783 to 1819. Compared with the Tables, 1821. 4to. 7s. 6d.
MACLEAR ON LACAILLE'S ARC OF MERIDIAN. 2 Vols. 20s. each.

ADMIRALTY PUBLICATIONS—*continued*.
MAYER'S DISTANCES of the MOON'S CENTRE from the PLANETS. 1822, 3s.; 1823, 4s. 6d. 1824 to 1835. 8vo. 4s. each.
—————— TABULÆ MOTUUM SOLIS ET LUNÆ. 1770. 5s.
—————— ASTRONOMICAL OBSERVATIONS MADE AT GOTTINGEN, from 1756 to 1761. 1826. Folio. 7s. 6d.
NAUTICAL ALMANACS, from 1767 to 1877, 80s. 2s. 6d. each.
—————— SELECTIONS FROM, up to 1812. 8vo. 5s. 1834-54. 5s.
—————— SUPPLEMENTS, 1828 to 1833, 1837 and 1838. 2s. each.
—————— TABLE requisite to be used with the N.A. 1781. 8vo. 5s.
SABINE'S PENDULUM EXPERIMENTS to DETERMINE THE FIGURE OF THE EARTH. 1825. 4to. 40s.
SHEPHERD'S TABLES for CORRECTING LUNAR DISTANCES. 1772. Royal 4to. 21s.
—————— TABLES, GENERAL, of the MOON'S DISTANCE from the SUN, and 10 STARS. 1787. Folio. 5s. 6d.
TAYLOR'S SEXAGESIMAL TABLE. 1780. 4to. 15s.
—————— TABLES OF LOGARITHMS. 4to. 60s.
TIARK'S ASTRONOMICAL OBSERVATIONS for the LONGITUDE of MADEIRA. 1822. 4to. 5s.
—————— CHRONOMETRICAL OBSERVATIONS for DIFFERENCES of LONGITUDE between DOVER, PORTSMOUTH, and FALMOUTH. 823. 4to. 5s.
VENUS and JUPITER: OBSERVATIONS of, compared with the TABLES. London, 1822. 4to. 2s.
WALES AND BAYLY'S ASTRONOMICAL OBSERVATIONS. 1777. 4to. 21s.
—————— REDUCTION OF ASTRONOMICAL OBSERVATIONS MADE IN THE SOUTHERN HEMISPHERE. 1764—1771. 1788. 4to. 10s. 6d.

BARBAULD (Mrs.). Hymns in Prose for Children. With Illustrations. Crown 8vo.

BARCLAY (JOSEPH, LL.D.). Selected Extracts from the Talmud, chiefly illustrating the Teaching of the Bible. With an Introduction. Illustrations. 8vo. 14s.

BARKLEY (H. C.). Five Years among the Bulgarians and Turks between the Danube and the Black Sea. Post 8vo. 10s. 6d.

—————— Bulgaria Before the War; during a Seven Years' Experience of European Turkey and its Inhabitants. Post 8vo. 10s. 6d.

—————— My Boyhood : a True Story. A Book for Schoolboys and others. With Illustrations. Post 8vo. 6s.

BARROW (SIR JOHN). Autobiographical Memoir, from Early Life to Advanced Age. Portrait. 8vo. 16s.

—————— (JOHN) Life, Exploits, and Voyages of Sir Francis Drake. Post 8vo. 2s.

BARRY (SIR CHARLES). Life and Works. By CANON BARRY. With Portrait and Illustrations. Medium 8vo. 15s.

BATES (H. W.) Records of a Naturalist on the River Amazons during eleven years of Adventure and Travel. Illustrations. Post 8vo. 7s. 6d.

BAX (CAPT. R.N.). Russian Tartary, Eastern Siberia, China, Japan, and Formosa. A Narrative of a Cruise in the Eastern Seas. With Map and Illustrations. Crown 8vo. 12s.

BELCHER (LADY). Account of the Mutineers of the 'Bounty,' and their Descendants: with their settlements in Pitcairn and Norfolk Islands. With Illustrations. Post 8vo. 12s.

BELL (SIR CHAS.). Familiar Letters. Portrait. Post 8vo. 12s.

B 2

BELL (DOYNE C.). Notices of the Historic Persons buried in the Chapel of St. Peter ad Vincula, in the Tower of London, with an account of the discovery of the supposed remains of Queen Anne Boleyn. With Illustrations. Crown 8vo. 14s.

BELT (THOS.). The Naturalist in Nicaragua, including a Residence at the Gold Mines of Chontales; with Journeys in the Savannahs and Forests; and Observations on Animals and Plants. Illustrations. Post 8vo. 12s.

BERTRAM (JAS. G.). Harvest of the Sea: an Account of British Food Fishes, including sketches of Fisheries and Fisher Folk. With 50 Illustrations. 8vo. 9s.

BIBLE COMMENTARY. THE OLD TESTAMENT. EXPLANATORY and CRITICAL. With a REVISION of the TRANSLATION. By BISHOPS and CLERGY of the ANGLICAN CHURCH. Edited by F. C. COOK, M.A., Canon of Exeter. 6 VOLS. Medium 8vo. 6l. 15s.

Vol. I. 30s. { GENESIS, EXODUS, LEVITICUS, NUMBERS, DEUTERONOMY.

Vols. II. and III. 36s. { JOSHUA, JUDGES, RUTH, SAMUEL, KINGS, CHRONICLES, EZRA, NEHEMIAH, ESTHER.

Vol. IV. 24s. { JOB, PSALMS, PROVERBS, ECCLESIASTES, SONG OF SOLOMON.

Vol. V. 20s. { ISAIAH, JEREMIAH.

Vol. VI. 25s. { EZEKIEL, DANIEL, MINOR PROPHETS.

THE NEW TESTAMENT. 4 VOLS. Medium 8vo.

Vol. I. 18s. { INTRODUCTION, ST. MATTHEW, ST. MARK, ST. LUKE.

Vol. II. { ST. JOHN, ACTS.

Vol. III. { ROMANS, CORINTHIANS, GALATIANS, PHILIPPIANS, EPHESIANS, COLOSSIANS, THESSALONIANS, PHILEMON, PASTORAL EPISTLES, HEBREWS.

Vol. IV. { ST. JAMES, ST. JOHN, ST. PETER, ST. JUDE, REVELATION.

BIGG-WITHER (T. P.). Pioneering in South Brazil; three years of forest and prairie life in the province of Parana. Map and Illustrations. 2 vols. Crown 8vo. 24s.

BIRCH (SAMUEL). A History of Ancient Pottery and Porcelain: Egyptian, Assyrian, Greek, Roman, and Etruscan. With Coloured Plates and 200 Illustrations. Medium 8vo. 42s.

BIRD (ISABELLA). The Hawaiian Archipelago; or Six Months among the Palm Groves, Coral Reefs, and Volcanoes of the Sandwich Islands. With Illustrations. Crown 8vo. 7s. 6d.

BISSET (GENERAL SIR JOHN). Sport and War in South Africa from 1834 to 1867, with a Narrative of the Duke of Edinburgh's Visit. With Map and Illustrations. Crown 8vo. 14s.

BLACKSTONE'S COMMENTARIES: adapted to the Present State of the Law. By R. MALCOLM KERR, LL.D. *Revised Edition*, incorporating all the Recent Changes in the Law. 4 vols. 8vo. 60s.

BLUNT (REV. J. J.). Undesigned Coincidences in the Writings of the Old and New Testaments, an Argument of their Veracity: containing the Books of Moses, Historical and Prophetical Scriptures, and the Gospels and Acts. Post 8vo. 6s.

—— History of the Church in the First Three Centuries. Post 8vo. 6s.

—— Parish Priest; His Duties, Acquirements and Obligations. Post 8vo. 6s.

—— University Sermons. Post 8vo. 6s.

—— Plain Sermons. 2 vols. Post 8vo. 12s.

BOSWELL'S Life of Samuel Johnson, LL.D. Including the Tour to the Hebrides. Edited by Mr. CROKER. *Seventh Edition.* Portraits. 1 vol. Medium 8vo. 12s.

BRACE (C. L.). Manual of Ethnology; or the Races of the Old World. Post 8vo. 6s.

BOOK OF COMMON PRAYER. Illustrated with Coloured Borders, Initial Letters, and Woodcuts. 8vo. 18s.

BORROW (GEORGE). Bible in Spain; or the Journeys, Adventures, and Imprisonments of an Englishman in an Attempt to circulate the Scriptures in the Peninsula. Post 8vo. 5s.

———— Gypsies of Spain; their Manners, Customs, Religion, and Language. With Portrait. Post 8vo. 5s.

———— Lavengro; The Scholar—The Gypsy—and the Priest. Post 8vo. 5s.

———— Romany Rye—a Sequel to "Lavengro." Post 8vo. 5s.

———— WILD WALES: its People, Language, and Scenery. Post 8vo. 5s.

———— Romano Lavo-Lil; Word-Book of the Romany, or English Gypsy Language; with Specimens of their Poetry, and an account of certain Gypsyries. Post 8vo. 10s. 6d.

BRAY (MRS.). Life of Thomas Stothard, R.A. With Portrait and 60 Woodcuts. 4to. 21s.

BRITISH ASSOCIATION REPORTS. 8vo.

York and Oxford, 1831-32, 13s. 6d.	Glasgow, 1855, 15s.
Cambridge, 1833, 12s.	Cheltenham, 1856, 18s.
Edinburgh, 1834, 15s.	Dublin, 1857, 15s.
Dublin, 1835, 13s. 6d.	Leeds, 1858, 20s.
Bristol, 1836, 12s.	Aberdeen, 1859, 15s.
Liverpool, 1837, 16s. 6d.	Oxford, 1860, 25s.
Newcastle, 1838, 15s.	Manchester, 1861, 15s.
Birmingham, 1839, 13s. 6d.	Cambridge, 1862, 20s.
Glasgow, 1840, 15s.	Newcastle, 1863, 25s.
Plymouth, 1841, 13s. 6d.	Bath, 1864, 18s.
Manchester, 1842, 10s. 6d.	Birmingham, 1865, 25s
Cork, 1843, 12s.	Nottingham, 1866, 24s.
York, 1844, 20s.	Dundee, 1867, 26s.
Cambridge, 1845, 12s.	Norwich, 1868, 25s.
Southampton, 1846, 15s.	Exeter, 1869, 22s.
Oxford, 1847, 18s.	Liverpool, 1870, 18s.
Swansea, 1848, 9s.	Edinburgh, 1871, 16s.
Birmingham, 1849, 10s.	Brighton, 1872, 24s.
Edinburgh, 1850, 15s.	Bradford, 1873, 25s.
Ipswich, 1851, 16s. 6d.	Belfast, 1874. 25s.
Belfast, 1852, 15s.	Bristol, 1875, 25s.
Hull, 1853, 10s. 6d.	Glasgow, 1876, 25s.
Liverpool, 1854, 18s.	

BROUGHTON (LORD). A Journey through Albania, Turkey in Europe and Asia, to Constantinople. Illustrations. 2 Vols. 8vo. 30s.

—— —— Visits to Italy. 2 Vols. Post 8vo. 18s.

BRUGSCH (PROFESSOR). A History of Egypt, from the earliest period. Derived from Monuments and Inscriptions. *New Edition.* Translated by the late H. DANBY SEYMOUR. 2 vols. 8vo. [*Nearly Ready.*

BUCKLEY (ARABELLA B.). A Short History of Natural Science, and the Progress of Discovery from the time of the Greeks to the present day, for Schools and young Persons. Illustrations. Post 8vo. 9s.

BURGON (Rev. J. W.). Christian Gentleman; or, Memoir of Patrick Fraser Tytler. Post 8vo. 9s.

BURN (Col.). Dictionary of Naval and Military Technical Terms, English and French—French and English. Crown 8vo. 15s.

BUXTON (Charles). Memoirs of Sir Thomas Fowell Buxton, Bart. With Selections from his Correspondence. Portrait. 8vo. 16s. *Popular Edition.* Fcap. 8vo. 5s.

—— Ideas of the Day. 8vo. 6s.

BURCKHARDT'S (Dr. Jacob) Cicerone; or Art Guide to Painting in Italy. Translated from the German by Mrs. A. Clough. Post 8vo. 6s.

BYLES (Sir John). Foundations of Religion in the Mind and Heart of Man. Post 8vo. 6s.

BYRON'S (Lord) LIFE AND WORKS:—

   Life, Letters, and Journals. By Thomas Moore. *Cabinet Edition.* Plates. 6 Vols. Fcap. 8vo. 18s.; or One Volume, Portraits. Royal 8vo., 7s. 6d.

   Life and Poetical Works. *Popular Edition.* Portraits. 2 vols. Royal 8vo. 15s.

   Poetical Works. *Library Edition.* Portrait. 6 Vols. 8vo. 45s.

   Poetical Works. *Cabinet Edition.* Plates. 10 Vols. 12mo. 30s.

   Poetical Works. *Pocket Ed.* 8 Vols. 16mo. In a case. 21s.

   Poetical Works. *Popular Edition.* Plates. Royal 8vo. 7s. 6d.

   Poetical Works. *Pearl Edition.* Crown 8vo. 2s. 6d.

   Childe Harold. With 80 Engravings. Crown 8vo. 12s.

   Childe Harold. 16mo. 2s. 6d.

   Childe Harold. Vignettes. 16mo. 1s.

   Childe Harold. Portrait. 16mo. 6d.

   Tales and Poems. 16mo. 2s. 6d.

   Miscellaneous. 2 Vols. 16mo. 5s.

   Dramas and Plays. 2 Vols. 16mo. 5s.

   Don Juan and Beppo. 2 Vols. 16mo. 5s.

   Beauties. Poetry and Prose. Portrait. Fcap. 8vo. 3s. 6d.

BUTTMANN'S Lexilogus; a Critical Examination of the Meaning of numerous Greek Words, chiefly in Homer and Hesiod. By Rev. J. R. Fishlake. 8vo. 12s.

———— Irregular Greek Verbs. With all the Tenses extant—their Formation, Meaning, and Usage, with Notes, by Rev. J. R. Fishlake. Post 8vo. 6s.

CALLCOTT (Lady). Little Arthur's History of England. *New Edition, brought down to 1872.* With Woodcuts. Fcap. 8vo. 1s. 6d.

CARNARVON (Lord). Portugal, Gallicia, and the Basque Provinces. Post 8vo. 3s. 6d.

CARTWRIGHT (W. C.). The Jesuits: their Constitution and Teaching. An Historical Sketch. 8vo. 9s.

CAMPBELL (LORD). Lord Chancellors and Keepers of the Great Seal of England. From the Earliest Times to the Death of Lord Eldon in 1838. 10 Vols. Crown 8vo. 6s. each.

—— Chief Justices of England. From the Norman Conquest to the Death of Lord Tenterden. 4 Vols. Crown 8vo. 6s. each.

—— Lives of Lyndhurst and Brougham. 8vo. 16s.

—— Lord Bacon. Fcap. 8vo. 2s. 6d.

—— (SIR GEORGE) Handy-Book on the Eastern Question; being a Very Recent View of Turkey. With Map. Post 8vo. 6s.

—— (THOS.) Essay on English Poetry. With Short Lives of the British Poets. Post 8vo. 3s. 6d.

CAVALCASELLE AND CROWE'S History of Painting in NORTH ITALY, from the 14th to the 16th Century. With Illustrations. 2 Vols. 8vo. 42s.

—— Early Flemish Painters, their Lives and Works. Illustrations. Post 8vo. 10s. 6d.; or Large Paper, 8vo. 15s.

—— Life and Times of Titian, with some Account of his Family. With Portrait and Illustrations. 2 vols. 8vo. 42s.

CESNOLA (GEN. L. P. DI). Cyprus; its Ancient Cities, Tombs, and Temples. A Narrative of Researches and Excavations during Ten Years' Residence in that Island. With Map and 400 Illustrations. Medium 8vo. 50s.

CHILD (CHAPLIN). Benedicite; or, Song of the Three Children; being Illustrations of the Power, Beneficence, and Design manifested by the Creator in his works. Post 8vo. 6s.

CHISHOLM (Mrs.). Perils of the Polar Seas; True Stories of Arctic Discovery and Adventure. Illustrations. Post 8vo. 6s.

CHURTON (ARCHDEACON). Poetical Remains, Translations and Imitations. Portrait. Post 8vo. 7s. 6d.

—— New Testament. Edited with a Plain Practical Commentary for Families and General Readers. With 100 Panoramic and other Views, from Sketches made on the Spot. 2 vols. 8vo. 21s.

CLASSIC PREACHERS OF THE ENGLISH CHURCH. St. James's Lectures, 1877. By Canon Lightfoot, Prof. Wace, Dean of Durham, Rev. W. R. Clark, Canon Farrar, and Dean of Norwich. With an Introduction by J. E. Kempe, M.A., Rector. Post 8vo. 7s. 6d.

CLIVE'S (LORD) Life. By REV. G. R. GLEIG. Post 8vo. 3s. 6d.

CLODE (C. M.). Military Forces of the Crown; their Administration and Government. 2 Vols. 8vo. 21s. each.

—— Administration of Justice under Military and Martial Law, as applicable to the Army, Navy, Marine, and Auxiliary Forces. 8vo. 12s.

COLERIDGE'S (SAMUEL TAYLOR) Table-Talk. Portrait. 12mo. 3s. 6d.

COLONIAL LIBRARY. [See Home and Colonial Library.]

COMPANIONS FOR THE DEVOUT LIFE. St. James' Lectures, 1875—6.

DE IMITATIONE CHRISTI. Canon Farrar.
PENSÉES OF BLAISE PASCAL. Dean Church.
S. FRANÇOIS DE SALES. Dean Goulburn.
BAXTER'S SAINTS' REST. Archbishop of Dublin.
S. AUGUSTINE'S CONFESSIONS. Bishop of Derry.
JEREMY TAYLOR'S HOLY LIVING AND DYING. Rev. Dr. Humphry.

THEOLOGIA GERMANICA. Can Ashwell.
FÉNELON's ŒUVRES SPIRITUELLES. Rev. T. T. Carter.
ANDREWES' DEVOTIONS. Bishop of Ely.
CHRISTIA YEAR. Canon Barry.
PARADISE LOST. Rev. E. H. Bickersteth.
PILGRIM'S PROGRESS. Dean Howson.
PRAYER BOOK. Dean Burgon.

With Preface by J. E. KEMPE, Rector. Crown 8vo. 6s.

COOK (Canon). Sermons Preached at Lincoln's Inn. 8vo. 9s.

COOKE (E. W.). Leaves from my Sketch-Book. Being a selection from sketches made during many tours. With Descriptive Text. 50 Plates. 2 vols. Small folio. 31s. 6d. each.

COOKERY (MODERN DOMESTIC). Founded on Principles of Economy and Practical Knowledge. By a Lady. Woodcuts. Fcap. 8vo. 5s.

COOPER (T. T.). Travels of a Pioneer of Commerce on an Overland Journey from China towards India. Illustrations. 8vo. 16s.

CRABBE (REV. GEORGE). Life and Poetical Works. With Illustrations. Royal 8vo. 7s.

CRAWFORD & BALCARRES (Earl of). Etruscan Inscriptions. Analyzed, Translated, and Commented upon. 8vo. 12s.

CRIPPS (WILFRED). Old English Plate : Ecclesiastical, Decorative, and Domestic, its makers and marks. Illustrations. Medium 8vo. 21s.

CROKER (J. W.). Progressive Geography for Children. 18mo. 1s. 6d.

—————— Stories for Children, Selected from the History of England. Woodcuts. 16mo. 2s. 6d.

—————— Boswell's Life of Johnson. Including the Tour to the Hebrides. *Seventh Edition.* Portraits. 8vo. 12s.

—————— Early Period of the French Revolution. 8vo. 15s.

—————— Historical Essay on the Guillotine. Fcap. 8vo. 1s.

CROWE AND CAVALCASELLE. Lives of the Early Flemish Painters. Woodcuts. Post 8vo, 10s. 6d.; or Large Paper, 8vo, 15s.

—————— History of Painting in North Italy, from 14th to 16th Century. Derived from Researches in that Country. With Illustrations. 2 Vols. 8vo. 42s.

—————— Life and Times of Titian, with some Account of his Family, chiefly from new and unpublished records. With Portrait and Illustrations. 2 vols. 8vo. 42s.

CUMMING (R. GORDON). Five Years of a Hunter's Life in the Far Interior of South Africa. Woodcuts. Post 8vo. 6s.

CUNYNGHAME (SIR ARTHUR). Travels in the Eastern Caucasus, on the Caspian and Black Seas, in Daghestan and the Frontiers of Persia and Turkey. With Map and Illustrations. 8vo. 18s.

CURTIUS' (PROFESSOR) Student's Greek Grammar, for the Upper Forms. Edited by DR. WM. SMITH. Post 8vo. 6s.

—————— Elucidations of the above Grammar. Translated by EVELYN ABBOT. Post 8vo. 7s. 6d.

—————— Smaller Greek Grammar for the Middle and Lower Forms. Abridged from the larger work. 12mo. 3s. 6d.

—————— Accidence of the Greek Language. Extracted from the above work. 12mo. 2s. 6d.

—————— Principles of Greek Etymology. Translated by A. S. WILKINS, M.A., and E. B. ENGLAND, B.A. 2 vols. 8vo. 15s. each.

CURZON (HON. ROBERT). Visits to the Monasteries of the Levant. Illustrations. Post 8vo. 7s. 6d.

CUST (GENERAL). Warriors of the 17th Century—The Thirty Years' War. 2 Vols. 16s. Civil Wars of France and England. 2 Vols. 16s. Commanders of Fleets and Armies. 2 Vols. 18s.

—————— Annals of the Wars—18th & 19th Century, 1700—1815. With Maps. 9 Vols. Post 8vo. 5s. each.

DAVY (Sir Humphry). Consolations in Travel; or, Last Days of a Philosopher. Woodcuts. Fcap. 8vo. 3s. 6d.

——— Salmonia; or, Days of Fly Fishing. Woodcuts. Fcap. 8vo. 3s. 6d.

DARWIN (Charles) WORKS:—

   Journal of a Naturalist during a Voyage round the World. Crown 8vo. 9s.

   Origin of Species by Means of Natural Selection; or, the Preservation of Favoured Races in the Struggle for Life. Woodcuts. Crown 8vo. 7s. 6d.

   Variation of Animals and Plants under Domestication. Woodcuts. 2 Vols. Crown 8vo. 18s.

   Descent of Man, and Selection in Relation to Sex. Woodcuts. Crown 8vo. 9s.

   Expressions of the Emotions in Man and Animals. With Illustrations. Crown 8vo. 12s.

   Various Contrivances by which Orchids are Fertilized by Insects. Woodcuts. Crown 8vo. 9s.

   Movements and Habits of Climbing Plants. Woodcuts, Crown 8vo. 6s.

   Insectivorous Plants. Woodcuts. Crown 8vo. 14s.

   Effects of Cross and Self-Fertilization in the Vegetable Kingdom. Crown 8vo. 12s.

   Different Forms of Flowers on Plants of the same Species. Crown 8vo. 10s. 6d.

   Facts and Argument for Darwin. By Fritz Muller. Translated by W. S. Dallas. Woodcuts. Post 8vo. 6s.

DE COSSON (E. A.). The Cradle of the Blue Nile; a Journey through Abyssinia and Soudan, and a residence at the Court of King John of Ethiopia. Map and Illustrations. 2 vols. Post 8vo. 21s.

DENNIS (George). The Cities and Cemeteries of Etruria. A new Edition, revised, recording all the latest Discoveries. With 20 Plans and 150 Illustrations. 2 vols. 8vo. 42s.

DENT (Emma). Annals of Winchcombe and Sudeley. With 120 Portraits, Plates and Woodcuts. 4to. 42s.

DERBY (Earl of). Iliad of Homer rendered into English Blank Verse. 10th Edition. With Portrait. 2 Vols. Post 8vo. 10s.

DERRY (Bishop of). Witness of the Psalms to Christ and Christianity. The Bampton Lectures for 1876. 8vo.

DEUTSCH (Emanuel). Talmud, Islam, The Targums and other Literary Remains. 8vo. 12s.

DILKE (Sir C. W.). Papers of a Critic. Selected from the Writings of the late Chas. Wentworth Dilke. With a Biographical Sketch. 2 Vols. 8vo. 24s.

DOG-BREAKING, with Odds and Ends for those who love the Dog and Gun. By Gen. Hutchinson. With 40 Illustrations. Crown 8vo. 7s. 6d.

DOMESTIC MODERN COOKERY. Founded on Principles of Economy and Practical Knowledge, and adapted for Private Families. Woodcuts. Fcap. 8vo. 5s.

DOUGLAS'S (Sir Howard) Life and Adventures. Portrait. 8vo. 15s.

―――― Theory and Practice of Gunnery. Plates. 8vo. 21s.

―――― Construction of Bridges and the Passage of Rivers in Military Operations. Plates. 8vo. 21s.

―――― (Wm.) Horse-Shoeing; As it Is, and As it Should be. Illustrations. Post 8vo. 7s. 6d.

DRAKE'S (Sir Francis) Life, Voyages, and Exploits, by Sea and Land. By John Barrow. Post 8vo. 2s.

DRINKWATER (John). History of the Siege of Gibraltar, 1779-1783. With a Description and Account of that Garrison from the Earliest Periods. Post 8vo. 2s.

DUCANGE'S Mediæval Latin-English Dictionary. Translated and Edited by Rev. E. A. Dayman and J. H. Hessels. Small 4to. [*In preparation.*]

DU CHAILLU (Paul B.). Equatorial Africa, with Accounts of the Gorilla, the Nest-building Ape, Chimpanzee, Crocodile, &c. Illustrations. 8vo. 21s.

―――― Journey to Ashango Land; and Further Penetration into Equatorial Africa. Illustrations. 8vo. 21s.

DUFFERIN (Lord). Letters from High Latitudes; a Yacht Voyage to Iceland, Jan Mayen, and Spitzbergen. Woodcuts. Post 8vo. 7s. 6d.

DUNCAN (Major). History of the Royal Artillery. Compiled from the Original Records. With Portraits. 2 Vols. 8vo. 30s.

―――― English in Spain; or, The Story of the War of Succession, 1834 and 1840. Compiled from the Reports of the British Commissioners With Illustrations. 8vo. 16s.

EASTLAKE (Sir Charles). Contributions to the Literature of the Fine Arts. With Memoir of the Author, and Selections from his Correspondence. By Lady Eastlake. 2 Vols. 8vo. 24s.

EDWARDS (W. H.). Voyage up the River Amazons, including a Visit to Para. Post 8vo. 2s.

EIGHT MONTHS AT ROME, during the Vatican Council, with a Daily Account of the Proceedings. By Pomponio Leto. Translated from the Original. 8vo. 12s.

ELDON'S (Lord) Public and Private Life, with Selections from his Correspondence and Diaries. By Horace Twiss. Portrait. 2 Vols. Post 8vo. 21s.

ELGIN (Lord). Letters and Journals. Edited by Theodore Walrond. With Preface by Dean Stanley. 8vo. 14s.

ELLESMERE (Lord). Two Sieges of Vienna by the Turks. Translated from the German. Post 8vo. 2s.

ELLIS (W.). Madagascar Revisited. Setting forth the Persecutions and Heroic Sufferings of the Native Christians. Illustrations. 8vo. 16s.

―――― Memoir. By His Son. With his Character and Work. By Rev. Henry Allon, D.D. Portrait. 8vo. 10s. 6d.

―――― (Robinson) Poems and Fragments of Catullus. 16mo. 5s.

ELPHINSTONE (Hon. Mountstuart). History of India—the Hindoo and Mahomedan Periods. Edited by Professor Cowell. Map. 8vo. 18s.

——— (H. W.) Patterns for Turning; Comprising Elliptical and other Figures cut on the Lathe without the use of any Ornamental Chuck. With 70 Illustrations. Small 4to. 15s.

ENGLAND. See Callcott, Croker, Hume, Markham, Smith, and Stanhope.

ESSAYS ON CATHEDRALS. With an Introduction. By Dean Howson. 8vo. 12s.

ELZE (Karl). Life of Lord Byron. With a Critical Essay on his Place in Literature. Translated from the German. With Portrait. 8vo. 16s.

FERGUSSON (James). History of Architecture in all Countries from the Earliest Times. With 1,600 Illustrations. 4 Vols. Medium 8vo.
Vol. I. & II. Ancient and Mediæval. 63s.
Vol. III. Indian & Eastern. 42s. Vol. IV. Modern. 31s. 6d.

——— Rude Stone Monuments in all Countries; their Age and Uses. With 230 Illustrations. Medium 8vo. 24s.

——— Holy Sepulchre and the Temple at Jerusalem. Woodcuts. 8vo. 7s. 6d.

——— Temples of the Jews and other buildings in the Haram Area at Jerusalem. With Illustrations. 4to. 42s.

FLEMING (Professor). Student's Manual of Moral Philosophy. With Quotations and References. Post 8vo. 7s. 6d.

FLOWER GARDEN. By Rev. Thos. James. Fcap. 8vo. 1s.

FORBES (Capt. C. J. F.S.) Sketches of Native Burmese; Life, Manners, Customs, and Religion. Crown 8vo. [In the Press.

FORD (Richard). Gatherings from Spain. Post 8vo. 3s. 6d.

FORSYTH (William). Hortensius; an Historical Essay on the Office and Duties of an Advocate. Illustrations. 8vo. 12s.

——— History of Ancient Manuscripts. Post 8vo. 2s. 6d.

——— Novels and Novelists of the 18th Century, in Illustration of the Manners and Morals of the Age. Post 8vo. 10s. 6d.

FORTUNE (Robert). Narrative of Two Visits to the Tea Countries of China, 1843-52. Woodcuts. 2 Vols. Post 8vo. 18s.

FORSTER (John). The Early Life of Jonathan Swift. 1667-1711. With Portrait. 8vo. 15s.

FOSS (Edward). Biographia Juridica, or Biographical Dictionary of the Judges of England, from the Conquest to the Present Time, 1066-1870. Medium 8vo. 21s.

FRANCE (History of). See Markham—Smith—Student's.

FRENCH IN ALGIERS; The Soldier of the Foreign Legion—and the Prisoners of Abd-el-Kadir. Translated by Lady Duff Gordon. Post 8vo. 2s.

FRERE (Sir Bartle). Indian Missions. Small 8vo. 2s. 6d.

——— Eastern Africa as a field for Missionary Labour. With Map. Crown 8vo. 5s.

——— Bengal Famine. How it will be Met and How to Prevent Future Famines in India. With Maps. Crown 8vo. 5s.

GALTON (FRANCIS). Art of Travel; or, Hints on the Shifts and Contrivances available in Wild Countries. Woodcuts. Post 8vo. 7s. 6d.

GEOGRAPHY. See CROKER—SMITH—STUDENTS.

GEOGRAPHICAL SOCIETY'S JOURNAL. (*Published Yearly.*)

GEORGE (ERNEST). The Mosel; a Series of Twenty Etchings, with Descriptive Letterpress. Imperial 4to. 42s.

——— Loire and South of France; a Series of Twenty Etchings, with Descriptive Text. Folio. 42s.

GERMANY (HISTORY OF). See MARKHAM.

GIBBON (EDWARD). History of the Decline and Fall of the Roman Empire. Edited by MILMAN and GUIZOT. Edited, with Notes, by Dr. WM. SMITH. Maps. 8 Vols. 8vo. 60s.

——— The Student's Edition; an Epitome of the above work, incorporating the Researches of Recent Commentators. By Dr. WM. SMITH. Woodcuts. Post 8vo. 7s. 6d.

GIFFARD (EDWARD). Deeds of Naval Daring; or, Anecdotes of the British Navy. Fcap. 8vo. 3s. 6d.

GLADSTONE (W. E.). Rome and the Newest Fashions in Religion. Three Tracts. 8vo. 7s. 6d.

GLEIG (G. R.). Campaigns of the British Army at Washington and New Orleans. Post 8vo. 2s.

——— Story of the Battle of Waterloo. Post 8vo. 3s. 6d.

——— Narrative of Sale's Brigade in Affghanistan. Post 8vo. 2s.

——— Life of Lord Clive. Post 8vo. 3s. 6d.

——— Sir Thomas Munro. Post 8vo. 3s. 6d.

GLYNNE (SIR STEPHEN R.). Notes on the Churches of Kent. With Preface by W. H. Gladstone, M.P. Illustrations. 8vo. 12s.

GOLDSMITH'S (OLIVER) Works. Edited with Notes by PETER CUNNINGHAM. Vignettes. 4 Vols. 8vo. 30s.

GORDON (SIR ALEX.). Sketches of German Life, and Scenes from the War of Liberation. Post 8vo. 3s. 6d.

——— (LADY DUFF) Amber-Witch: A Trial for Witchcraft. Post 8vo. 2s.

——— French in Algiers. 1. The Soldier of the Foreign Legion. 2. The Prisoners of Abd-el-Kadir. Post 8vo. 2s.

GRAMMARS. See CURTIUS; HALL; HUTTON; KING EDWARD; MATTHIE; MAETZNER; SMITH.

GREECE (HISTORY OF). See GROTE—SMITH—Student.

GUIZOT (M.). Meditations on Christianity. 3 Vols. Post 8vo. 30s.

GROTE'S (GEORGE) WORKS :—

HISTORY OF GREECE. From the Earliest Times to the close of the generation contemporary with the death of Alexander the Great. *Library Edition.* Portrait, Maps, and Plans. 10 Vols. 8vo. 120s. *Cabinet Edition.* Portrait and Plans. 12 Vols. Post 8vo. 6s. each.

PLATO, and other Companions of Socrates. 3 Vols. 8vo. 45s.

ARISTOTLE. 2 Vols. 8vo. 32s.

MINOR WORKS. With Critical Remarks. By ALEX. BAIN. Portrait. 8vo. 14s.

FRAGMENTS ON ETHICAL SUBJECTS. With Introduction. By ALEXANDER BAIN. 8vo. 7s. 6d.

LETTERS ON SWITZERLAND IN 1847. 6s.

PERSONAL LIFE. Compiled from Family Documents, Original Letters, &c. By Mrs. GROTE. Portrait. 8vo. 12s.

HALL (T. D.) AND Dr. WM. SMITH'S School Manual of English Grammar. With Copious Exercises. 12mo. 3s. 6d.

———— Primary English Grammar for Elementary Schools. Based on the above work. 16mo. 1s.

———— Child's First Latin Book, including a Systematic Treatment of the New Pronunciation, and a full Praxis of Nouns, Adjectives, and Pronouns. 16mo. 1s. 6d.

HALLAM'S (HENRY) WORKS:—
> THE CONSTITUTIONAL HISTORY OF ENGLAND, from the Accession of Henry the Seventh to the Death of George the Second. *Library Edition.* 3 Vols. 8vo. 30s. *Cabinet Edition.* 3 Vols. Post 8vo. 12s.
>
> Student's Edition of the above work. Edited by WM. SMITH, D.C.L. Post 8vo. 7s. 6d.
>
> HISTORY OF EUROPE DURING THE MIDDLE AGES. *Library Edition.* 3 Vols. 8vo. 30s. *Cabinet Edition,* 3 Vols. Post 8vo. 12s.
>
> Student's Edition of the above work. Edited by WM. SMITH, D.C.L. Post 8vo. 7s. 6d.
>
> LITERARY HISTORY OF EUROPE DURING THE 15TH, 16TH, AND 17TH CENTURIES. *Library Edition.* 3 Vols. 8vo. 36s. *Cabinet Edition.* 4 Vols. Post 8vo. 16s.

HALLAM'S (ARTHUR) Literary Remains; in Verse and Prose. Portrait. Fcap. 8vo. 3s. 6d.

HAMILTON (GEN. SIR F. W.). History of the Grenadier Guards. From Original Documents in the Rolls' Records, War Office, Regimental Records, &c. With Illustrations. 3 Vols. 8vo. 63s.

HART'S ARMY LIST. (*Published Quarterly and Annually.*)

HAY (SIR J. H. DRUMMOND). Western Barbary, its Wild Tribes and Savage Animals. Post 8vo. 2s.

HEAD'S (SIR FRANCIS) WORKS:—
> THE ROYAL ENGINEER. Illustrations. 8vo. 12s.
>
> LIFE OF SIR JOHN BURGOYNE. Post 8vo. 1s.
>
> RAPID JOURNEYS ACROSS THE PAMPAS. Post 8vo. 2s.
>
> BUBBLES FROM THE BRUNNEN OF NASSAU. Illustrations. Post 8vo. 7s. 6d.
>
> STOKERS AND POKERS; or, the London and North Western Railway. Post 8vo. 2s.

HEAD (SIR EDMUND) Shall and Will; or, Future Auxiliary Verbs. Fcap. 8vo. 4s.

HEBER'S (BISHOP) Journals in India. 2 Vols. Post 8vo. 7s.

———— Poetical Works. Portrait. Fcap. 8vo. 3s. 6d.

———— Hymns adapted to the Church Service. 16mo. 1s. 6d.

FOREIGN HANDBOOKS.

HAND-BOOK—TRAVEL-TALK. English, French, German, and Italian. 18mo. 3s. 6d.

———— HOLLAND AND BELGIUM. Map and Plans. Post 8vo. 6s.

———— NORTH GERMANY and THE RHINE,— The Black Forest, the Hartz, Thüringerwald, Saxon Switzerland, Rügen the Giant Mountains, Taunus, Odenwald, Elass, and Lothringen. Map and Plans. Post 8vo. 10s.

———— SOUTH GERMANY,— Wurtemburg, Bavaria, Austria, Styria, Salzburg, the Austrian and Bavarian Alps, Tyrol, Hungary, and the Danube, from Ulm to the Black Sea. Map. Post 8vo. 10s.

———— PAINTING. German, Flemish, and Dutch Schools. Illustrations. 2 Vols. Post 8vo. 24s.

———— LIVES OF EARLY FLEMISH PAINTERS. By CROWE and CAVALCASELLE. Illustrations. Post 8vo. 10s. 6d.

———— SWITZERLAND, Alps of Savoy, and Piedmont. Maps. Post 8vo. 9s.

———— FRANCE, Part I. Normandy, Brittany, the French Alps, the Loire, the Seine, the Garonne, and Pyrenees. Post 8vo. 7s. 6d.

———— Part II. Central France, Auvergne, the Cevennes, Burgundy, the Rhone and Saone, Provence, Nimes, Arles, Marseilles, the French Alps, Alsace, Lorraine, Champagne, &c. Maps. Post 8vo. 7s. 6d.

———— MEDITERRANEAN ISLANDS—Malta, Corsica, Sardinia, and Sicily. Maps. Post 8vo. [*In the Press.*

———— ALGERIA. Algiers, Constantine, Oran, the Atlas Range. Map. Post 8vo. 9s.

———— PARIS, and its Environs. Map. 16mo. 3s. 6d.

———— SPAIN, Madrid, The Castiles, The Basque Provinces, Leon, The Asturias, Galicia, Estremadura, Andalusia, Ronda, Granada, Murcia, Valencia, Catalonia, Aragon, Navarre, The Balearic Islands, &c. &c. Maps. Post 8vo. 20s.

———— PORTUGAL, LISBON, Porto, Cintra, Mafra, &c. Map. Post 8vo. 12s.

———— NORTH ITALY, Turin, Milan, Cremona, the Italian Lakes, Bergamo, Brescia, Verona, Mantua, Vicenza, Padua, Ferrara, Bologna, Ravenna, Rimini, Piacenza, Genoa, the Riviera, Venice, Parma, Modena, and Romagna. Map. Post 8vo. 10s.

———— CENTRAL ITALY, Florence, Lucca, Tuscany, The Marches, Umbria, and late Patrimony of St. Peter's. Map. Post 8vo. 10s.

———— ROME AND ITS ENVIRONS. Map. Post 8vo. 10s.

———— SOUTH ITALY, Naples, Pompeii, Herculaneum, and Vesuvius. Map. Post 8vo. 10s.

———— PAINTING. The Italian Schools. Illustrations. 2 Vols. Post 8vo. 30s.

———— LIVES OF ITALIAN PAINTERS, FROM CIMABUE to BASSANO. By Mrs. JAMESON. Portraits. Post 8vo. 12s.

———— NORWAY, Christiania, Bergen, Trondhjem. The Fjelds and Fjords. Map. Post 8vo. 9s.

———— SWEDEN, Stockholm, Upsala, Gothenburg, the Shores of the Baltic, &c. Post 8vo. 6s.

———— DENMARK, Sleswig, Holstein, Copenhagen, Jutland, Iceland. Map. Post 8vo. 6s.

HAND-BOOK—RUSSIA, St. Petersburg, Moscow, Poland, and Finland. Maps. Post 8vo. 18s.

——— GREECE, the Ionian Islands, Continental Greece, Athens, the Peloponnesus, the Islands of the Ægean Sea, Albania, Thessaly, and Macedonia. Maps. Post 8vo. 15s.

——— TURKEY IN ASIA—Constantinople, the Bosphorus, Dardanelles, Brousa, Plain of Troy, Crete, Cyprus, Smyrna, Ephesus, the Seven Churches, Coasts of the Black Sea, Armenia, Mesopotamia, &c. Maps. Post 8vo. 15s.

——— EGYPT, including Descriptions of the Course of the Nile through Egypt and Nubia, Alexandria, Cairo, and Thebes, the Suez Canal, the Pyramids, the Peninsula of Sinai, the Oases, the Fyoom, &c. Map. Post 8vo. 15s.

——— HOLY LAND—Syria, Palestine, Peninsula of Sinai, Edom, Syrian Deserts, Petra, Damascus; and Pa'myra. Maps. Post 8vo. 20s. *⁎* Travelling Map of Palestine. In a case. 12s.

——— INDIA — Bombay and Madras. Map. 2 Vols. Post 8vo. 12s. each.

ENGLISH HANDBOOKS.

HAND-BOOK—MODERN LONDON. Map. 16mo. 3s. 6d.

——— ENVIRONS OF LONDON within a circuit of 20 miles. 2 Vols. Crown 8vo. 21s.

——— EASTERN COUNTIES, Chelmsford, Harwich, Colchester, Maldon, Cambridge, Ely, Newmarket, Bury St. Edmunds, Ipswich, Woodbridge, Felixstowe, Lowestoft, Norwich, Yarmouth, Cromer, &c. Map and Plans. Post 8vo. 12s.

——— CATHEDRALS of Oxford, Peterborough, Norwich, Ely, and Lincoln. With 90 Illustrations. Crown 8vo. 18s.

——— KENT, Canterbury, Dover, Ramsgate, Sheerness, Rochester, Chatham, Woolwich. Map. Post 8vo. 7s. 6d.

——— SUSSEX, Brighton, Chichester, Worthing, Hastings, Lewes, Arundel, &c. Map. Post 8vo. 6s.

——— SURREY AND HANTS, Kingston, Croydon, Reigate, Guildford, Dorking, Boxhill, Winchester, Southampton, New Forest, Portsmouth, and Isle of Wight. Maps. Post 8vo. 10s.

——— BERKS, BUCKS, AND OXON, Windsor, Eton, Reading, Aylesbury, Uxbridge, Wycombe, Henley, the City and University of Oxford, Blenheim, and the Descent of the Thames. Map. Post 8vo. 7s. 6d.

——— WILTS, DORSET, AND SOMERSET, Salisbury, Chippenham, Weymouth, Sherborne, Wells, Bath, Bristol, Taunton, &c. Map. Post 8vo. 10s.

——— DEVON AND CORNWALL, Exeter, Ilfracombe, Linton, Sidmouth, Dawlish, Teignmouth, Plymouth, Devonport, Torquay, Launceston, Truro, Penzance, Falmouth, the Lizard, Land's End, &c. Maps. Post 8vo. 12s.

——— CATHEDRALS of Winchester, Salisbury, Exeter, Wells, Chichester, Rochester, Canterbury, and St. Albans. With 130 Illustrations. 2 Vols. Crown 8vo. 36s. St. Albans separately, crown 8vo. 6s.

——— GLOUCESTER, HEREFORD, and WORCESTER Cirencester, Cheltenham, Stroud, Tewkesbury, Leominster, Ross, Malvern, Kidderminster, Dudley, Bromsgrove, Evesham. Map. Post 8vo. 9s.

——— CATHEDRALS of Bristol, Gloucester, Hereford, Worcester, and Lichfield. With 50 Illustrations. Crown 8vo. 16s.

LIST OF WORKS

HAND-BOOK—NORTH WALES, Bangor, Carnarvon, Beaumaris, Snowdon, Llanberis, Dolgelly, Cader Idris, Conway, &c. Map. Post 8vo. 7s.

—————— SOUTH WALES, Monmouth, Llandaff, Merthyr, Vale of Neath, Pembroke, Carmarthen, Tenby, Swansea, The Wye, &c. Map. Post 8vo. 7s.

—————— CATHEDRALS OF BANGOR, ST. ASAPH, Llandaff, and St. David's. With Illustrations. Post 8vo. 15s.

—————— NORTHAMPTONSHIRE AND RUTLAND— Northampton, Peterborough, Towcester, Daventry, Market Harborough, Kettering, Wallingborough, Thrapston, Stamford, Uppingham, Oakham. Maps. Post 8vo.

—————— DERBY, NOTTS, LEICESTER, STAFFORD, Matlock, Bakewell, Chatsworth, The Peak, Buxton, Hardwick, Dove Dale, Ashborne, Southwell, Mansfield, Retford, Burton, Belvoir Melton Mowbray, Wolverhampton, Lichfield, Walsall, Tamworth. Map. Post 8vo. 9s.

—————— SHROPSHIRE, CHESHIRE and LANCASHIRE —Shrewsbury, Ludlow, Bridgnorth, Oswestry, Chester, Crewe, Alderley, Stockport, Birkenhead, Warrington, Bury, Manchester, Liverpool, Burnley, Clitheroe, Bolton, Blackburn, Wigan, Preston, Rochdale, Lancaster, Southport, Blackpool, &c. Map. Post 8vo. 10s.

—————— YORKSHIRE, Doncaster, Hull, Selby, Beverley, Scarborough, Whitby, Harrogate, Ripon, Leeds, Wakefield, Bradford, Halifax, Huddersfield, Sheffield. Map and Plans. Post 8vo. 12s.

—————— CATHEDRALS of York, Ripon, Durham, Carlisle, Chester, and Manchester. With 60 Illustrations. 2 Vols. Crown 8vo. 21s.

—————— DURHAM AND NORTHUMBERLAND, Newcastle, Darlington, Gateshead, Bishop Auckland, Stockton, Hartlepool, Sunderland, Shields, Berwick-on-Tweed, Morpeth, Tynemouth, Coldstream, Alnwick, &c. Map. Post 8vo. 9s.

—————— WESTMORLAND AND CUMBERLAND—Lancaster, Furness Abbey, Ambleside, Kendal, Windermere, Coniston, Keswick, Grasmere, Ulswater, Carlisle, Cockermouth, Penrith, Appleby. Map. Post 8vo. 6s.

*** MURRAY'S MAP OF THE LAKE DISTRICT, on canvas. 3s. 6d.

—————— ENGLAND AND WALES. Alphabetically arranged and condensed into one volume. Post 8vo. [In the Press.

—————— SCOTLAND, Edinburgh, Melrose, Kelso, Glasgow, Dumfries, Ayr, Stirling, Arran, The Clyde, Oban, Inverary, Loch Lomond, Loch Katrine and Trossachs, Caledonian Canal, Inverness, Perth, Dundee, Aberdeen, Braemar, Skye, Caithness, Ross, Sutherland, &c. Maps and Plans. Post 8vo. 9s.

—————— IRELAND, Dublin, Belfast, Donegal, Galway, Wexford, Cork, Limerick, Waterford, Killarney, Munster, &c. Maps. Post 8vo.

HERODOTUS. A New English Version. Edited, with Notes and Essays, historical, ethnographical, and geographical, by CANON RAWLINSON, assisted by SIR HENRY RAWLINSON and SIR J. G. WILKINSON. Maps and Woodcuts. 4 Vols. 8vo. 48s.

HERSCHEL'S (CAROLINE) Memoir and Correspondence. By MRS. JOHN HERSCHEL. With Portraits. Crown 8vo. 12s.

HATHERLEY (LORD). The Continuity of Scripture, as Declared by the Testimony of our Lord and of the Evangelists and Apostles. 8vo. 6s. *Popular Edition.* Post 8vo. 2s. 6d.

HOLLWAY (J. G.). A Month in Norway. Fcap. 8vo. 2s.

HONEY BEE. By REV. THOMAS JAMES. Fcap. 8vo. 1s.

HOOK (DEAN). Church Dictionary. 8vo. 16s.

PUBLISHED BY MR. MURRAY. 17

HOME AND COLONIAL LIBRARY. A Series of Works adapted for all circles and classes of Readers, having been selected for their acknowledged interest, and ability of the Authors. Post 8vo. Published at 2s. and 3s. 6d. each, and arranged under two distinctive heads as follows:—

CLASS A.

HISTORY, BIOGRAPHY, AND HISTORIC TALES.

1. SIEGE OF GIBRALTAR. By JOHN DRINKWATER. 2s.
2. THE AMBER-WITCH. By LADY DUFF GORDON. 2s.
3. CROMWELL AND BUNYAN. By ROBERT SOUTHEY. 2s.
4. LIFE OF SIR FRANCIS DRAKE. By JOHN BARROW. 2s.
5. CAMPAIGNS AT WASHINGTON. By REV. G. R. GLEIG. 2s.
6. THE FRENCH IN ALGIERS. By LADY DUFF GORDON. 2s.
7. THE FALL OF THE JESUITS. 2s.
8. LIVONIAN TALES. 2s.
9. LIFE OF CONDÉ. By LORD MAHON. 3s. 6d.
10. SALE'S BRIGADE. By REV. G. R. GLEIG. 2s.
11. THE SIEGES OF VIENNA. By LORD ELLESMERE. 2s.
12. THE WAYSIDE CROSS. By CAPT. MILMAN. 2s.
13. SKETCHES OF GERMAN LIFE. By SIR A. GORDON. 3s. 6d.
14. THE BATTLE OF WATERLOO. By REV. G. R. GLEIG. 3s. 6d.
15. AUTOBIOGRAPHY OF STEFFENS. 2s.
16. THE BRITISH POETS. By THOMAS CAMPBELL. 3s. 6d.
17. HISTORICAL ESSAYS. By LORD MAHON. 3s. 6d.
18. LIFE OF LORD CLIVE. By REV. G. R. GLEIG. 3s. 6d.
19. NORTH-WESTERN RAILWAY. By SIR F. B. HEAD. 2s.
20. LIFE OF MUNRO. By REV. G. R. GLEIG. 3s. 6d.

CLASS B.

VOYAGES, TRAVELS, AND ADVENTURES.

1. BIBLE IN SPAIN. By GEORGE BORROW. 3s. 6d.
2. GYPSIES OF SPAIN. By GEORGE BORROW. 3s. 6d.
3 & 4. JOURNALS IN INDIA. By BISHOP HEBER. 2 Vols. 7s.
5. TRAVELS IN THE HOLY LAND. By IRBY and MANGLES. 2s.
6. MOROCCO AND THE MOORS. By J. DRUMMOND HAY. 2s.
7. LETTERS FROM THE BALTIC. By a LADY.
8. NEW SOUTH WALES. By MRS. MEREDITH. 2s.
9. THE WEST INDIES. By M. G. LEWIS. 2s.
10. SKETCHES OF PERSIA. By SIR JOHN MALCOLM. 3s. 6d.
11. MEMOIRS OF FATHER RIPA. 2s.
12 & 13. TYPEE AND OMOO. By HERMANN MELVILLE. 2 Vols. 7s.
14. MISSIONARY LIFE IN CANADA. By REV. J. ABBOTT. 2s.
15. LETTERS FROM MADRAS. By a LADY. 2s.
16. HIGHLAND SPORTS. By CHARLES ST. JOHN. 3s. 6d.
17. PAMPAS JOURNEYS. By SIR F. B. HEAD. 2s.
18. GATHERINGS FROM SPAIN. By RICHARD FORD. 3s. 6d.
19. THE RIVER AMAZON. By W. H. EDWARDS. 2s.
20. MANNERS & CUSTOMS OF INDIA. By REV. C. ACLAND. 2s.
21. ADVENTURES IN MEXICO. By G. F. RUXTON. 3s. 6d.
22. PORTUGAL AND GALICIA. By LORD CARNARVON. 3s. 6d.
23. BUSH LIFE IN AUSTRALIA. By REV. H. W. HAYGARTH. 2s.
24. THE LIBYAN DESERT. By BAYLE ST. JOHN. 2s.
25. SIERRA LEONE. By A LADY. 3s. 6d.

⁎ Each work may be had separately.

C

HOOK'S (THEODORE) Life. By J. G. LOCKHART. Fcap. 8vo. 1s.

HOPE (T. C.). ARCHITECTURE OF AHMEDABAD, with Historical Sketch and Architectural Notes. With Maps, Photographs, and Woodcuts. 4to. 5l. 5s.

—— (A. J. BERESFORD) Worship in the Church of England. 8vo. 9s., or, *Popular Selections from.* 8vo. 2s. 6d.

HORACE; a New Edition of the Text. Edited by DEAN MILMAN. With 100 Woodcuts. Crown 8vo. 7s. 6d.

—————— Life of. By DEAN MILMAN. Illustrations. 8vo. 9s.

HOUGHTON'S (LORD) Monographs, Personal and Social. With Portraits. Crown 8vo. 10s. 6d.

—————— POETICAL WORKS. *Collected Edition.* With Portrait. 2 Vols. Fcap. 8vo. 12s.

HUME (The Student's). A History of England, from the Invasion of Julius Cæsar to the Revolution of 1688. Corrected and continued to 1868. Woodcuts. Post 8vo. 7s. 6d.

HUTCHINSON (GEN.) Dog Breaking, with Odds and Ends for those who love the Dog and the Gun. With 40 Illustrations. 6th edition. 7s. 6d.

HUTTON (H. E.). Principia Græca; an Introduction to the Study of Greek. Comprehending Grammar, Delectus, and Exercise-book, with Vocabularies. *Sixth Edition.* 12mo. 3s. 6d.

IRBY AND MANGLES' Travels in Egypt, Nubia, Syria, and the Holy Land. Post 8vo. 2s.

JACOBSON (BISHOP). Fragmentary Illustrations of the History of the Book of Common Prayer; from Manuscript Sources (Bishop SANDERSON and Bishop WREN). 8vo. 5s.

JAMES' (REV. THOMAS) Fables of Æsop. A New Translation, with Historical Preface. With 100 Woodcuts by TENNIEL and WOLF. Post 8vo. 2s. 6d.

JAMESON (MRS.). Lives of the Early Italian Painters—and the Progress of Painting in Italy—Cimabue to Bassano. With 50 Portraits. Post 8vo. 12s.

JENNINGS (LOUIS J.). Field Paths and Green Lanes in Surrey and Sussex. Illustrations. Post 8vo. 10s. 6d.

JERVIS (REV. W. H.). The Gallican Church, from the Concordat of Bologna, 1516, to the Revolution. With an Introduction. Portraits. 2 Vols. 8vo. 28s.

JESSE (EDWARD). Gleanings in Natural History. Fcp. 8vo. 3s. 6d.

JEX-BLAKE (REV. T. W.). Life in Faith: Sermons Preached at Cheltenham and Rugby. Fcap. 8vo. 3s. 6d.

JOHNS (REV. B. G.). Blind People; their Works and Ways. With Sketches of the Lives of some famous Blind Men. With Illustrations. Post 8vo. 7s. 6d.

JOHNSON'S (DR. SAMUEL) Life. By James Boswell. Including the Tour to the Hebrides. Edited by MR. CROKER. 1 vol. Royal 8vo. 12s. *New Edition.* Portraits. 4 Vols. 8vo. [*In Preparation.*

—————— Lives of the most eminent English Poets, with Critical Observations on their Works. Edited with Notes, Corrective and Explanatory, by PETER CUNNINGHAM. 3 vols. 8vo. 22s. 6d.

JUNIUS' HANDWRITING Professionally investigated. By Mr. CHABOT, Expert. With Preface and Collateral Evidence, by the Hon. EDWARD TWISLETON With Facsimiles, Woodcuts, &c. 4to. £3 3s.

KEN'S (BISHOP) Life. By a LAYMAN. Portrait. 2 Vols. 8vo. 18s.
——— Exposition of the Apostles' Creed. 16mo. 1s. 6d.
KERR (ROBERT). GENTLEMAN'S HOUSE; OR, HOW TO PLAN ENGLISH RESIDENCES FROM THE PARSONAGE TO THE PALACE. With Views and Plans. 8vo. 21s.
——— Small Country House. A Brief Practical Discourse on the Planning of a Residence from 2000l. to 5000l. With Supplementary Estimates to 7000l. Post 8vo. 3s.
——— Ancient Lights; a Book for Architects, Surveyors, Lawyers, and Landlords. 8vo. 5s. 6d.
——— (R. MALCOLM) Student's Blackstone. A Systematic Abridgment of the entire Commentaries, adapted to the present state of the law. Post 8vo. 7s. 6d.
KING EDWARD VITH's Latin Grammar. 12mo. 3s. 6d.
——— First Latin Book. 12mo. 2s. 6d.
KING (R. J.). Archæology, Travel and Art; being Sketches and Studies, Historical and Descriptive. 8vo. 12s.
KIRK (J. FOSTER). History of Charles the Bold, Duke of Burgundy. Portrait. 3 Vols. 8vo. 45s.
KIRKES' Handbook of Physiology. Edited by W. MORRANT BAKER, F.R.C.S. With 400 Illustrations. Post 8vo. 14s.
KUGLER'S Handbook of Painting.—The Italian Schools. Revised and Remodelled from the most recent Researches. By LADY EASTLAKE. With 140 Illustrations. 2 Vols. Crown 8vo. 30s.
——— Handbook of Painting.—The German, Flemish, and Dutch Schools. Revised and in part re-written. By J. A. CROWE. With 60 Illustrations. 2 Vols. Crown 8vo. 24s.
LANE E. W.). Account of the Manners and Customs of Modern Egyptians. With Illustrations. 2 Vols. Post 8vo. 12s.
LAWRENCE (SIR GEO.). Reminiscences of Forty-three Years' Service in India; including Captivities in Cabul among the Affghans and among the Sikhs, and a Narrative of the Mutiny in Rajputana. Crown 8vo. 10s. 6d.
LAYARD (A. H.). Nineveh and its Remains. Being a Narrative of Researches and Discoveries amidst the Ruins of Assyria. With an Account of the Chaldean Christians of Kurdistan; the Yezedis, or Devil-worshippers; and an Enquiry into the Manners and Arts of the Ancient Assyrians. Plates and Woodcuts. 2 Vols. 8vo. 36s.
** A POPULAR EDITION of the above work. With Illustrations. Post 8vo. 7s. 6d.
——— Nineveh and Babylon; being the Narrative of Discoveries in the Ruins, with Travels in Armenia, Kurdistan and the Desert, during a Second Expedition to Assyria. With Map and Plates. 8vo. 21s.
** A POPULAR EDITION of the above work. With Illustrations Post 8vo. 7s. 6d.
LEATHES' (STANLEY) Practical Hebrew Grammar. With the Hebrew Text of Genesis i.—vi., and Psalms i.—vi. Grammatical Analysis and Vocabulary. Post 8vo. 7s. 6d.
LENNEP (REV. H. J. VAN). Missionary Travels in Asia Minor. With Illustrations of Biblical History and Archæology. With Map and Woodcuts. 2 Vols. Post 8vo. 24s.
——— Modern Customs and Manners of Bible Lands in Illustration of Scripture. With Coloured Maps and 300 Illustrations. 2 Vols. 8vo. 21s.

LESLIE (C. R.). Handbook for Young Painters. With Illustrations. Post 8vo. 7s. 6d.
———— Life and Works of Sir Joshua Reynolds. Portraits and Illustrations. 2 Vols. 8vo. 42s.
LETO (Pomponio). Eight Months at Rome during the Vatican Council. With a daily account of the proceedings. Translated from the original. 8vo. 12s.
LETTERS From the Baltic. By a Lady. Post 8vo. 2s.
———— Madras. By a Lady. Post 8vo. 2s.
———— Sierra Leone. By a Lady. Post 8vo. 3s. 6d.
LEVI (Leone). History of British Commerce; and of the Economic Progress of the Nation, from 1763 to 1870. 8vo. 16s.
LIDDELL (Dean). Student's History of Rome, from the earliest Times to the establishment of the Empire. Woodcuts. Post 8vo. 7s. 6d.
LLOYD (W. Watkiss). History of Sicily to the Athenian War; with Elucidations of the Sicilian Odes of Pindar. With Map. 8vo. 14s.
LISPINGS from LOW LATITUDES; or, the Journal of the Hon. Impulsia Gushington. Edited by Lord Dufferin. With 24 Plates. 4to. 21s.
LITTLE ARTHUR'S History of England. By Lady Callcott. *New Edition, continued to* 1872. With Woodcuts. Fcap. 8vo. 1s. 6d.
LIVINGSTONE (Dr.). Popular Account of his First Expedition to Africa, 1840-56. Illustrations. Post 8vo. 7s. 6d.
———— Second Expedition to Africa, 1858-64. Illustrations. Post 8vo. 7s. 6d.
———— Last Journals in Central Africa, from 1865 to his Death. Continued by a Narrative of his last moments and sufferings. By Rev. Horace Waller. Maps and Illustrations. 2 Vols. 8vo. 28s.
LIVINGSTONIA. Journal of Adventures in Exploring Lake Nyassa, and Establishing a Missionary Settlement there. By E. D. Young, R.N. Revised by Rev. Horace Waller. Maps Post 8vo. 7s. 6d.
LIVONIAN TALES. By the Author of "Letters from the Baltic." Post 8vo. 2s.
LOCH (H. B.). Personal Narrative of Events during Lord Elgin's Second Embassy to China. With Illustrations. Post 8vo. 9s.
LOCKHART (J. G.). Ancient Spanish Ballads. Historical and Romantic. Translated, with Notes. With Portrait and Illustrations. Crown 8vo. 5s.
———— Life of Theodore Hook. Fcap. 8vo. 1s.
LOUDON (Mrs.). Gardening for Ladies. With Directions and Calendar of Operations for Every Month. Woodcuts. Fcap. 8vo. 3s. 6d.
LYELL (Sir Charles). Principles of Geology; or, the Modern Changes of the Earth and its Inhabitants considered as illustrative of Geology. With Illustrations. 2 Vols. 8vo. 32s.
———— Student's Elements of Geology. With Table of British Fossils and 600 Illustrations. Post 8vo. 9s.
———— Geological Evidences of the Antiquity of Man, including an Outline of Glacial Post-Tertiary Geology, and Remarks on the Origin of Species. Illustrations. 8vo. 14s.
———— (K. M.). Geographical Handbook of Ferns. With Tables to show their Distribution. Post 8vo. 7s. 6d.
LYTTON (Lord). A Memoir of Julian Fane. With Portrait. Post 8vo. 5s.
McCLINTOCK (Sir L.). Narrative of the Discovery of the Fate of Sir John Franklin and his Companions in the Arctic Seas. With Illustrations. Post 8vo. 7s. 6d.
MACDOUGALL (Col.). Modern Warfare as Influenced by Modern Artillery. With Plans. Post 8vo. 12s.

PUBLISHED BY MR. MURRAY. 21

MACGREGOR (J.). Rob Roy on the Jordan, Nile, Red Sea, Gennesareth, &c. A Canoe Cruise in Palestine and Egypt and the Waters of Damascus. With Map and 70 Illustrations. Crown 8vo. 7s. 6d.

MAETZNER'S ENGLISH GRAMMAR. A Methodical, Analytical, and Historical Treatise on the Orthography, Prosody, Inflections, and Syntax of the English Tongue. Translated from the German. By CLAIR J. GRECE, LL.D. 3 Vols. 8vo. 36s.

MAHON (LORD), see STANHOPE.

MAINE (SIR H. SUMNER). Ancient Law: its Connection with the Early History of Society, and its Relation to Modern Ideas. 8vo. 12s.

—— Village Communities in the East and West. 8vo. 12s.

—— Early History of Institutions. 8vo. 12s.

MALCOLM (SIR JOHN). Sketches of Persia. Post 8vo. 3s. 6d.

MANSEL (DEAN). Limits of Religious Thought Examined. Post 8vo. 8s. 6d.

———— Letters, Lectures, and Papers, including the Phrontisterion, or Oxford in the XIXth Century. Edited by H. W. CHANDLER, M.A. 8vo. 12s.

———— Gnostic Heresies of the First and Second Centuries. With a sketch of his life and character. By Lord CARNARVON. Edited by Canon LIGHTFOOT. 8vo. 10s. 6d.

MANUAL OF SCIENTIFIC ENQUIRY. For the Use of Travellers. Edited by REV. R. MAIN. Post 8vo. 3s. 6d. (*Published by order of the Lords of the Admiralty.*)

MARCO POLO. The Book of Ser Marco Polo, the Venetian. Concerning the Kingdoms and Marvels of the East. A new English Version. Illustrated by the light of Oriental Writers and Modern Travels. By COL. HENRY YULE. Maps and Illustrations. 2 Vols. Medium 8vo. 63s.

MARKHAM (CLEMENTS R.). The Introduction of Bark Culture into the British Dominions, containing a narrative of Journeys in Peru and India, and some account of the Chincona Plantations already formed. Illustrations. 8vo.

———— (MRS.) History of England. From the First Invasion by the Romans to 1867. Woodcuts. 12mo. 3s. 6d.

———— History of France. From the Conquest by the Gauls to 1861. Woodcuts. 12mo. 3s. 6d.

———— History of Germany. From the Invasion by Marius to 1867. Woodcuts. 12mo. 3s. 6d.

MARLBOROUGH'S (SARAH, DUCHESS OF) Letters. Now first published from the Original MSS. at Madresfield Court. With an Introduction. 8vo. 10s. 6d.

MARRYAT (JOSEPH). History of Modern and Mediæval Pottery and Porcelain. With a Description of the Manufacture. Plates and Woodcuts. 8vo. 42s.

MARSH (G. P.). Student's Manual of the English Language. Edited with Additions. By DR. WM. SMITH. Post 8vo. 7s. 6d.

MASTERS in English Theology. The King's College Lectures, 1877. By Canon Barry, Dean of S*. Paul's; Prof. Plumptre, Canon Westcott, Canon Farrar, and Prof. Cheetham. With Introduction by Canon Barry. Post 8vo. 7s. 6d.

MATTHIÆ'S GREEK GRAMMAR. Abridged by BLOMFIELD. Revised by E. S. CROOKE. 12mo. 4s.

MAUREL'S Character, Actions, and Writings of Wellington. Fcap. 8vo. 1s. 6d.

MAYO (LORD). Sport in Abyssinia; or, the March and Tackazzee. With Illustrations. Crown 8vo. 12s.

MEADE (Hon. Herbert). Ride through the Disturbed Districts of New Zealand, with a Cruise among the South Sea Islands. With Illustrations. Medium 8vo. 12s.

MELVILLE (Hermann). Marquesas and South Sea Islands. 2 Vols. Post 8vo. 7s.

MEREDITH (Mrs. Charles). Notes and Sketches of New South Wales. Post 8vo. 2s.

MICHAEL ANGELO, Sculptor, Painter, and Architect. His Life and Works. By C. Heath Wilson. Illustrations. Royal 8vo. 26s.

MILLINGTON (Rev. T. S.). Signs and Wonders in the Land of Ham, or the Ten Plagues of Egypt, with Ancient and Modern Illustrations. Woodcuts. Post 8vo. 7s. 6d.

MILMAN'S (Dean) WORKS:—
History of the Jews, from the earliest Period down to Modern Times. 3 Vols. Post 8vo. 18s.
Early Christianity, from the Birth of Christ to the Abolition of Paganism in the Roman Empire. 3 Vols. Post 8vo. 18s.
Latin Christianity, including that of the Popes to the Pontificate of Nicholas V. 9 Vols. Post 8vo. 54s.
Annals of St. Paul's Cathedral, from the Romans to the funeral of Wellington. Illustrations. 8vo.
Character and Conduct of the Apostles considered as an Evidence of Christianity. 8vo. 10s. 6d.
Quinti Horatii Flacci Opera. With 100 Woodcuts. Small 8vo. 7s. 6d.
Life of Quintus Horatius Flaccus. With Illustrations. 8vo. 9s.
Poetical Works. The Fall of Jerusalem—Martyr of Antioch—Balshazzar—Tamor—Anne Boleyn—Fazio, &c. With Portrait and Illustrations. 3 Vols. Fcap. 8vo. 18s.
Fall of Jerusalem. Fcap. 8vo. 1s.

MILMAN (Capt. E. A.) Wayside Cross. Post 8vo. 2s.

MIVART (St. George). Lessons from Nature; as manifested in Mind and Matter. 8vo. 15s.

MODERN DOMESTIC COOKERY. Founded on Principles of Economy and Practical Knowledge. *New Edition.* Woodcuts. Fcap. 8vo. 5s.

MONGREDIEN (Augustus). Trees and Shrubs for English Plantation. A Selection and Description of the most Ornamental which will flourish in the open air in our climate. With Classified Lists. With 30 Illustrations. 8vo. 10s.

MOORE (Thomas). Life and Letters of Lord Byron. *Cabinet Edition.* With Plates. 6 Vols. Fcap. 8vo. 18s.; *Popular Edition,* with Portraits. Royal 8vo. 7s. 6d.

MORESBY (Capt.), R.N. Discoveries in New Guinea, Polynesia, Torres Straits, &c., during the cruise of H.M.S. Basilisk. Map and Illustrations. 8vo. 15s.

MOTLEY (J. L.). History of the United Netherlands: from the Death of William the Silent to the Twelve Years' Truce, 1609. *Library Edition.* Portraits. 4 Vols. Post 8vo. 6s. each.

—————— Life and Death of John of Barneveld, Advocate of Holland. With a View of the Primary Causes and Movements of the Thirty Years' War. *Library Edition.* Illustrations. 2 Vols. 8vo. 28s. *Cabinet Edition.* 2 vols. Post 8vo. 12s.

MOSSMAN (Samuel). New Japan; the Land of the Rising Sun; its Annals and Progress during the past Twenty Years, recording the remarkable Progress of the Japanese in Western Civilisation. With Map. 8vo. 15s.

MOZLEY (Canon). Treatise on the Augustinian doctrine of Predestination. Crown 8vo. 9s.

———— Primitive Doctrine of Baptismal Regeneration. Post 8vo.

MUIRHEAD (Jas.). The Vaux-de-Vire of Maistre Jean Le Houx, Advocate of Vire. Translated and Edited. With Portrait and Illustrations. 8vo. 21s.

MUNRO'S (General) Life and Letters. By Rev. G. R. Gleig. Post 8vo. 3s. 6d.

MURCHISON (Sir Roderick). Siluria; or, a History of the Oldest rocks containing Organic Remains. Map and Plates. 8vo. 18s.

———— Memoirs. With Notices of his Contemporaries, and Rise and Progress of Palæozoic Geology. By Archibald Geikie. Portraits. 2 Vols. 8vo. 30s.

MURRAY'S RAILWAY READING. Containing:—

Wellington. By Lord Ellesmere. 6d.
Nimrod on the Chase. 1s.
Music and Dress. 1s.
Milman's Fall of Jerusalem. 1s.
Mahon's "Forty-Five." 3s.
Life of Theodore Hook. 1s.
Deeds of Naval Daring. 3s. 6d.
The Honey Bee. 1s.
Æsop's Fables. 2s. 6d.
Nimrod on the Turf. 1s. 6d.
Mahon's Joan of Arc. 1s.
Head's Emigrant. 2s. 6d.
Nimrod on the Road. 1s.
Croker on the Guillotine. 1s.
Hollway's Norway. 2s.
Maurel's Wellington. 1s. 6d.
Campbell's Life of Bacon. 2s. 6d.
The Flower Garden. 1s.
Rejected Addresses. 1s.
Penn's Hints on Angling. 1s.

MUSTERS' (Capt.) Patagonians; a Year's Wanderings over Untrodden Ground from the Straits of Magellan to the Rio Negro. Illustrations. Post 8vo. 7s. 6d.

NAPIER (Sir Wm.). English Battles and Sieges of the Peninsular War. Portrait. Post 8vo. 9s.

NAPOLEON at Fontainebleau and Elba. A Journal of Occurrences and Notes of Conversations. By Sir Neil Campbell, C.B. With a Memoir. By Rev. A. N. C. Maclachlan, M.A. Portrait 8vo. 15s.

NARES (Sir George), R.N. Official Report to the Admiralty of the recent Arctic Expedition. Map. 8vo. 2s. 6d.

NASMYTH and CARPENTER. The Moon. Considered as a Planet, a World, and a Satellite. With Illustrations from Drawings made with the aid of Powerful Telescopes, Woodcuts, &c. 4to. 30s.

NAUTICAL ALMANAC (The). (By Authority.) 2s. 6d.

NAVY LIST. (Monthly and Quarterly.) Post 8vo.

NEW TESTAMENT. With Short Explanatory Commentary. By Archdeacon Churton, M.A., and Archdeacon Basil Jones, M.A. With 110 authentic Views, &c. 2 Vols. Crown 8vo 21s. bound.

NEWTH (Samuel). First Book of Natural Philosophy; an Introduction to the Study of Statics, Dynamics, Hydrostatics, Light, Heat, and Sound, with numerous Examples. New and enlarged edition. Small 8vo. 3s. 6d.

———— Elements of Mechanics, including Hydrostatics, with numerous Examples. Small 8vo. 8s. 6d.

———— Mathematical Examples. A Graduated Series of Elementary Examples in Arithmetic, Algebra, Logarithms, Trigonometry, and Mechanics. Small 8vo. 8s. 6d.

NICHOLS' (J. G.) Pilgrimages to Walsingham and Canterbury. By Erasmus. Translated, with Notes. With Illustrations. Post 8vo. 6s.

———— (Sir George) History of the English Poor Laws. 2 Vols. 8vo.

NICOLAS (Sir Harris) Historic Peerage of England. Exhibiting the Origin, Descent, and Present State of every Title of Peerage which has existed in this Country since the Conquest. By William Courthope. 8vo. 30s.

NIMROD, On the Chace—Turf—and Road. With Portrait and Plates. Crown 8vo. 5s. Or with Coloured Plates, 7s. 6d.

NORDHOFF (Chas.). Communistic Societies of the United States; including Detailed Accounts of the Shakers, The Amana, Oneida, Bethell, Aurora, Icarian and other existing Societies; with Particulars of their Religious Creeds, Industries, and Present Condition. With 40 Illustrations. 8vo. 15s.

NORTHCOTE'S (Sir John) Notebook in the Long Parliament. Containing Proceedings during its First Session, 1640. Edited, with a Memoir, by A. H. A. Hamilton. Crown 8vo. 9s.

OWEN (Lieut.-Col.). Principles and Practice of Modern Artillery, including Artillery Material, Gunnery, and Organisation and Use of Artillery in Warfare. With Illustrations. 8vo. 15s.

OXENHAM (Rev. W.). English Notes for Latin Elegiacs; designed for early Proficients in the Art of Latin Versification, with Prefatory Rules of Composition in Elegiac Metre. 12mo. 3s. 6d.

PALGRAVE (R. H. I.). Local Taxation of Great Britain and Ireland. 8vo. 5s.
——————Notes on Banking in Great Britain and Ireland, Sweden, Denmark, and Hamburg, with some Remarks on the amount of Bills in circulation, both Inland and Foreign. 8vo. 6s.

PALLISER (Mrs.). Brittany and its Byeways, its Inhabitants, and Antiquities. With Illustrations. Post 8vo. 12s.
——————Mottoes for Monuments, or Epitaphs selected for General Use and Study. With Illustrations. Crown 8vo. 7s. 6d.

PARIS (Dr.) Philosophy in Sport made Science in Earnest; or, the First Principles of Natural Philosophy inculcated by aid of the Toys and Sports of Youth. Woodcuts. Post 8vo. 7s. 6d.

PARKYNS' (Mansfield) Three Years' Residence in Abyssinia: with Travels in that Country. With Illustrations. Post 8vo. 7s. 6d.

PEEK PRIZE ESSAYS. The Maintenance of the Church of England as an Established Church. By Rev. Charles Hole—Rev. R. Watson Dixon—and Rev. Julius Lloyd. 8vo. 10s. 6d.

PEEL'S (Sir Robert) Memoirs. 2 Vols. Post 8vo. 15s.

PENN (Richard). Maxims and Hints for an Angler and Chess-player. Woodcuts. Fcap. 8vo. 1s.

PERCY (John, M.D.). Metallurgy. 1st Division.—Fuel, Wood, Peat, Coal, Charcoal, Coke. Fire-Clays. *New Edition*. With Illustrations. 8vo. 30s.
—————— 2nd Division.—Copper, Zinc, and Brass. *New Edition*. With Illustrations. [*In the Press*.
—————— 3rd Division.—Iron and Steel. *New Edition*. With Illustrations. [*In Preparation*.
—————— 4th Division.—Lead, including part of Silver. With Illustrations. 30s.
—————— 5th Division.—Silver. With Illustrations. [*Nearly Ready*.
—————— 6th Division.—Gold, Mercury, Platinum, Tin, Nickel, Cobalt, Antimony, Bismuth, Arsenic, and other Metals. With Illustrations. [*In Preparation*.

PHILLIPS' (JOHN) Memoirs of William Smith. 8vo. 7s. 6d.
———— Geology of Yorkshire, The Coast, and Limestone District. Plates. 2 Vols. 4to. 31s. 6d. each.
———— Rivers, Mountains, and Sea Coast of Yorkshire. With Essays on the Climate, Scenery, and Ancient Inhabitants. Plates. 8vo. 15s.
———— (SAMUEL). Literary Essays from "The Times." With Portrait. 2 Vols. Fcap. 8vo. 7s.
POPE'S (ALEXANDER) Works. With Introductions and Notes, by REV. WHITWELL ELWIN. Vols. I., II., VI., VII., VIII. With Portraits. 8vo. 10s. 6d. each.
PORTER (REV. J. L.). Damascus, Palmyra, and Lebanon. With Travels among the Giant Cities of Bashan and the Hauran. Map and Woodcuts. Post 8vo. 7s. 6d.
PRAYER-BOOK (ILLUSTRATED), with Borders, Initials, Vignettes, &c. Edited, with Notes, by REV. THOS. JAMES. Medium 8vo. 18s. cloth; 31s. 6d. calf; 36s. morocco.
PRINCESS CHARLOTTE OF WALES. A Brief Memoir. With Selections from her Correspondence and other unpublished Papers. By LADY ROSE WEIGALL. With Portrait. 8vo. 8s. 6d.
PUSS IN BOOTS. With 12 Illustrations. By OTTO SPECKTER. 16mo. 1s. 6d. Or coloured, 2s. 6d.
PRIVY COUNCIL JUDGMENTS in Ecclesiastical Cases relating to Doctrine and Discipline. With Historical Introduction, by G. C. BRODRICK and W. H. FREMANTLE. 8vo. 10s. 6d.
QUARTERLY REVIEW (THE). 8vo. 6s.
RAE (EDWARD). Country of the Moors. A Journey from Tripoli in Barbary to the Holy City of Kairwan. Map and Etchings. Crown 8vo. 10s. 6d.
RAMBLES in the Syrian Deserts. Post 8vo. 10s. 6d.
RASSAM (HORMUZD). Narrative of the British Mission to Abyssinia. With Notices of the Countries Traversed from Massowah to Magdala. Illustrations. 2 Vols. 8vo. 28s.
RAWLINSON'S (CANON) Herodotus. A New English Version. Edited with Notes and Essays. Maps and Woodcut. 4 Vols. 8vo. 48s.
———————— Five Great Monarchies of Chaldæa, Assyria, Media, Babylonia, and Persia. With Maps and Illustrations. 3 Vols. 8vo. 42s.
———————— (SIR HENRY) England and Russia in the East; a Series of Papers on the Political and Geographical Condition of Central Asia. Map. 8vo. 12s.
REED (E. J.). Shipbuilding in Iron and Steel; a Practical Treatise, giving full details of Construction, Processes of Manufacture, and Building Arrangements. With Illustrations. 8vo.
———— Iron-Clad Ships; their Qualities, Performances, and Cost. With Chapters on Turret Ships, Iron-Clad Rams, &c. With Illustrations. 8vo. 12s.
———— Letters from Russia in 1875. 8vo. 5s.
REJECTED ADDRESSES (THE). By JAMES AND HORACE SMITH. Woodcuts. Post 8vo. 3s. 6d.; or Popular Edition, Fcap. 8vo. 1s.
REYNOLDS' (SIR JOSHUA) Life and Times. By C. R. LESLIE, R.A. and TOM TAYLOR. Portraits. 2 Vols. 8vo. 42s.
RICARDO'S (DAVID) Political Works. With a Notice of his Life and Writings. By J. R. M'CULLOCH. 8vo. 16s.
RIPA (FATHER). Thirteen Years' Residence at the Court of Peking. Post 8vo. 2s.

ROBERTSON (Canon). History of the Christian Church, from the Apostolic Age to the Reformation, 1517. *Library Edition*. 4 Vols. 8vo. *Cabinet Edition*. 8 Vols. Post 8vo. 6s. each.

ROBINSON (Rev. Dr.). Biblical Researches in Palestine and the Adjacent Regions, 1838—52. Maps. 3 Vols. 8vo. 42s.

—— Physical Geography of the Holy Land. Post 8vo. 10s. 6d.

—— (Wm.) Alpine Flowers for English Gardens. With 70 Illustrations. Crown 8vo. 12s.

—— Wild Garden; or, our Groves and Shrubberies made beautiful by the Naturalization of Hardy Exotic Plants. With Frontispiece. Small 8vo. 6s.

—— Sub-Tropical Garden; or, Beauty of Form in the Flower Garden. With Illustrations. Small 8vo. 7s. 6d.

ROBSON (E. R.). School Architecture. Being Practical Remarks on the Planning, Designing, Building, and Furnishing of School-houses. With 300 Illustrations. Medium 8vo. 18s.

ROME (History of). *See* Liddell and Smith.

ROWLAND (David). Laws of Nature the Foundation of Morals. Post 8vo. 6s.

RUXTON (Geo. F.). Travels in Mexico; with Adventrs. among Wild Tribes and Animals of the Prairies and Rocky Mountains. Post 8vo. 3s. 6d.

SALE'S (Sir Robert) Brigade in Affghanistan. With an Account of the Defence of Jellalabad. By Rev. G. R. Gleig. Post 8vo. 2s.

SCEPTICISM IN GEOLOGY; and the Reasons for It. An assemblage of facts from Nature combining to invalidate and refute the theory of "Causes now in Action." By Verifier. Woodcuts. Crown 8vo. 6s.

SCHLIEMANN (Dr. Henry). Troy and Its Remains. A Narrative of Researches and Discoveries made on the Site of Ilium, and in the Trojan Plain. With Maps, Views, and 500 Illustrations. Medium 8vo. 42s.

—— Discoveries on the Sites of Ancient Mycenæ and Tiryns. With Maps and 500 Illustrations. Medium 8vo. 50s.

SCOTT (Sir G. G.). Secular and Domestic Architecture, Present and Future. 8vo. 9s.

—— (Dean) University Sermons. Post 8vo. 8s. 6d.

SCROPE (G. P.). Geology and Extinct Volcanoes of Central France. Illustrations. Medium 8vo. 30s.

SELBORNE (Lord). Notes on some Passages in the Liturgical History of the Reformed English Church. 8vo. 6s.

SHADOWS OF A SICK ROOM. With a Preface by Canon Liddon. 16mo. 2s. 6d.

SHAH OF PERSIA'S Diary during his Tour through Europe in 1873. Translated from the Original. By J. W. Redhouse. With Portrait and Coloured Title. Crown 8vo. 12s.

SMILES' (Samuel) WORKS:—

British Engineers; from the Earliest Period to the death of the Stephensons. With Illustrations. 5 Vols. Crown 8vo. 7s. 6d. each.

Life of a Scotch Naturalist. With Portrait and Illustrations. Crown 8vo. 10s. 6d.

Huguenots in England and Ireland. Crown 8vo. 7s. 6d.

Self-Help. With Illustrations of Conduct and Perseverance. Post 8vo. 6s. Or in French, 5s.

Character. A Sequel to "Self-Help." Post 8vo. 6s.

Thrift. A Book of Domestic Counsel. Post 8vo. 6s.

Industrial Biography; or, Iron Workers and Tool Makers. Post 8vo. 6s.

Boy's Voyage Round the World. Illustrations. Post 8vo. 6s.

SMITH'S (Dr. Wm.). DICTIONARIES:—
   DICTIONARY OF THE BIBLE; its Antiquities, Biography, Geography, and Natural History. Illustrations. 3 Vols. 8vo. 105s.
   CONCISE BIBLE DICTIONARY. With 300 Illustrations. Medium 8vo. 21s.
   SMALLER BIBLE DICTIONARY. With Illustrations. Post 8vo. 7s. 6d.
   CHRISTIAN ANTIQUITIES. Comprising the History, Institutions, and Antiquities of the Christian Church. With Illustrations. Vol. I. 8vo. 31s. 6d. (To be completed in 2 vols.)
   CHRISTIAN BIOGRAPHY, LITERATURE, SECTS, AND DOCTRINES; from the Times of the Apostles to the Age of Charlemagne. Vol. I. 8vo. 31s. 6d. (To be completed in 3 vols.)
   GREEK AND ROMAN ANTIQUITIES. With 500 Illustrations. Medium 8vo. 28s.
   GREEK AND ROMAN BIOGRAPHY AND MYTHOLOGY. With 600 Illustrations. 3 Vols. Medium 8vo. 4l. 4s.
   GREEK AND ROMAN GEOGRAPHY. 2 Vols. With 500 Illustrations. Medium 8vo. 56s.
   ATLAS OF ANCIENT GEOGRAPHY—BIBLICAL AND CLASSICAL. Folio. 6l. 6s.
   CLASSICAL DICTIONARY OF MYTHOLOGY, BIOGRAPHY, AND GEOGRAPHY. 1 Vol. With 750 Woodcuts. 8vo. 18s.
   SMALLER CLASSICAL DICTIONARY. With 200 Woodcuts. Crown 8vo. 7s. 6d.
   SMALLER GREEK AND ROMAN ANTIQUITIES. With 200 Woodcuts. Crown 8vo. 7s. 6d.
   COMPLETE LATIN-ENGLISH DICTIONARY. With Tables of the Roman Calendar, Measures, Weights, and Money. 8vo. 21s.
   SMALLER LATIN-ENGLISH DICTIONARY. 12mo. 7s. 6d.
   COPIOUS AND CRITICAL ENGLISH-LATIN DICTIONARY. 8vo. 21s.
   SMALLER ENGLISH-LATIN DICTIONARY. 12mo. 7s. 6d.

SMITH'S (Dr. Wm.) ENGLISH COURSE:—
   SCHOOL MANUAL OF ENGLISH GRAMMAR, WITH COPIOUS EXERCISES. Post 8vo. 3s. 6d.
   SCHOOL MANUAL OF MODERN GEOGRAPHY, PHYSICAL AND POLITICAL. Post 8vo. 5s.
   PRIMARY ENGLISH GRAMMAR. 16mo. 1s.
   PRIMARY HISTORY OF BRITAIN. 12mo. 2s. 6d.

SMITH'S (Dr. Wm.) FRENCH COURSE:—
   FRENCH PRINCIPIA. Part I. A First Course, containing a Grammar, Delectus, Exercises, and Vocabularies. 12mo. 3s. 6d.
   FRENCH PRINCIPIA. Part II. A Reading Book, containing Fables, Stories, and Anecdotes, Natural History, and Scenes from the History of France. With Grammatical Questions, Notes and copious Etymological Dictionary. 12mo. 4s. 6d.
   FRENCH PRINCIPIA. Part III. Prose Composition, containing a Systematic Course of Exercises on the Syntax, with the Principal Rules of Syntax. 12mo. [In the Press.
   STUDENT'S FRENCH GRAMMAR. By C. HERON-WALL. With Introduction by M. Littré. Post 8vo. 7s. 6d.
   SMALLER GRAMMAR OF THE FRENCH LANGUAGE. Abridged from the above. 12mo. 3s. 6d.

LIST OF WORKS

SMITH'S (Dr. Wm.) GERMAN COURSE:—

GERMAN PRINCIPIA. Part I. A First German Course, containing a Grammar, Delectus, Exercise Book, and Vocabularies. 12mo. 3s. 6d.

GERMAN PRINCIPIA. Part II. A Reading Book; containing Fables, Stories, and Anecdotes, Natural History, and Scenes from the History of Germany. With Grammatical Questions, Notes, and Dictionary. 12mo. 3s. 6d.

PRACTICAL GERMAN GRAMMAR. Post 8vo. 3s. 6d.

SMITH'S (Dr. Wm.) LATIN COURSE:—

PRINCIPIA LATINA. Part I. First Latin Course, containing a Grammar, Delectus, and Exercise Book, with Vocabularies. 12mo. 3s. 6d.
** In this Edition the Cases of the Nouns, Adjectives, and Pronouns are arranged both as in the ORDINARY GRAMMARS and as in the PUBLIC SCHOOL PRIMER, together with the corresponding Exercises.

APPENDIX TO PRINCIPIA LATINA Part I.; being Additional Exercises, with Examination Papers. 12mo. 2s. 6d.

PRINCIPIA LATINA. Part II. A Reading-book of Mythology, Geography, Roman Antiquities, and History. With Notes and Dictionary. 12mo. 3s. 6d.

PRINCIPIA LATINA. Part III. A Poetry Book. Hexameters and Pentameters; Eclog. Ovidianæ; Latin Prosody. 12mo. 3s. 6d.

PRINCIPIA LATINA. Part IV. Prose Composition. Rules of Syntax with Examples, Explanations of Synonyms, and Exercises on the Syntax. 12mo. 3s. 6d.

PRINCIPIA LATINA. Part V. Short Tales and Anecdotes for Translation into Latin. 12mo. 3s.

LATIN-ENGLISH VOCABULARY AND FIRST LATIN-ENGLISH DICTIONARY FOR PHÆDRUS, CORNELIUS NEPOS, AND CÆSAR. 12mo. 3s. 6d.

STUDENT'S LATIN GRAMMAR. Post 8vo. 6s.

SMALLER LATIN GRAMMAR. 12mo. 3s. 6d.

TACITUS, GERMANIA, AGRICOLA, &c. With English Notes. 12mo. 3s. 6d.

SMITH'S (Dr. Wm.) GREEK COURSE:—

INITIA GRÆCA. Part I. A First Greek Course, containing a Grammar, Delectus, and Exercise-book. With Vocabularies. 12mo. 3s. 6d.

INITIA GRÆCA. Part II. A Reading Book. Containing Short Tales, Anecdotes, Fables, Mythology, and Grecian History. 12mo. 3s. 6d.

INITIA GRÆCA. Part III. Prose Composition. Containing the Rules of Syntax, with copious Examples and Exercises. 12mo. 3s. 6d.

STUDENT'S GREEK GRAMMAR. By CURTIUS. Post 8vo. 6s.

SMALLER GREEK GRAMMAR. 12mo. 3s. 6d.

GREEK ACCIDENCE. 12mo. 2s. 6d.

PLATO, APOLOGY OF SOCRATES, &c. With Notes. 12mo. 3s. 6d.

SMITH'S (Dr. Wm.) SMALLER HISTORIES:—

SCRIPTURE HISTORY. Woodcuts. 16mo. 3s. 6d.

ANCIENT HISTORY. Woodcuts. 16mo. 3s. 6d.

ANCIENT GEOGRAPHY. Woodcuts. 16mo. 3s. 6d.

ROME. Woodcuts. 16mo. 3s. 6d.

GREECE. Woodcuts. 16mo. 3s. 6d.

CLASSICAL MYTHOLOGY. Woodcuts. 16mo. 3s. 6d.

ENGLAND. Woodcuts. 16mo. 3s. 6d.

ENGLISH LITERATURE. 16mo. 3s. 6d.

SPECIMENS OF ENGLISH LITERATURE. 16mo. 3s. 6d.

SHAW (T. B.). Student's Manual of English Literature. Post 8vo. 7s. 6d.

—— Specimens of English Literature. Selected from the Chief Writers. Post 8vo. 7s. 6d.

—— (ROBERT). Visit to High Tartary, Yarkand, and Kashgar (formerly Chinese Tartary), and Return Journey over the Karakorum Pass. With Map and Illustrations. 8vo. 16s.

SIERRA LEONE; Described in Letters to Friends at Home. By A LADY. Post 8vo. 3s. 6d.

SIMMONS (CAPT.). Constitution and Practice of Courts-Martial. *Seventh Edition.* 8vo. 15s.

SMITH (PHILIP). A History of the Ancient World, from the Creation to the Fall of the Roman Empire, A.D. 476. *Fourth Edition.* 3 Vols. 8vo. 31s. 6d.

SPALDING (CAPTAIN). The Tale of Frithiof. Translated from the Swedish of ESIAS TEGNER. Post 8vo. 7s. 6d.

STANLEY'S (DEAN) WORKS:—

SINAI AND PALESTINE, in connexion with their History. Map. 8vo. 14s.

BIBLE IN THE HOLY LAND; Extracted from the above Work. Woodcuts. Fcap. 8vo. 2s. 6d.

EASTERN CHURCH. Plans. 8vo. 12s.

JEWISH CHURCH. From the Earliest Times to the Christian Era. 3 Vols. 8vo. 38s.

EPISTLES OF ST. PAUL TO THE CORINTHIANS. 8vo. 18s.

LIFE OF DR. ARNOLD, OF RUGBY. With selections from his Correspondence. With portrait. 2 vols. Crown 8vo. 12s.

CHURCH OF SCOTLAND. 8vo. 7s. 6d.

MEMORIALS OF CANTERBURY CATHEDRAL. Woodcuts. Post 8vo. 7s. 6d.

WESTMINSTER ABBEY. With Illustrations. 8vo. 15s.

SERMONS DURING A TOUR IN THE EAST. 8vo. 9s.

ADDRESSES AND CHARGES OF THE LATE BISHOP STANLEY. With Memoir. 8vo. 10s. 6d.

STEPHEN (REV. W. R.). Life and Times of St. Chrysostom. With Portrait. 8vo. 15s.

ST. JOHN (CHARLES). Wild Sports and Natural History of the Highlands. Post 8vo. 3s. 6d.

—— (BAYLE) Adventures in the Libyan Desert. Post 8vo. 2s.

SUMNER'S (BISHOP) Life and Episcopate during 40 Years. By Rev. G. H. SUMNER. Portrait. 8vo. 14s.

STREET (G. E.) Gothic Architecture in Spain. From Personal Observations made during several Journeys. With Illustrations. Royal 8vo. 30s.

—————— Italy, chiefly in Brick and Marble. With Notes of Tours in the North of Italy. With 60 Illustrations. Royal 8vo. 26s.

LIST OF WORKS

STUDENTS' MANUALS:—

OLD TESTAMENT HISTORY; from the Creation to the Return of the Jews from Captivity. Maps and Woodcuts. Post 8vo. 7s. 6d.

NEW TESTAMENT HISTORY. With an Introduction connecting the History of the Old and New Testaments. Maps and Woodcuts. Post 8vo. 7s. 6d.

ECCLESIASTICAL HISTORY. A History of the Christian Church during the First Ten Centuries; From its Foundation to the full establishment of the Holy Roman Empire and the Papal Power. Post 8vo. 7s. 6d.

ENGLISH CHURCH HISTORY, from the accession of Henry VIII. to the silencing of Convocation in the 18th Century. By Rev. G. G. PERRY. Post 8vo. 7s. 6d.

ANCIENT HISTORY OF THE EAST; Egypt, Assyria, Babylonia, Media, Persia, Asia Minor, and Phœnicia. Woodcuts. Post 8vo. 7s. 6d.

ANCIENT GEOGRAPHY. By REV. W. L. BEVAN. Woodcuts. Post 8vo. 7s. 6d.

HISTORY OF GREECE; from the Earliest Times to the Roman Conquest. By WM. SMITH, D.C.L. Woodcuts. Crown 8vo. 7s. 6d.
⁎ Questions on the above Work, 12mo. 2s.

HISTORY OF ROME; from the Earliest Times to the Establishment of the Empire. By DEAN LIDDELL. Woodcuts. Crown 8vo. 7s. 6d.

GIBBON'S DECLINE AND FALL OF THE ROMAN EMPIRE. Woodcuts. Post 8vo. 7s. 6d.

HALLAM'S HISTORY OF EUROPE during the Middle Ages. Post 8vo. 7s. 6d.

HALLAM'S HISTORY OF ENGLAND; from the Accession of Henry VII. to the Death of George II. Post 8vo. 7s. 6d.

HUME'S HISTORY OF ENGLAND from the Invasion of Julius Cæsar to the Revolution in 1688. Continued down to 1868. Woodcuts. Post 8vo. 7s. 6d.
⁎ Questions on the above Work, 12mo. 2s.

HISTORY OF FRANCE: from the Earliest Times to the Establishment of the Second Empire, 1852. By REV. H. W. JERVIS. Woodcuts. Post 8vo. 7s. 6d.

ENGLISH LANGUAGE. By GEO. P. MARSH. Post 8vo. 7s. 6d.

ENGLISH LITERATURE. By T. B. SHAW, M.A. Post 8vo. 7s. 6d.

SPECIMENS OF ENGLISH LITERATURE from the Chief Writers. By T. B. SHAW. Post 8vo. 7s. 6d.

MODERN GEOGRAPHY; Mathematical, Physical and Descriptive. By REV. W. L. BEVAN. Woodcuts. Post 8vo. 7s. 6d.

MORAL PHILOSOPHY. By WILLIAM FLEMING, D.D. Post 8vo. 7s. 6d.

BLACKSTONE'S COMMENTARIES ON THE LAWS OF ENGLAND. By R. MALCOLM KERR, LL.D. Post 8vo. 7s. 6d.

STYFFE (KNUTT). Strength of Iron and Steel. Plates. 8vo. 12s.

SOMERVILLE (MARY). Personal Recollections from Early Life to Old Age. With her Correspondence. Portrait. Crown 8vo. 12s.

———————— Physical Geography. Portrait. Post 8vo. 9s.

———————— Connexion of the Physical Sciences. Portrait. Post 8vo. 9s.

———————— Molecular and Microscopic Science. Illustrations. 2 Vols. Post 8vo. 21s.

STANHOPE'S (EARL) WORKS :—
   HISTORY OF ENGLAND FROM THE REIGN OF QUEEN ANNE TO THE PEACE OF VERSAILLES, 1701-83. 9 vols. Post 8vo. 5s. each.
   BRITISH INDIA, FROM ITS ORIGIN TO 1783. 8vo. 3s. 6d.
   HISTORY OF "FORTY-FIVE." Post 8vo. 3s.
   HISTORICAL AND CRITICAL ESSAYS. Post 8vo. 3s. 6d.
   FRENCH RETREAT FROM MOSCOW, AND OTHER ESSAYS. Post 8vo. 7s. 6d.
   LIFE OF BELISARIUS. Post 8vo. 10s. 6d.
   LIFE OF CONDÉ. Post 8vo. 3s. 6d.
   LIFE OF WILLIAM PITT. Portraits. 4 Vols. 8vo. 24s.
   MISCELLANIES. 2 Vols. Post 8vo. 13s.
   STORY OF JOAN OF ARC. Fcap. 8vo. 1s.
   ADDRESSES ON VARIOUS OCCASIONS. 16mo. 1s.

SOUTHEY (ROBERT). Lives of Bunyan and Cromwell. Post 8vo. 2s.

SWAINSON (CANON). Nicene and Apostles' Creeds; Their Literary History; together with some Account of "The Creed of St. Athanasius." 8vo. 16s.

SYBEL (VON) History of Europe during the French Revolution, 1789-1795. 4 Vols. 8vo. 48s.

SYMONDS' (REV. W.) Records of the Rocks; or Notes on the Geology, Natural History, and Antiquities of North and South Wales, Siluria, Devon, and Cornwall. With Illustrations. Crown 8vo. 12s.

THIBAUT'S (ANTOINE) Purity in Musical Art. Translated from the German. With a prefatory Memoir by W. H. Gladstone, M.P. Post 8vo. 6s.

THIELMANN (BARON). Journey through the Caucasus to Tabreez, Kurdistan, down the Tigris and Euphrates to Nineveh and Babylon, and across the Desert to Palmyra. Translated by CHAS. HENEAGE. Illustrations. 2 Vols. Post 8vo. 18s.

THOMS (W. J.). Longevity of Man: its Facts and its Fiction. Including Observations on the more Remarkable Instances. Post 8vo. 10s. 6d.

THOMSON (ARCHBISHOP). Lincoln's Inn Sermons. 8vo. 10s. 6d.
———— Life in the Light of God's Word. Post 8vo. 5s.

TITIAN'S LIFE AND TIMES. With some account of his Family, chiefly from new and unpublished Records. By CROWE and CAVALCASELLE. With Portrait and Illustrations. 2 Vols. 8vo. 42s.

TOCQUEVILLE'S State of Society in France before the Revolution, 1789, and on the Causes which led to that Event. Translated by HENRY REEVE. 8vo. 14s.

TOMLINSON (CHARLES): The Sonnet; Its Origin, Structure, and Place in Poetry. With translations from Dante, Petrarch, &c. Post 8vo. 9s.

TOZER (REV. H. F.) Highlands of Turkey, with Visits to Mounts Ida, Athos, Olympus, and Pelion. 2 Vols. Crown 8vo. 24s.
———— Lectures on the Geography of Greece. Map. Post 8vo. 9s.

TRISTRAM (CANON) Great Sahara. Illustrations. Crown 8vo. 15s.
———— Land of Moab; Travels and Discoveries on the East Side of the Dead Sea and the Jordan. Illustrations. Crown 8vo. 15s.

LIST OF WORKS PUBLISHED BY MR. MURRAY.

TWENTY YEARS' RESIDENCE among the Greeks, Albanians, Turks, Armenians, and Bulgarians. By an ENGLISH LADY. Edited by STANLEY LANE POOLE. 2 Vols. Crown 8vo.

TWISLETON (EDWARD). The Tongue not Essential to Speech, with Illustrations of the Power of Speech in the case of the African Confessors. Post 8vo. *6s.*

TWISS' (HORACE) Life of Lord Eldon. 2 Vols. Post 8vo. 21*s.*

TYLOR (E. B.) Early History of Mankind, and Development of Civilization. 8vo. 12*s.*

―――――― Primitive Culture; the Development of Mythology, Philosophy, Religion, Art, and Custom. 2 Vols. 8vo. 24*s.*

VAMBERY (ARMINIUS) Travels from Teheran across the Turkoman Desert on the Eastern Shore of the Caspian. Illustrations. 8vo. 21*s.*

VAN LENNEP (HENRY J.) Travels in Asia Minor. With Illustrations of Biblical Literature, and Archæology. With Woodcuts. 2 Vols. Post 8vo. 24*s.*

―――――― Modern Customs and Manners of Bible Lands, in illustration of Scripture. With Maps and 300 Illustrations. 2 Vols. 8vo. 21*s.*

VIRCHOW (PROFESSOR). The Freedom of Science in the Modern State. Fcap. 8vo. 2*s.*

WELLINGTON'S Despatches during his Campaigns in India, Denmark, Portugal, Spain, the Low Countries, and France. 8 Vols. 8vo. 20*s.* each.

―――――― Supplementary Despatches, relating to India, Ireland, Denmark, Spanish America, Spain, Portugal, France, Congress of Vienna, Waterloo and Paris. 14 Vols. 8vo. 20*s.* each. *⁎⁎* An *Index.* 8vo. 20*s.*

―――――― Civil and Political Correspondence. Vols. I. to VII. 8vo. 20*s.* each.

―――――― Speeches in Parliament. 2 Vols. 8vo. 42*s.*

WHEELER (G.). Choice of a Dwelling; a Practical Handbook of Useful Information on Building a House. Plans. Post 8vo. 7*s. 6d.*

WHITE (W. H.). Manual of Naval Architecture, for the use of Naval Officers, Shipowners, Shipbuilders, and Yachtsmen. Illustrations. 8vo. 24*s.*

WILBERFORCE'S (BISHOP) Life of William Wilberforce. Portrait. Crown 8vo. *6s.*

WILKINSON (SIR J. G.). Manners and Customs of the Ancient Egyptians, their Private Life, Government, Laws, Arts, Manufactures, Religion, &c. A new edition, with additions by the late Author. Edited by SAMUEL BIRCH, LL.D. Illustrations. 3 Vols 8vo.

―――――― Popular Account of the Ancient Egyptians. With 500 Woodcuts. 2 Vols. Post 8vo. 12*s.*

WOOD'S (CAPTAIN) Source of the Oxus. With the Geography of the Valley of the Oxus. By COL. YULE. Map. 8vo. 12*s.*

WORDS OF HUMAN WISDOM. Collected and Arranged by E. S. With a Preface by CANON LIDDON. Fcap. 8vo. 3*s. 6d.*

WORDSWORTH'S (BISHOP) Athens and Attica. Plates. 8vo. 5*s.*

YULE'S (COLONEL) Book of Marco Polo. Illustrated by the Light of Oriental Writers and Modern Travels. With Maps and 80 Plates. 2 Vols. Medium 8vo. 63*s.*

www.ingramcontent.com/pod-product-compliance
Lightning Source LLC
Chambersburg PA
CBHW031432230426
43668CB00007B/508